KUSTOM KULTURE

KUSTOM KULTURE

Von Dutch,
Ed "Big Daddy" Roth,
Robert Williams and Others

C.R. Stecyk, Guest Curator
with Bolton Colburn

Laguna Art Museum
in association with
Last Gasp of San Francisco

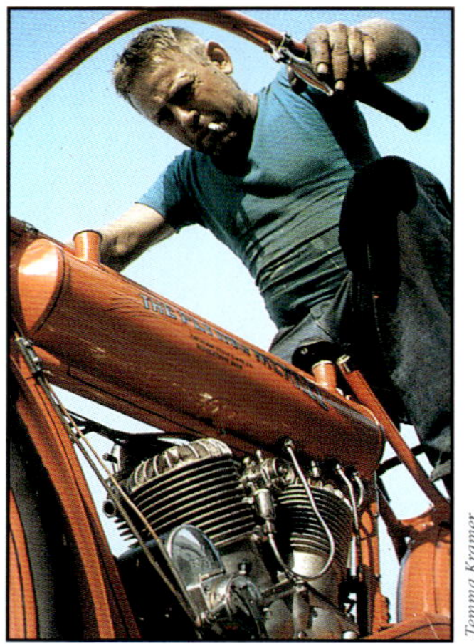

The American Custom Car culture has many fathers, one of whom, Kenneth Robert Howard —known to most people by his assumed name, Von Dutch—died on 19 September 1992. The mother of the American custom car culture is the automobile herself—a Machine Age icon that is eternal. Both the person and the symbol are honored in this book and exhibition.

This book is published by the Laguna Art Museum, in association with Last Gasp of San Francisco, on the occasion of an exhibition of the same title organized by the Museum. The exhibition was presented at the Laguna Art Museum (17 July - 7 November 1993), the Maryland Institute College of Art, Baltimore (3 December 1993 - 23 January 1994) and the Center on Contemporary Art, Seattle (29 May - 17 July 1994).

Works in the exhibition are indicated by the Iron Cross symbol (✠).

This project was made possible by generous donations from
M. Dolores Milhous
and
Judy and Stuart Spence.

Catalogue design: Jeff Girard, Victoria Street Graphic Design, Dana Point, CA
Photography: C.R. Stecyk, unless otherwise credited
Cover art: James Cleveland
Thanks to Brian Pike, Cindy Love, Catherine Girard

Library of Congress Cataloging-in-Publication Data

Kustom Kulture: Von Dutch, Ed "Big Daddy" Roth, Robert Williams and others.
p. cm.
Contents: Direct descent: Von Dutch to Robert Williams / Pat Ganahl -- Origins of a sub-species / C.R. Stecyk -- Rites of passage, customized / Temma Kramer -- The Kandy-Kolored Tangerine-Flake Streamline Baby / Tom Wolfe -- Rubberneck manifesto / Robert Williams -- Some others / Bolton Colburn.
ISBN 0-86719-405-7
1. Automobiles--Customizing--Exhibitions. 2. Automobiles--Decoration--Exhibitions. 3. Automobiles in art--Exhibitions. 4. Art, Modern--20th century--California--Exhibitions.
I. Dutch, Von 1929-1992 II. Roth, Ed. III. Williams, Robert IV. Title: Custom Culture.
TL7.U62L344 1993
629.26--dc20

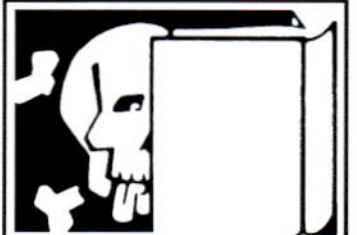

Last Gasp of San Francisco
P.O. Box 410067
San Francisco, California 94141-0067
Publisher: Ron Turner

6th printing

Printed in Hong Kong by Prolong Press Ltd.

CONTENTS

PREFACE

Charles Desmarais
Director

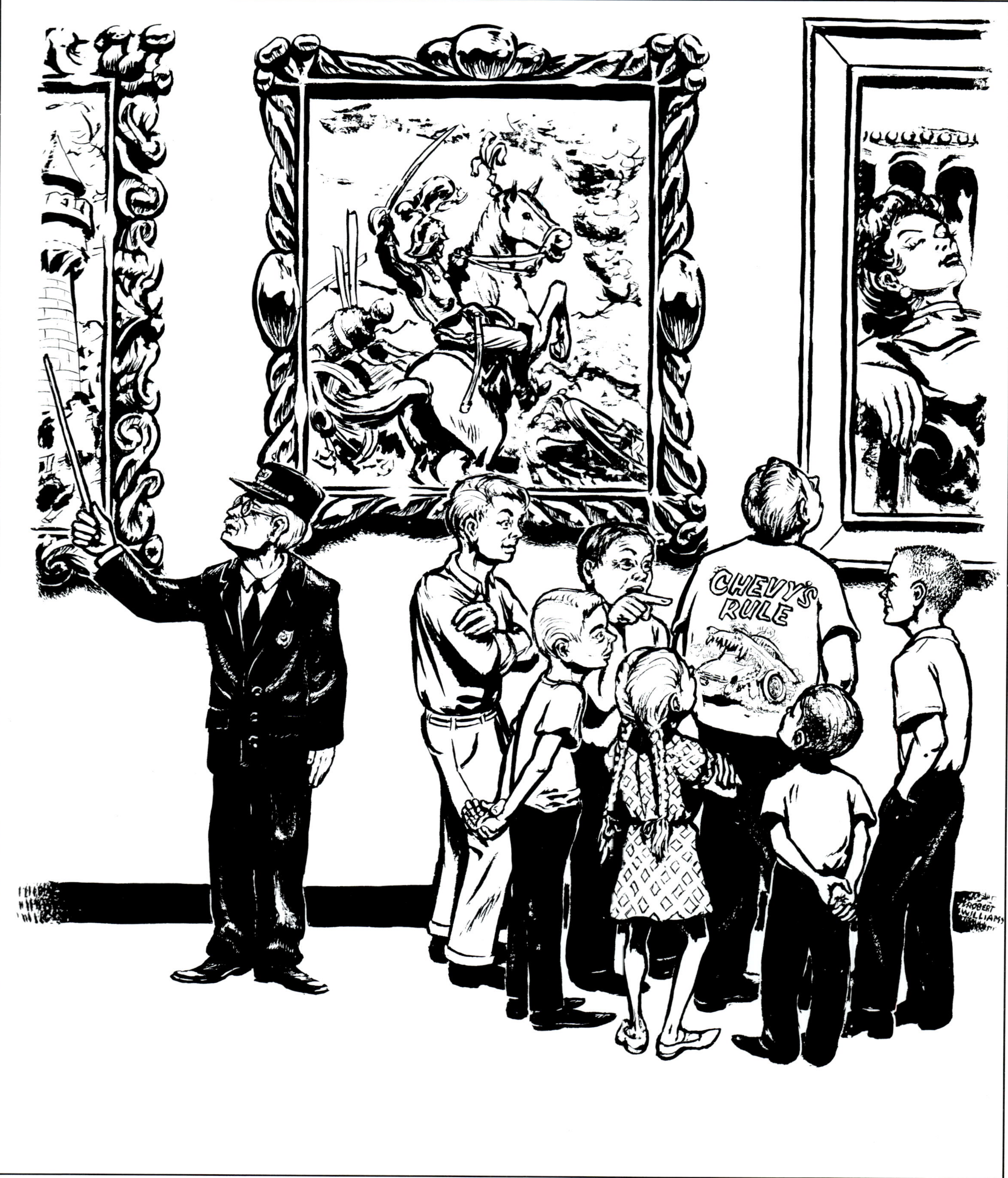

It was a guy thing.

Cars and comix. Sleek, sexy bodies and base humor.

If these were all the custom car craze of the early 1960s had left behind, it might hold some sociological interest. But some other things happened at the same time, in the same place, and thus it became more than just a guy thing—it was a youth thing, a California thing.

California's own adolescence coincided with that of half of America. American art, too, was growing up and taking a predominant place on the international scene.

With floods of cultural hormones pulsing through Southern California's veins, the region became a focal point for American youth—a metaphor for post-pubescent energy and anxiousness and creativity. And so, a craze became something else, with its own language, mores, traditions and art—a culture, customized for its age and geography: Kustom Kulture.

This book and the exhibition it accompanies are a look at Kustom Kulture through the work of three of its central figures and some thirty-five "others" who immersed themselves in it. The project is exactly the sort of innovative approach to the history of art in California upon which the Laguna Art Museum prides itself. I want to thank the many people who have contributed yet another high point in the seventy-five year history of our institution.

First among such contributors is Craig Stecyk, who selected the primary works for the exhibition and wrote the principal text, and whose instincts about the history of the car culture have led to the remarkable product now in the reader's hands. Also essential to this effort were Laguna Art Museum trustee Greg Escalante, without whose organizational genius and witty intelligence this project never would have happened, and Bolton Colburn, LAM Curator of Collections, who chose and wrote about many of the works in the show.

For the members and trustees of the Laguna Art Museum, I thank the major donors who made this work possible: M. Dolores Milhous and Judy and Stuart Spence. All three of these special people have made important contributions in the past, and we thank them for their continued belief in the art of our time and the Museum's dedication to it.

Jim and Dan Brucker have devoted many years and substantial resources to supporting and collecting the art of Von Dutch, Ed Roth and Robert Williams. We thank them and the other lenders to this project for preserving this important work, and for sharing it with a larger public.

The Laguna Art Museum board and staff rarely receive proper acknowledgement of their many contributions to the Museum and its various efforts, yet nothing the Museum does would be possible without them. We owe a debt of gratitude to them all. Among the staff, I would particularly thank Susan M. Anderson, Curator of Exhibitions, who coordinated the exhibition at the Museum. I would also like to thank Curatorial Assistant Lisa Buck and Colleen Callinan, Assistant to the Director, for their assistance.

Finally, we thank Ed Roth, Robert Williams, the late Von Dutch and the other artists who agreed to participate. It is they who have defined Kustom Kulture.

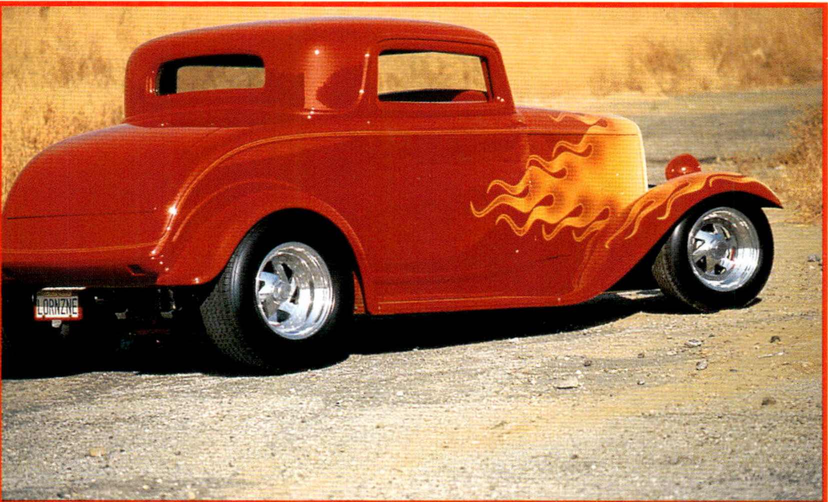

Contemporary vehicle by Boyd Coddington reveals the influence of Von Dutch's paint treatment. Photo courtesy Rod and Custom.

(Opposite) Robert Williams illustration for Ed Roth Studios, 1967.

DIRECT DESCENT: VON DUTCH TO ROBERT WILLIAMS

Pat Ganahl

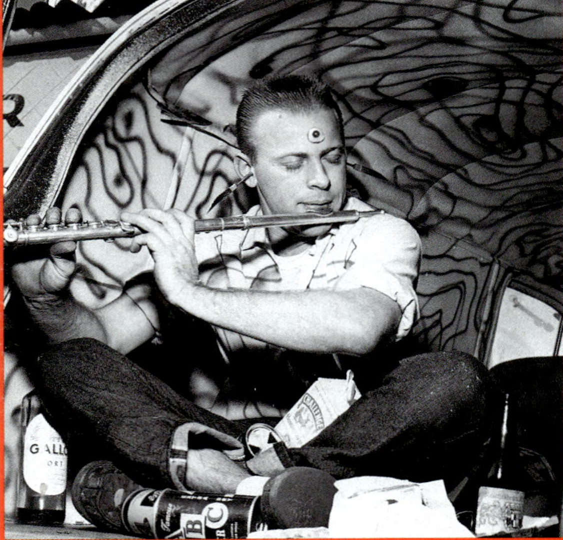

Von Dutch in the back of his delivery van/domicile, 1950s. Photo courtesy Rod and Custom.

(Opposite) Von Dutch pinstripe design, c. 1956. Photo courtesy Rod and Custom.

Museums and galleries usually get this wrong. When they assemble shows with titles like "The Car and Culture" or "Art and the Automobile," they too often tend to ascribe elements of art to the vehicles themselves. This is especially true when the topic turns to hot rods and custom cars.

There is nothing artistic about automobiles. They are functional machines skinned with bodies designed to promote their salability on showroom floors. Sure, some buyers literally love these designs, but that doesn't make them art.

A hot rodder strips this mass-produced vehicle to its bare essentials, pumps the engine full of horsepower, and possibly adds a few innovative embellishments to mark it unmistakably as his hot rod—immediately identifiable as such at first sighting on the street. The customizer smooths and sleekens the factory body, removes excess ornamentation—especially brand emblems (again, to personalize and mystify the car)—lowers it as much as possible, and coats it in luscious, custom-mixed paint. Neither the hot rodder nor the customizer is an artist; what they do to their cars is a craft.

Of course, there's more to it than that. Hot rodding is a culture, with rites and customs that have been passed from generation to generation. In fact, from its beginnings in the early Depression years, hot rodding has had strong overtones of counterculture. Not being able to afford flashy new cars, the rodders stripped down cheap Model T and A Ford roadsters to make them lighter and faster, souped up the engines with homemade speed equipment, and then flaunted this speed on the street. The cars were fenderless, hoodless and topless; they were loud; and some were painted with flames or other menacing designs. Clubs formed with names such as Outriders, Low Flyers, Bungholers, Knight Riders and Sidewinders. Street racing was a common, dangerous, outlaw activity.

Naturally, hot rodding has evolved, engendered diverse offshoots and even gentrified over the past sixty years. But the culture is still core: do it yourself, make it better than—or at least different from—the mass-produced offerings, individualize it, be a renegade. Most cling to the outlaw image—some, like Robert Williams, more than others. All look to legends such as Von Dutch and Ed Roth for inspiration.

OK. What we have here has little to do with cars, but plenty to do with hot rod culture. Von Dutch turned the craft of pinstriping—used for centuries as ornamentation on furniture, musical instruments, carriages, bicycles and early motor vehicles—into a completely new, enigmatic and intriguing art form that did more than simply decorate hot rods and customs. Although he was a superb craftsman who restored motorcycles and built one-off vehicles, he was never known for building rods or customs of his own. Ed Roth started his career lettering and pinstriping hot rods, but made his fame—as far as rodders were concerned—from the amazing, hand-formed, fiberglass-bodied, bubble-topped cars that he built in the sixties. Although definitely hot rod inspired, these vehicles remain in a category completely unto themselves—nobody had conceived of anything remotely like them before or since. Although ostensibly functional, they were built strictly for display (some being undrivable). If any rods or customs approach rolling art, the Roth cars do. And Robert Williams, who began his career as a Roth employee drawing monster shirt designs and magazine ads, now brings hot rod culture directly to two- dimensional, oil-on-canvas art. His primered Deuce and chopped '34 are for escape.

Pat Ganahl is Senior Editor of *Rod & Custom* magazine

That's looking at it from a hot rod perspective. From an art viewpoint, there's an even more direct descent. Besides his baroque, freeform, pinstripe designs, Von Dutch sometimes painted small, grotesque, misshapen Hieronymus Bosch-type figures on the dashboard, nose or undercarriage of rods or race cars. He often included his signature flying eyeball, as well. Just as Von Dutch single-handedly created the hot rod style of pinstriping that bred countless imitators immediately and that continues to proliferate today, he was also the first, as far as I can tell, to paint these "weirdo" or "monster" figures on hot rods, customs and race cars. (Not incidentally, his witting weirdo demeanor was also adopted by the cadre of hot rod pinstripers, each of whom goes by something other than his real name. Also, you will notice in the famous photo of Von Dutch, with an eyeball pasted to his forehead, playing the flute in the back of his panel truck, that not only is the entire inside of his truck airbrush-painted with a manic design, but his shirt is also airbrushed with a design of triangles and circles (what you can't see is the large flying eyeball airbrushed on the back). As far as I know, Von Dutch was the first to airbrush anything, let alone weird designs, on shirts.

The one who popularized it to the point of creating a craze, though, was Ed "Big Daddy" Roth. Self-admittedly not much of an artistic technician, Roth would take his easel and airbrush and a pile of T-shirts to car shows where his latest vehicle was on display and dash off exaggerated cartoon-style monsters with giant heads popping out of zany coupes or roadsters with big supercharged engines and smoking rear tires. Eager customers snapped up the shirts—it was a way for Roth to pay his expenses while traveling around the country from show to show. He'd title the shirts "Wild Child" or "Mother's Worry," and the young rodders would wear them as further proof of their rebellious yet fun attitude. Soon the demand for Roth's monster shirts outstripped his airbrushing capacity, so he hired talented artists to ink new designs, which he silkscreened onto the shirts.

One of these artists was Robert Williams, who drove out to California in his 406, 4-speed Ford Galaxy to study at Chouinard Art Institute and who ended up working at the Roth Studios. He not only drew new T-shirt designs, but also created weird, rebellious, humorous and zany full-page Roth T-shirt ads for Car Craft magazine that are sixties classics. Williams didn't have to learn to draw hot rod weirdo monsters. Although his artistic influences are many, he will tell you that Von Dutch was one of the first. The hot rod culture has been part of Williams's life since he was a youngster. The fact that he drew T-shirt monsters for Ed Roth was probably more than coincidental. The influence of the hot rod weirdo/monster cult on Williams's current art is apparent; the influence of hot rod culture in general on his art work is more wide ranging.

I can't begin to explain hot rod culture here. Like most cultures, it must be lived or personally experienced to be properly understood. Von Dutch, Ed Roth and Robert Williams are all intimate with hot rod culture. Dutch and Roth—though each is eccentric within that culture—certainly helped define it. Art or artifact, their work will speak for itself. Whether this museum gets it right will remain to be seen.

Harvey Shaken By Cross Breeding

ORIGINS OF A SUB-SPECIES

By C.R. Stecyk

C.R. Stecyk is a Los Angeles artist.

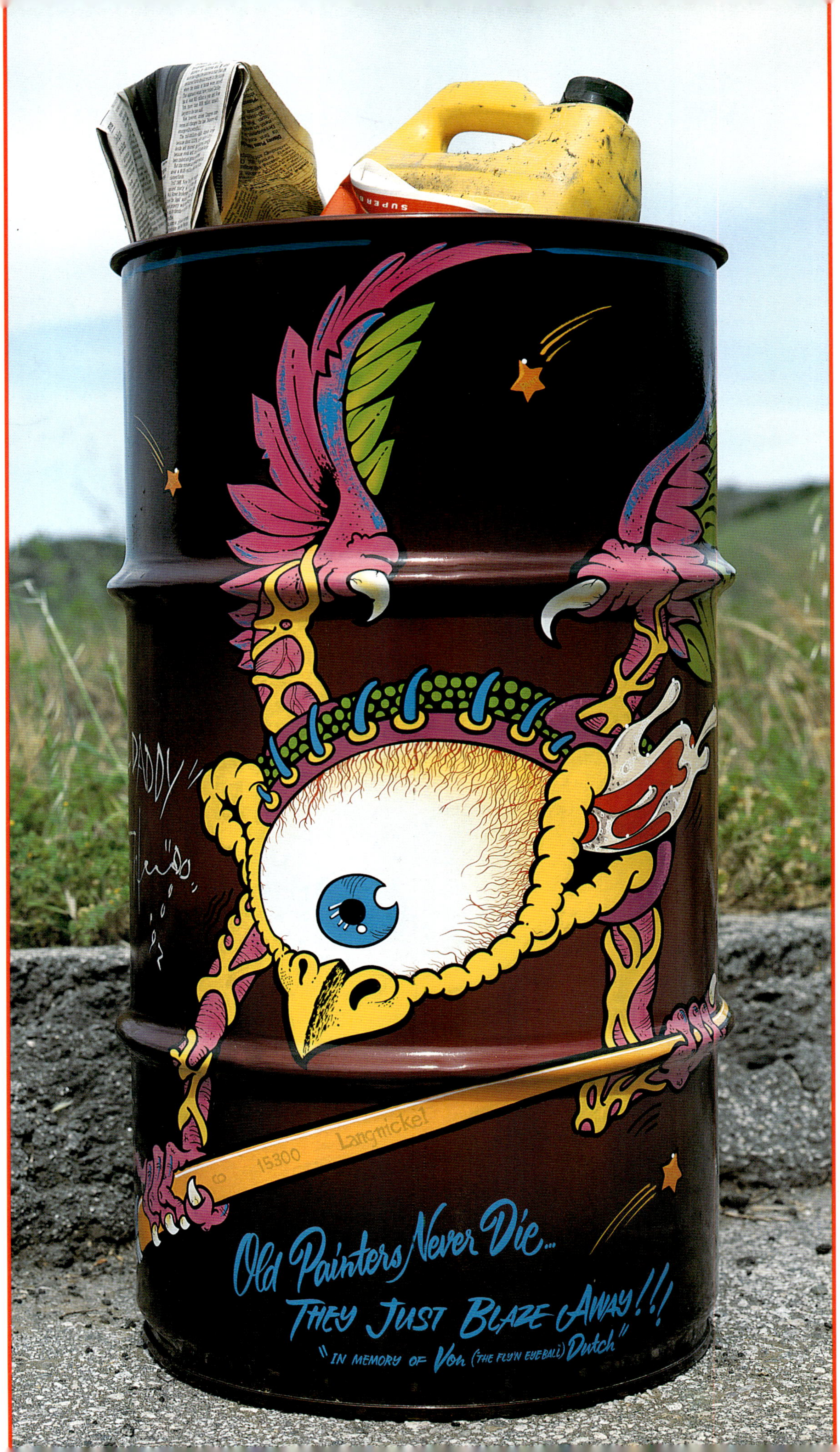

Dawn. 19 December 1992. Santa Fe Springs, California. Here in a suburban LA community the day's first light hits a chrome yellow building emblazoned with a pair of giant eyes. This is the home of Dean Moon's specialty hot rod equipment company. In the parking lot, Ed "Big Daddy" Roth awakens from his slumber in the front seat of the red Peterbilt minitruck. Ed likes to live on the road. He never stays in a hotel 'cause he feels it isolates him from the veracity of the travel experience. Besides, it saves money and Roth is, above all, practical.

Today's BDR enterprise is the Rat Fink Reunion, an annual charity benefit that Roth hosts. The Reunion is, in equal parts, a gathering of the tribes and an industrial spectacle. By noon hundreds of rods and customs line the streets for blocks in any direction. The range of vehicles is astounding. World class leadsleds sit side by side with primered A-Bone beaters, such arcana as 1965 Harley Davidson motor scooters, and obvious icons like the Jocko's Porting Streamliner. It's street theater, and uninitiated passersbys stare in slack-jawed wonder.

Many prominent personages from the modified car world can be seen here joining with Roth in an informal art/jam session to create works that will be auctioned off to benefit the Shriners Children's Hospital. The event is noteworthy for several reasons. The reputation of the Rat Fink get together brings in hundreds of individuals. The guest list boasts notable types from Southern California's various counter cultures: artists, film makers, politicians, real estate moguls, movie stars, industrial designers, welders, machinists, engineers, body men, sheet metal fabricators, mechanics—this is an audience of aficionados, and the accent is on excellence in execution. And, in a throwback, Big Daddy feeds everyone for free.

If one were to employ standard anthropological methodology, establishing the existence of shared cultural values, distinctive clothing, oral historical narratives, unique iconography and communicated beliefs, it would be apparent that the RF party qualifies as a clan ceremony. Now, when such things occur out in some sweaty tropical paradise, the czars of cultural anthropology tend to get real worked up over it all. But this is the good 'ole USA and a situation like the Reunion is dismissed as mere hot rod hi-jinx. Such rejection, if anything, would just serve to make it all better—a poll of those present would reveal a general mistrust of the workings of the alleged cultural hierarchy. For example, merely mention the fine art scene and you'll hear cursing about the canonization of the technically inept. In this social structure, deed is far more persuasive than the wordy ramblings of any self-promoters. Here the collective assessment of the peer group determines the pecking order; one cannot buy, bluff or blitz his way onto the acropolis.

Ed Roth had stature among this group years before Tom Wolfe extolled his virtues in *The Kandy-Kolored Tangerine-Flake Streamline Baby*. Robert Williams was recognized by these cognoscenti as a brilliant social satirist long before his accreditation by LA's Museum of Contemporary Art. Today Williams is in attendance at the RF convocation. Von Dutch, the paterfamilias of the auto-as-art movement, is not. He died two months ago as a result of complications caused by cirrhosis of the liver.

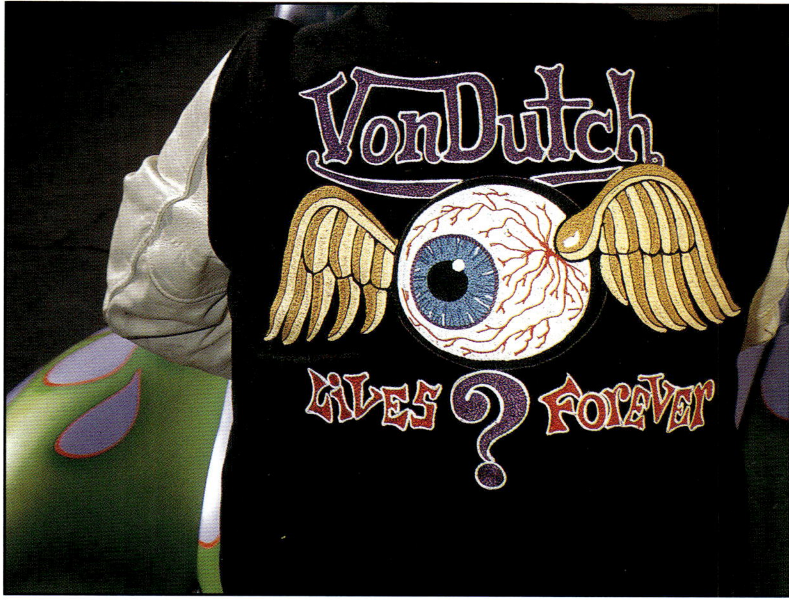

Franco Costanzo's embroidered jacket tribute to Von Dutch at the 1992 Rat Fink Reunion.

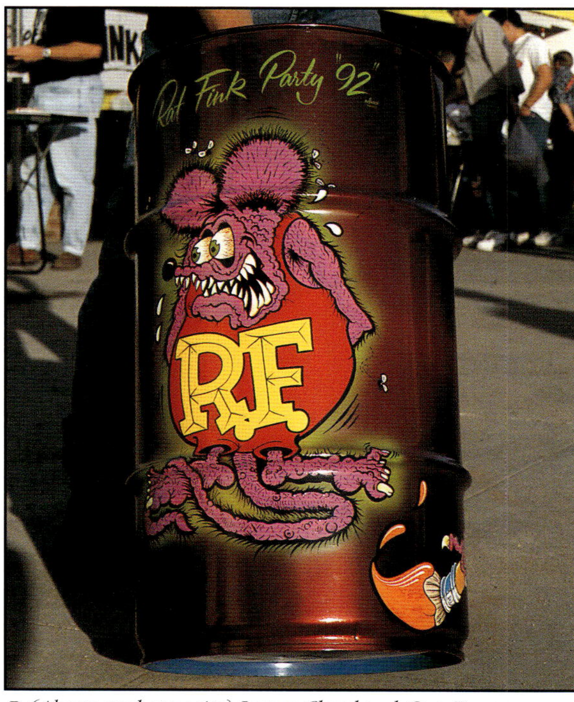

✠ *(Above and opposite) James Cleveland,* OLD PAINTERS NEVER DIE...THEY JUST BLAZE AWAY!!! (IN MEMORY OF VON "THE FLY'N EYEBALL" DUTCH), *1992 (enamel on oil drum, 27 x 14¾ dia. in.; collection of Greg and Kristin Escalante).*

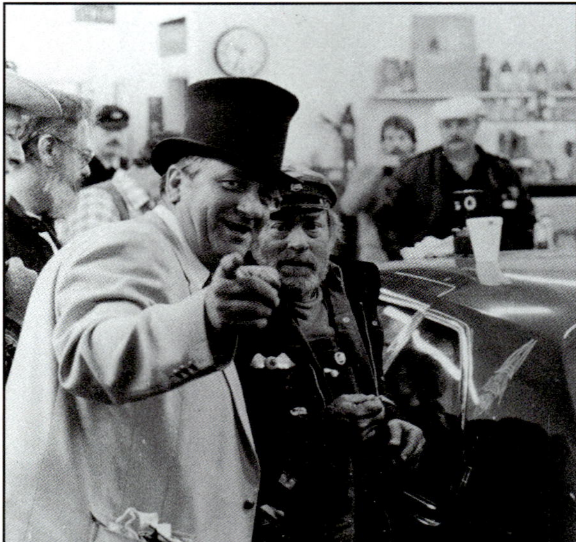

Ed Roth and Von Dutch at 1987 Rat Fink Reunion. Photo by Pat Ganahl.

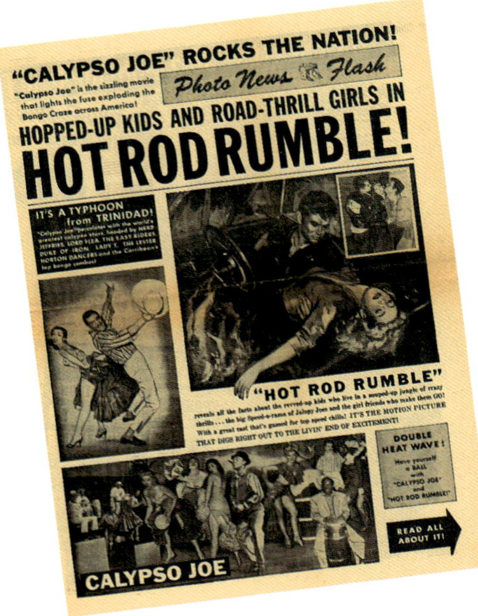

"CALYPSO JOE" ROCKS THE NATION!

"Calypso Joe" is the sizzling movie that lights the fuse exploding the Bongo Craze across America!

Photo News Flash

HOPPED-UP KIDS AND ROAD-THRILL GIRLS IN

HOT ROD RUMBLE!

IT'S A TYPHOON from TRINIDAD!

"Calypso Joe" percolates with the world's greatest calypso stars, headed by HERB JEFFRIES, LORD FLEA, THE EASY RIDERS, DUKE OF IRON, LADY T, THE LESTER HORTON DANCERS and the Carribean's top bongo combos!

"HOT ROD RUMBLE"

reveals all the facts about the revved-up kids who live in a souped-up jungle of crazy thrills . . . the big Speed-o-rama of Jalopy Joes and the girl friends who make them GO! With a great cast that's geared for top speed chills! IT'S THE MOTION PICTURE THAT DIGS RIGHT OUT TO THE LIVIN' END OF EXCITEMENT!

DOUBLE HEAT WAVE! Have yourself a BALL with "CALYPSO JOE" and "HOT ROD RUMBLE!"

READ ALL ABOUT IT!

CALYPSO JOE

Promotional tabloid for teen exploitation film Hot Rod Rumble, *1950s.*

(Opposite) Von Dutch, Hollywood, California, mid-1950s. Photo courtesy Rod and Custom.

Dutch lived hard and he died harder. During the last couple years of his life he dealt with a rupture in his abdominal wall. The dripping fistula he carried around was a visual indication of the man's constant pain and physical distress. Von Dutch worked on his art constantly up to the end and he never lost his mental acuity. Those present at his deathbed report that he maintained his sense of humor right up to the end. Despite the incredible pain, Dutch never whimpered or allowed himself to be attended by a doctor. As he told me a couple of weeks before he finally succumbed, "I put myself into this condition and I'll get out of it or die trying."

It is an unspoken fact that this Rat Fink event is dedicated to the fallen master. Without Von Dutch's virtuosity, none of this would ever have happened. He was the first, he was the best, and he was an utter original. The philosophy that Dutch espoused—for example, his often repeated assertion that "the work is all that matters"—and his conspicuous avoidance of the limelight are at the core of this group's psyche.

On this crisp, cool Saturday no one could fail to be impressed by the abundant demonstrations of remarkable technical skills—the Von Dutch heritage—as the painters execute quick, off-hand works around the barbecue area with a decided absence of pretense. Consider the toilet seat pinstriped by Bob Bond: could anyone listed in *Who's Who in American Art* even come close to equaling the economy of line, the sense of proportion, the implied movement and its lyrical perfection? Forget the conceptualized rhetoric of the minimal masters. This is work done for the sheer joy of it. How about Jimmy Cleveland's trash can? Think any of the New Image or Neo Geo types could touch this? Check out the paint handling and the overt image overload.

Is any of this really art? I've been asked the same about my own work. When I try to explain, I'm told, "Oh, yeah, that's right, you're from California." Blame it on the Left Coast.

World War II created a high technology economic base in California when military and defense contractors set up shop to take advantage of a benign climate that would allow year-round manufacturing. The state's strategic location in relation to the Pacific theater of war also helped to bring California into political prominence.

The presence of numerous facilities for building military aircraft, ships and vehicles created massive employment opportunities. Young workers flocked to the region, lured by the high paying jobs. In the plants, these workers accumulated skills in metal fabrication, welding and machining; they were also exposed to such revolutionary new materials as plastics and exotic metals.

The employees built up their bank accounts, but could find little to spend their money on due to wartime shortages of consumer goods. Cars were a priority item on everyone's list, since civilian auto production had been halted at the beginning of the conflict. A new car connoted luxury, status and the return to peacetime normalcy. Using skills honed in the defense plants, some workers began extensively modifying old cars to create something new and different. These efforts, combined with the longstanding practice of "hopping up" a car to radically increase its speed, performance and handling capabilities, marked the beginning of the modified vehicle trend. In the years following World War II the hot rod and custom craze would first sweep the nation, and eventually the world.

Though the development of the automobile had been largely an international affair, America's contributions, beginning with the work of Eli Whitney, the inventor of interchangeable parts, and Henry Ford, the pioneer of the moving assembly line, helped to create a modern automobile industry.

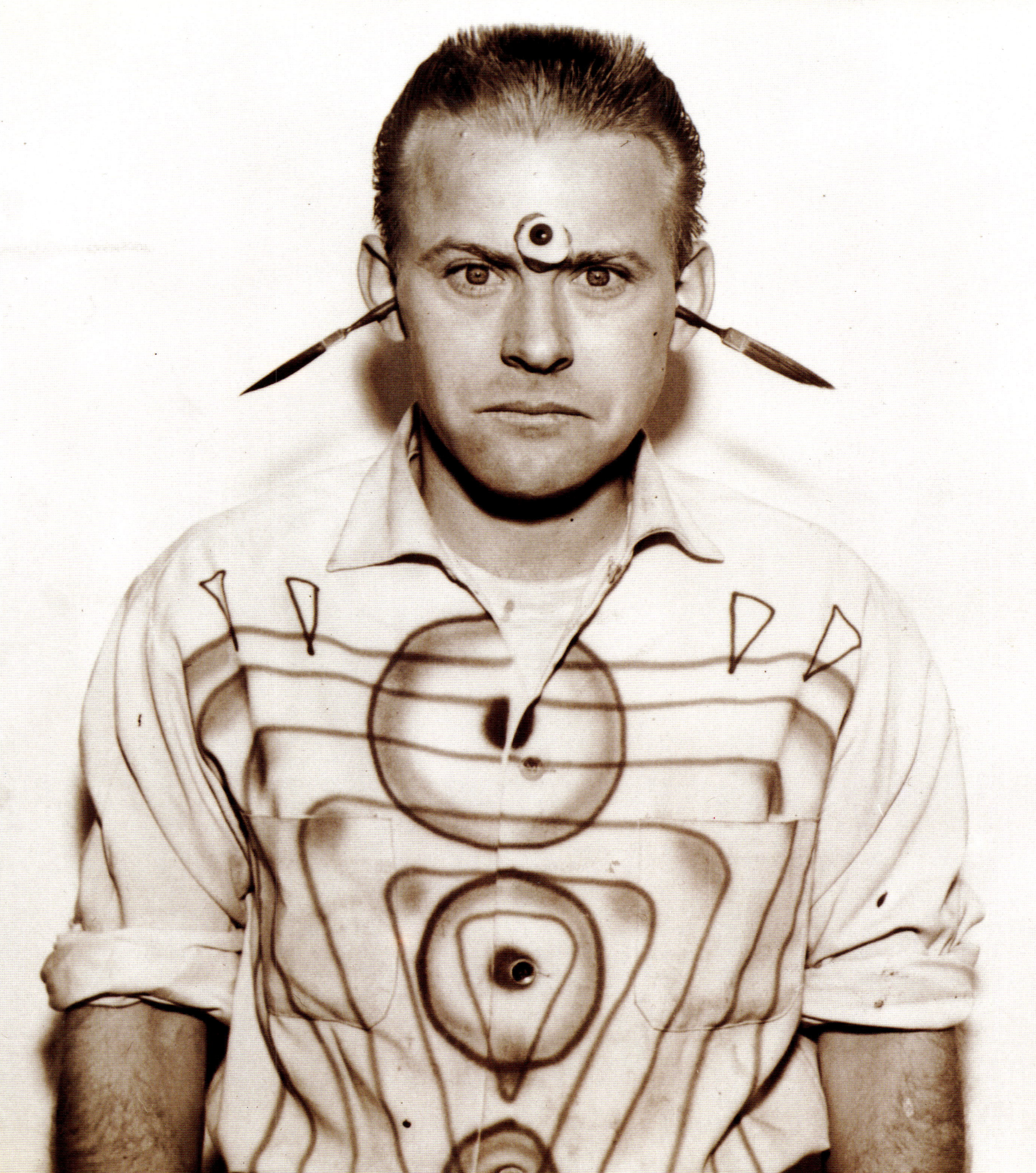

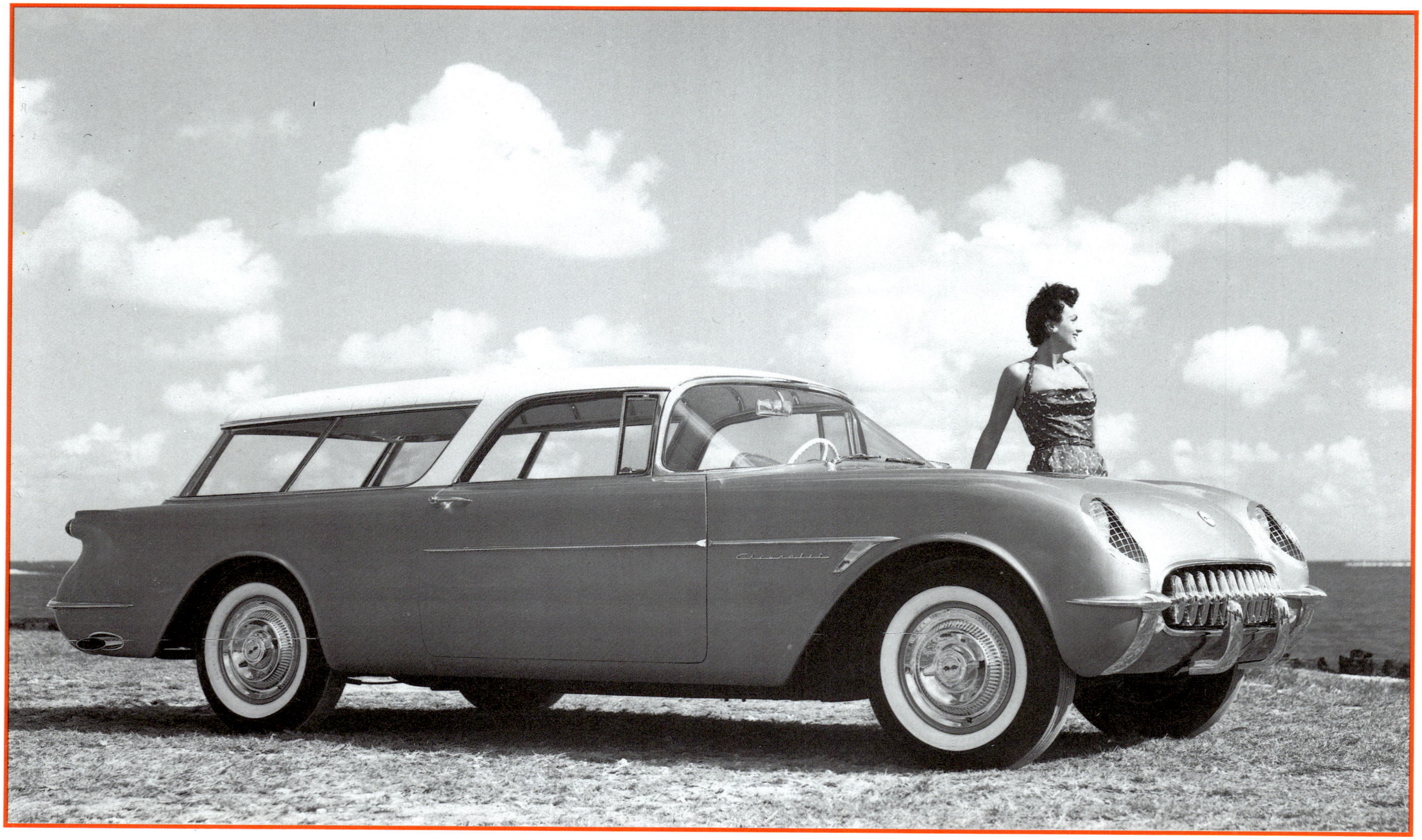

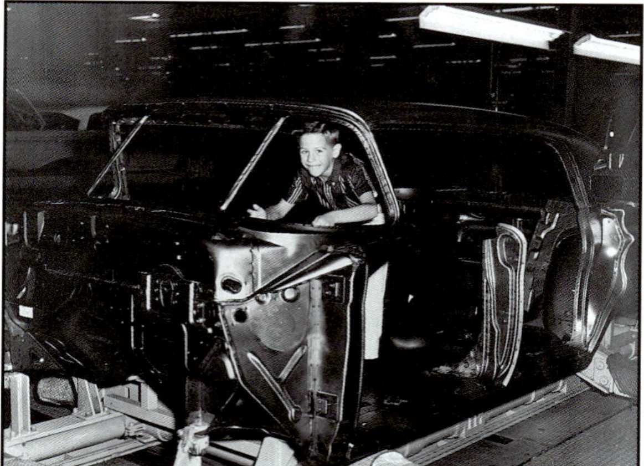

Author C.R. Stecyk on the assembly line in 1957 at the Lincoln-Mercury plant in Lynwood, California. Photo by Milton Curtis.

Prior to these innovations, only the wealthy could afford the exclusive, entirely hand-built motorized conveyances. Ford created the mass market with the hegemony of his Model T. Inauguration of the five-dollar-a-day wage enabled his workers to afford the products that they worked on. To Ford, the beauty of the Model T lay in the perfection of endless replication. The more he produced, the cheaper he could sell them. Any unnecessary changes in production were to be avoided because they impeded efficiency. Ford theorized that by continually lowering the cost of his utilitarian Model T design he would achieve perpetual sales. Eventually, his avoidance of cosmetic alterations created massive opportunities in the marketplace.

By 1925 the majority of auto owners were coming around to purchasing their second car. The General Motors Corporation began to cater to the desires of this more discerning market. Under Alfred P. Sloan, the head of the corporation, GM's plan was to offer a distinctive range of vehicles attractive to all buyers, from the farm boy to the millionaire. Ford continued to build his generic Model Ts, while the General Motors combine aggressively used style and color as the cornerstone of its marketing strategy. As Henry Ford uttered the famous words, "Give them any color they want as long as it's black," GM searched for ways to make its products more attractive to the consumer. To this end, the corporation discovered and

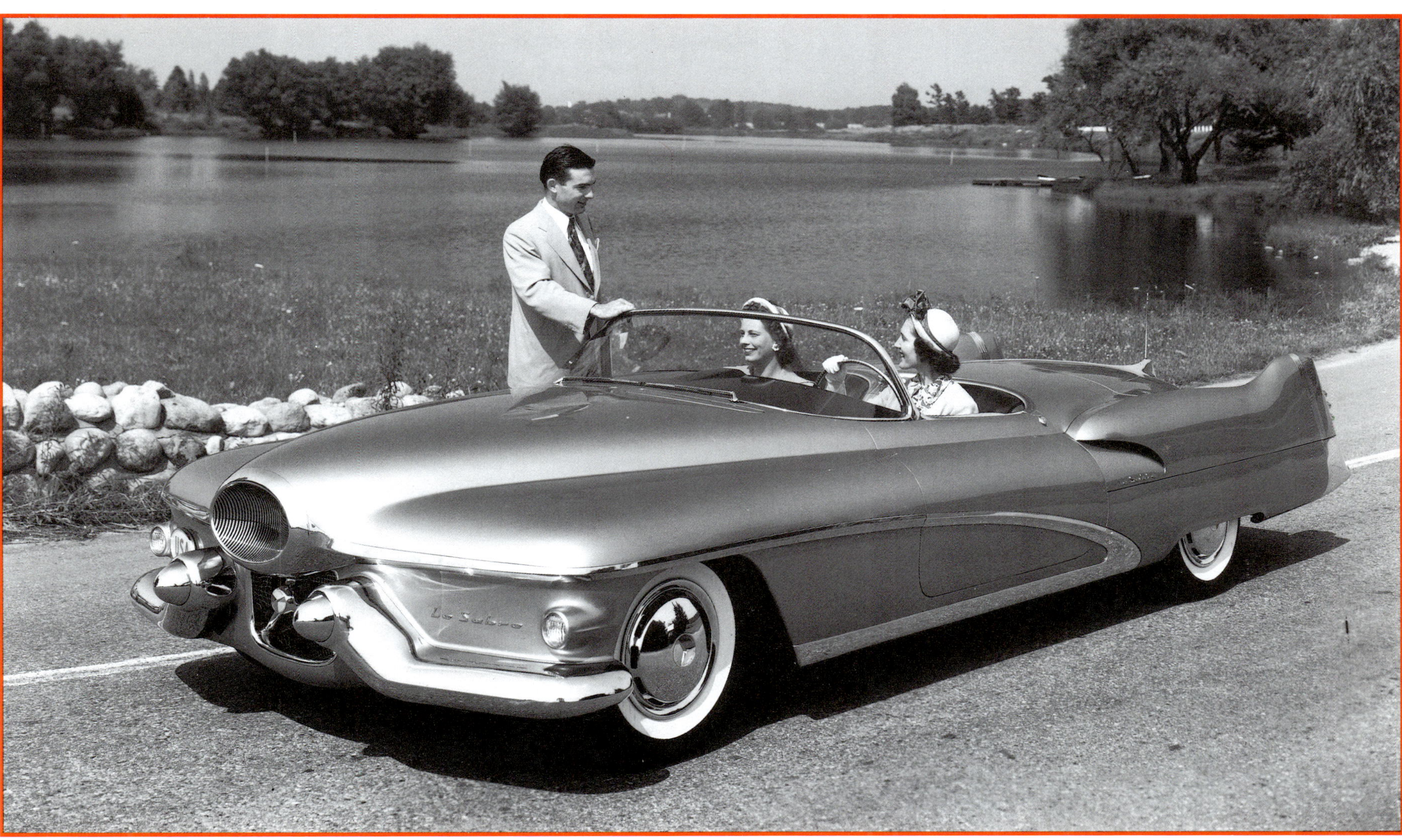

nurtured the work of a young automotive stylist in Los Angeles, Harley D. Earl.

In the initial stages of the horseless carriage business, most of the fabricators were wagon and coach makers. Studebaker, for example, was a firm that successfully transitioned from building prairie schooner wagons to crafting modern motorcars. The Earl Carriage Works started as a small wagon building concern located on Main Street in downtown LA. Eventually, the presence of the movie industry in Hollywood provided the Earl company a market for movie props. Another sideline was making fuselages for the Martin Aircraft company.

Harley Earl had grown up in this family business and he was a naturally talented designer. Young Earl began styling custom bodies for autos as a replacement for the clunky, wagonlike, stock bodies of the day. Eventually these works attracted a luxury clientele, largely composed of the Hollywood elite. Western film star Tom Mix commissioned Harley to design a long, low, sport runabout that featured the cowboy star's brand, cowhide covered seats and swooping cattle longhorns mounted on the radiator shell. Roscoe "Fatty" Arbuckle paid $28,000 for his Earl custom.

In time, General Motors lured the young man to Detroit and set him up as the chief designer. Harley Earl thus became history's first professional auto designer. GM under Earl's reign was the source of many of

(Opposite, top) Early 1950s design exercise by Harley Earl for General Motors. This vehicle presages both the later Corvette and Chevrolet Nomad Sport Wagon.

(Above) The 1951 Le Sabre show car was a particular favorite of its designer, Harley Earl, who used it for his personal transportation. Photos reprinted with permission of General Motors Corporation.

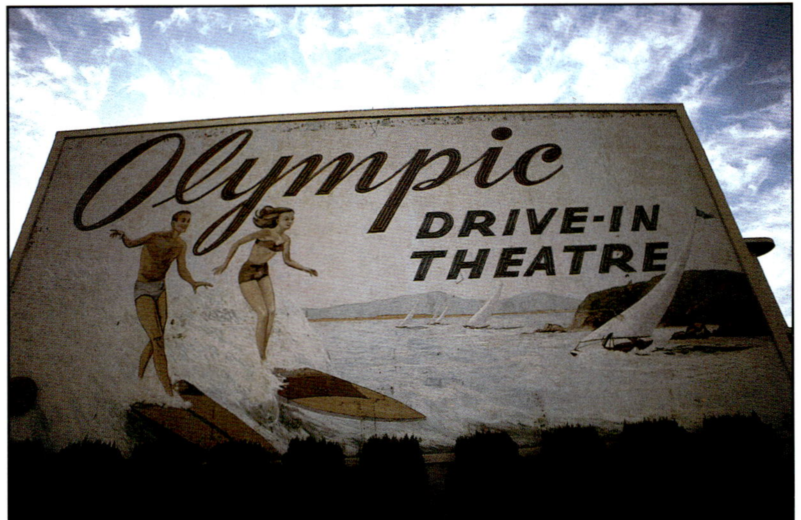

The Olympic Drive-in Theatre in West Los Angeles featured this mural tribute to California kitsch. The now-defunct Olympic is generally regarded as the world's first drive-in movie theater.

the clichés of car design that we take for granted today. Chrome-laden behemoths, two-tone paint schemes, wraparound windshields, the hardtop and the tail fin were all pioneered by Harley Earl.

The fact that Earl sprang forth from Los Angeles is significant. Detroit's earlier *de facto* designers were mired in the rigid precepts of the manufacturing process. Earl represents the freedom, glamour, and upstart braggadocio of Hollywood. Where else were there people with incredible financial resources whose very existence required the mounting of conspicuous displays? (And what better way was there to draw attention to one's status and stardom than by arriving in a sumptuously opulent motorcar?) The greater LA basin was populated by those who daily witnessed fantasy as reality. Movie crews were constantly working in the streets, where they could be readily observed making the present the historical past or imagined future. The locals enthusiastically sought out eccentric behavior and bizarre product as a matter of course. Just a tour of the city's major thoroughfares was a trip to Fantasyland, years before Walt. Olympic Boulevard, for example, passed through the Twentieth Century Fox back lot. Here, in a four block stretch, the driver would experience King Arthur's Camelot, the Wild West, the Arctic wilderness, New York City and the future of Buck Rogers. D.W. Griffith's set of Babylon towered over the small wood framed bungalows of Hollywood; when David O. Selznick torched the back lot in Culver City for *Gone with the Wind*, the conflagration was visible in the night sky from any point in LA. To stand out in this environment, you needed a little more flash. Harley Earl produced it in spades. After conquering the streets of Tinseltown, the highways of America were child's play.

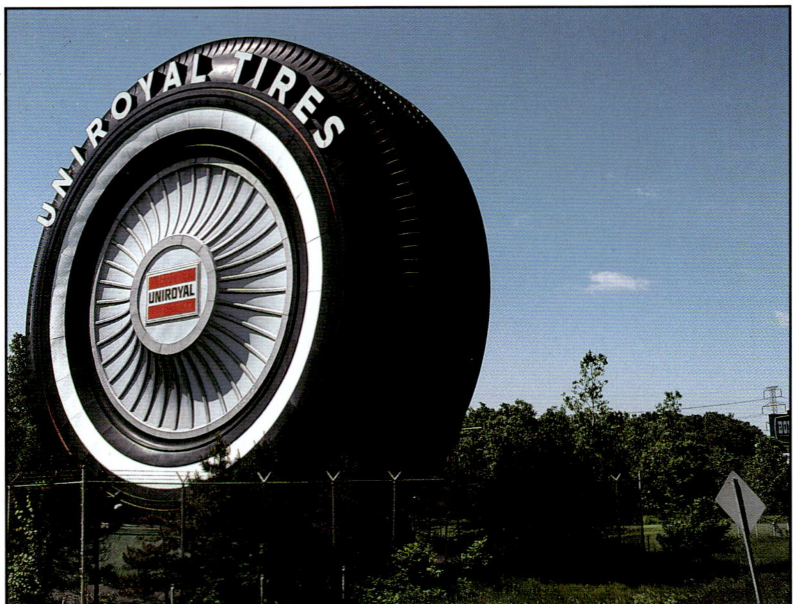

Programmatic advertising on the highway, Detroit, Michigan, 1975.

From the emergence of Earl on, Los Angeles has been the center of the modified auto world. LA was the first major city largely designed around the automobile. Its extensive roadway construction projects provided endless avenues for motorized pleasure. Local oil baron Earl Gilmore created the first service station when he went down to the dirt road that was to become Wilshire Boulevard and sold his first bucket of gas to a passing motorist. Gilmore would later construct a large auto racing track and sponsor numerous car entries in the Indianapolis 500. The Olympic Drive-In Theatre was another LA

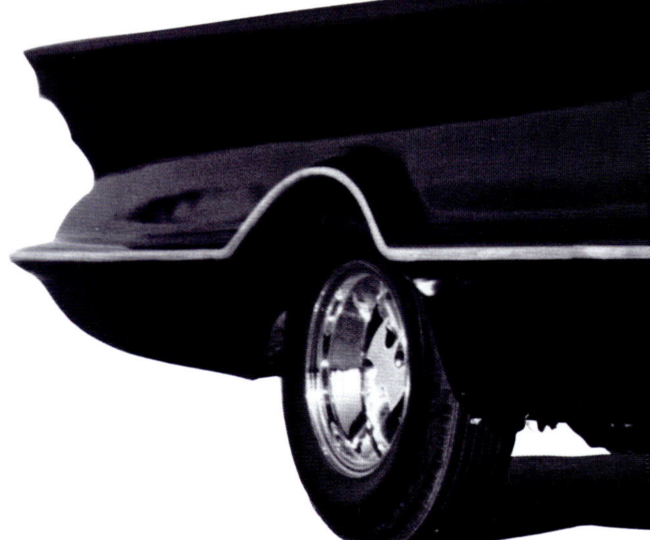

auto first. Entertainment could now be had without ever vacating one's car. Dry cleaners, churches, eateries, dairies, etc. would soon offer Angelenos drive-in services. Programmatic designs in which a building's form reflected its function were created to make such structures more easily visible to customers whizzing past at sixty miles per hour. Who could fail to grasp the purpose of a Paul Bunyan-scaled donut building selling donuts, or a camera-shaped facade fronting film supplies?

After World War II, Los Angeles underwent a period of tremendous expansion. The So-Cal economic environment was healthy due to a population boom of ex-GIs seeking the good life. The embryonic aerospace industry and the more established entertainment industries were augmented by a real estate boom. Local businessmen worked overtime providing goods and services to this dynamic new market.

America after the war was psychologically buoyed by its tremendous victory. As the stewards of the new social order settled in, they devoted their lives to making up for time lost during the conflict. The V8 luxury offered by Detroit was considered an inalienable right. Men and women had fought and died for the right to possess chrome. Lady Liberty had transformed herself into a winged-goddess hood ornament.

This obsession with the auto was at its most extreme in LA. Many specialty automotive firms developed to cater to those who demanded more than the industrial giants could provide. Some of the more noteworthy customizers and specialty shops included the Barris Brothers, Carson Auto Tops, Coach Craft, Valley Custom (Neil Emory and Clay Jensen), the Ayala Brothers, Dean Jefferies, Larry Watson, Iskendarian Cams, Vic Edelrock and the Moon Equipment Company.

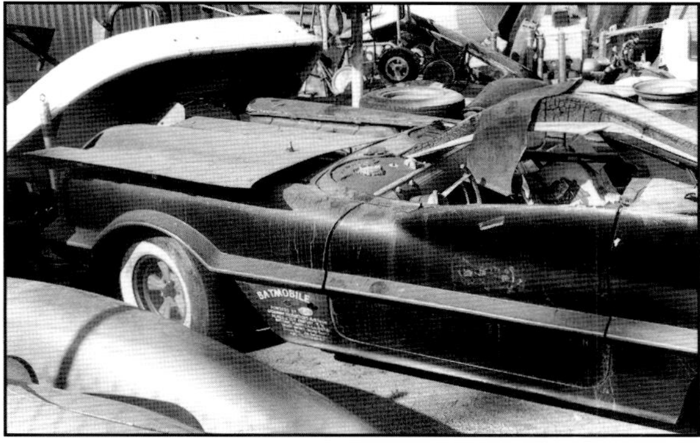

Two views of the Batmobile: (above) the remains behind the Barris Kustom Industries shop in 1978; (below) on the set of the television series in 1966.
Photo courtesy George Barris.

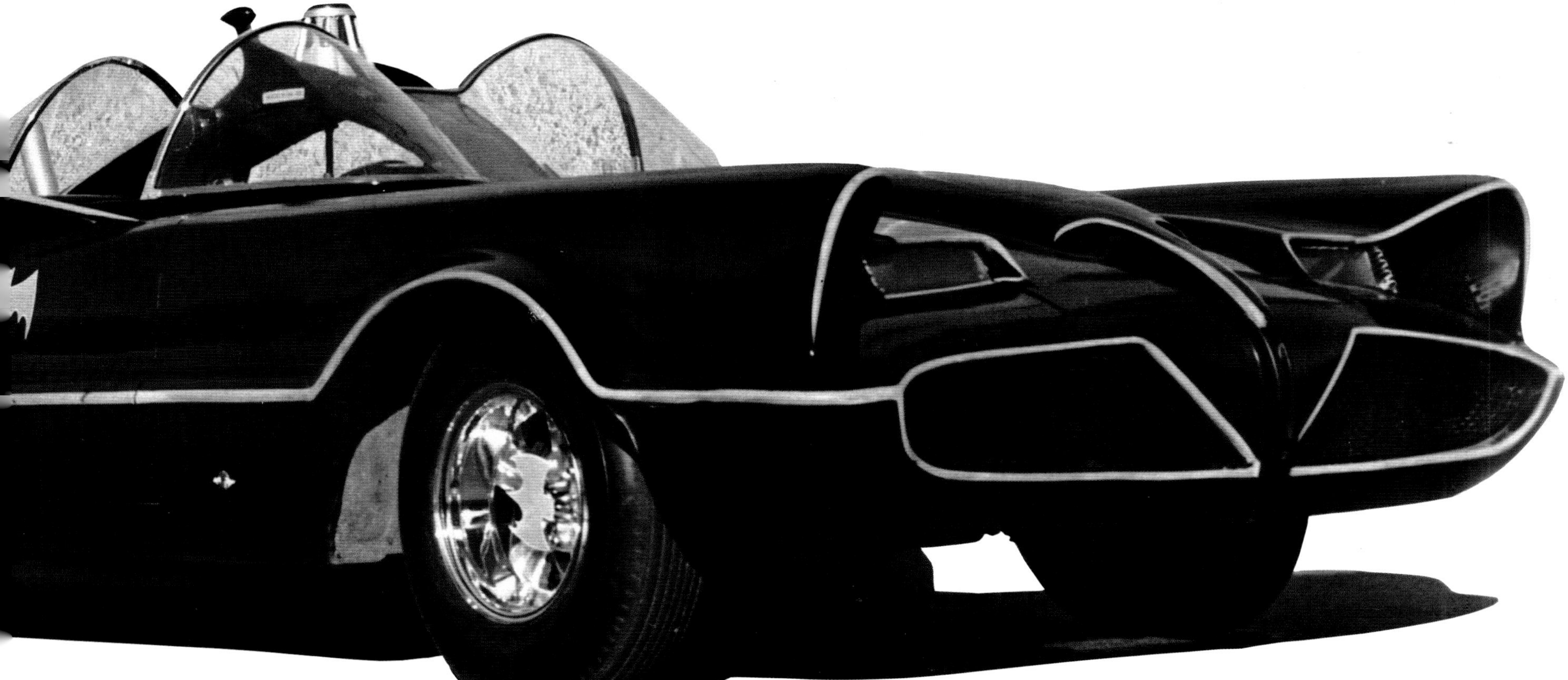

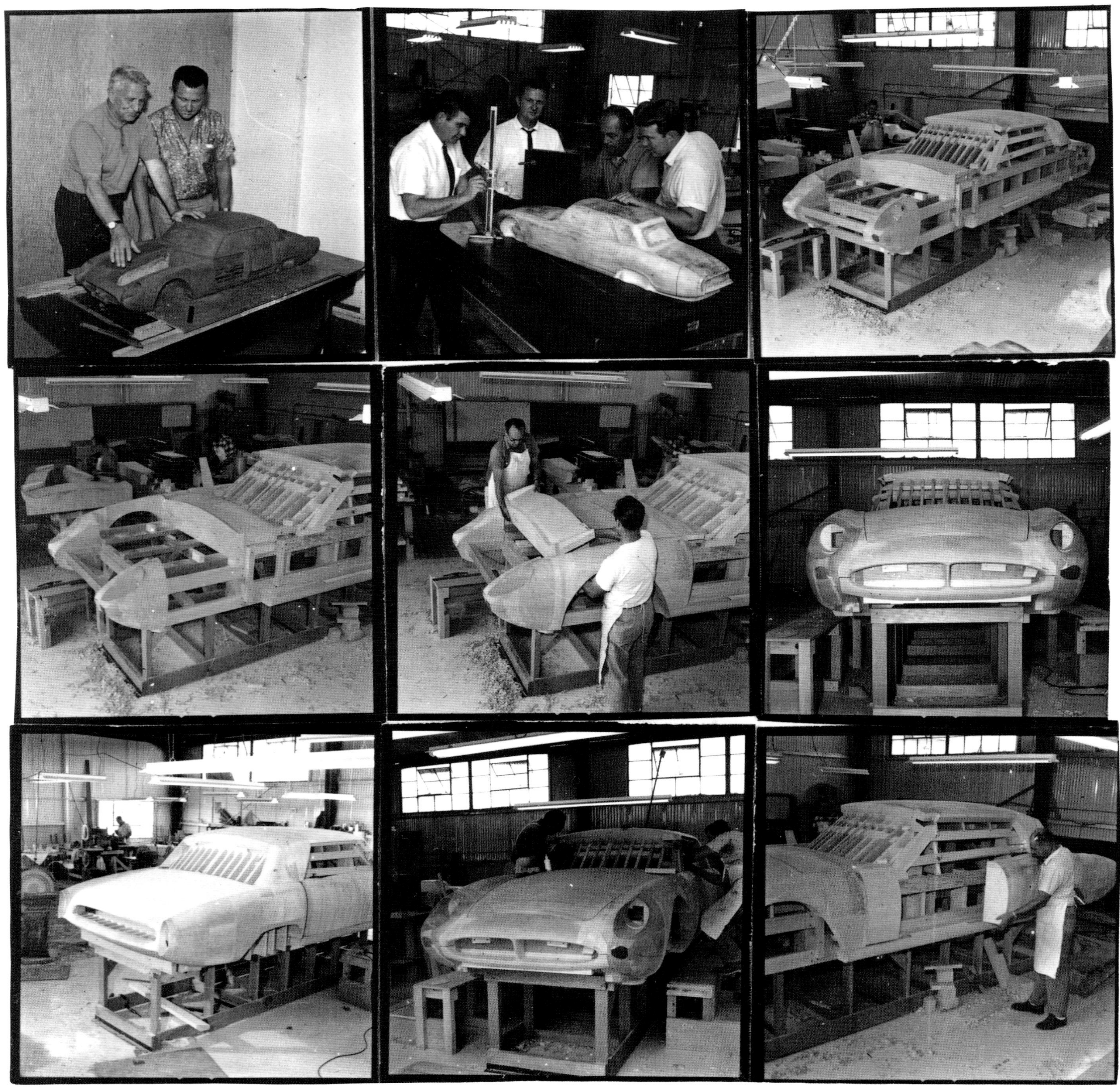

Other area stylists like Howard "Dutch" Darrin (no relation to Von Dutch) were more oriented to the well-heeled customer. Darrin's "salon" served individuals such as Errol Flynn, the Rothschilds and the King of Spain, in addition to corporations like Packard, Willys, Jeep, Citröen and Kaiser. Elsewhere in the Golden State similar interests thrived. Joe Bailon operated out of Hayward, Frank De Rosa worked near Pittsburgh, Gene Winfield customized in Modesto and Joe Wilhelm labored in San Jose. These individuals, much like the Barris and Ayala Brothers, carried forth the implicit direction of 1940s West Coast restyling masters Harry Westergard, Jimmy Summers and Linc Paola, as well as the industrial impresarios Earl and Darrin.

Early on in the field of custom painting, Von Dutch set the standards—he literally invented the form. In the sculpting of "one-off" show cars, the highest art of the auto world, Ed Roth had no equals. Later, after serving an apprenticeship with Roth and also working with Von Dutch, Robert Williams became recognized as the foremost fine art chronicler of the rod world. Civilized society has been fundamentally impacted by the labors and viewpoints of these men.

The work of Von Dutch, Roth and Williams shares both a high respect for craftsmanship and a certain hard-edged, cynical bent. If this were an art historical diatribe it would be easy to equate their efforts to a number of recognized personages. I suppose the Roth studio, with its collaborative work environment, would be the nitro-injected, twentieth-century version of the Della Robbia atelier.

The hideously distorted figures produced by the trio would most resemble the Ghost of Carravagio being buggered by Basil Wolverton. The broadening of focus common to Von Dutch, Roth and Williams could be correlated to the work of Pierre Auguste Renoir and Jean Renoir: just as papa R's impressionism became the son's *cinema verité* stylization, Von Dutch's linear iconoclasm begot Roth's exuberant automotive forms, which in turn led to Williams's exaggerated commentaries on his life and times. Similarly, just as the work of the second Renoir evolved beyond the confines of the art world, the triad's innovations gradually fanned out from its nuclear automotive audience to entangle popular culture. But whereas both Renoirs pay homage to the formulas of fine art, our three have continually attempted to sidestep it.

In the early 1950s a La Cienega gallery wanted to represent Von Dutch's surrealistic oil paintings. At first open to the possibility, Dutch put a couple of pieces on display. One immediately sold. As he later recalled, "It was a completely nonsensical thing, just something I had made up that didn't have any meaning at all. The lady that bought it asked me to explain the story of the painting. I made up the biggest line of ridiculous crap I could think of and laid it out for her. She lapped it all up and believed every word. I knew then and there that the art scene was just bullshit. I left the gallery and never again had anything to do with any of it." To the end, Von Dutch was committed purely to his own aesthetic satisfaction. He contended that all ideas come from some great collective subconscious. Execution was perfection and that was the be all and end all. In 1984 he lamented to Ed Roth, "Although Picasso dug my stuff I always felt guilty that I couldn't find anything nice to say about his." Above all else, Dutch was honest, even if one of his frequent factual assessments would almost certainly lead to social ostracism. Von Dutch never chased a dollar and he never allowed money to chase him either. He remained pure to his ironclad convictions.

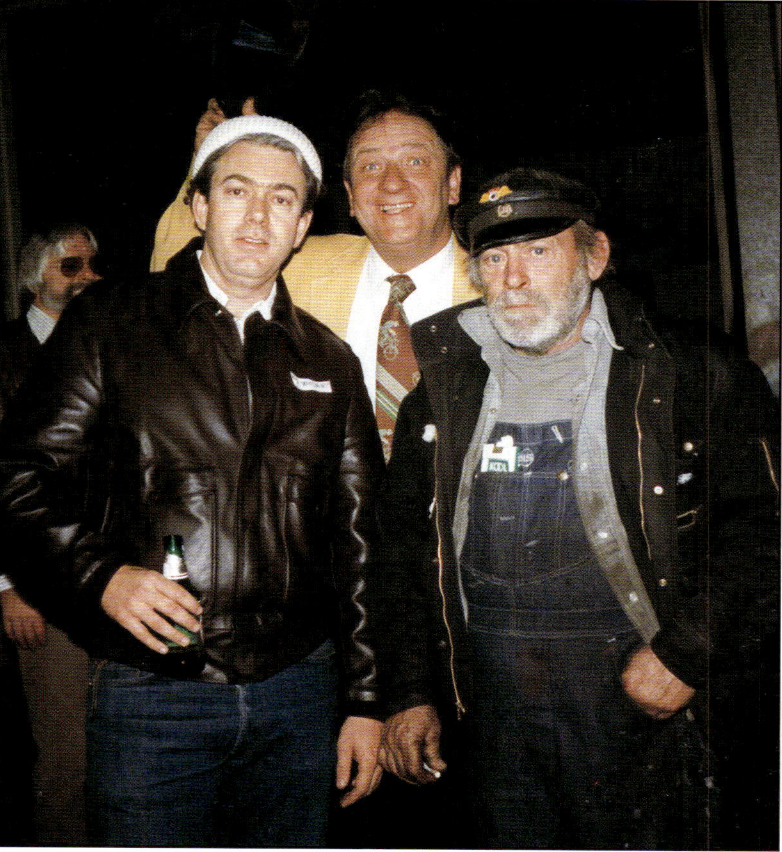

Williams, Roth and Von Dutch at 1985 Rat Fink Reunion. Photo by Suzanne Williams.

(Opposite) Howard A. Darrin's automotive styling salon, mid-1950s. Photo courtesy Pat Darrin.

Von Dutch

Von Dutch automotive graphic, 1950s.

Von Dutch was born Kenneth Howard in Los Angeles on 7 September 1929. His father, Wally, was a well respected sign painter who had created the famous Western Exterminator logo. The senior Howard was also on call to gold leaf the names on the doors of LA's City Hall. By the age of ten the younger Howard was able to paint and letter on a professional level. The nickname "Dutch" was given him early on by family members, who found him "stubborn as a Dutchman." Living in the suburb of Compton, Von Dutch was exposed to numerous influences. As a youth he would bring bits of tile and broken bottles for Simon Rodia to use in building the Watts Towers folk art environment. Local nightclubs in the area such as the Barrel House were showcases for the then-emergent musical form of modern jazz. (Throughout his life, Von Dutch was an avid music aficionado and an accomplished flautist.)

At Compton High School, he excelled in track and field and later recalled being called "the fastest man in LA."

Artistically he astounded all watchers with his seemingly innate technical proficiency. By the late-1930s he had developed a personal logo—the flying eyeball. His first professional striping job came as the result of a bet. A motorcycle at Birops Shop, where he worked as a cleanup boy, required painting. Figuring that he'd seen his dad paint signs often enough, the brash youth volunteered to stripe the cycle. With paint and a brush from his father's tool box, he returned after hours and painted the motorbike by himself. The next day, when the shop opened, no one believed that the job had been done by a kid. Von Dutch bet that he could execute another one while they watched. He did, and pinstriping was never the same again.

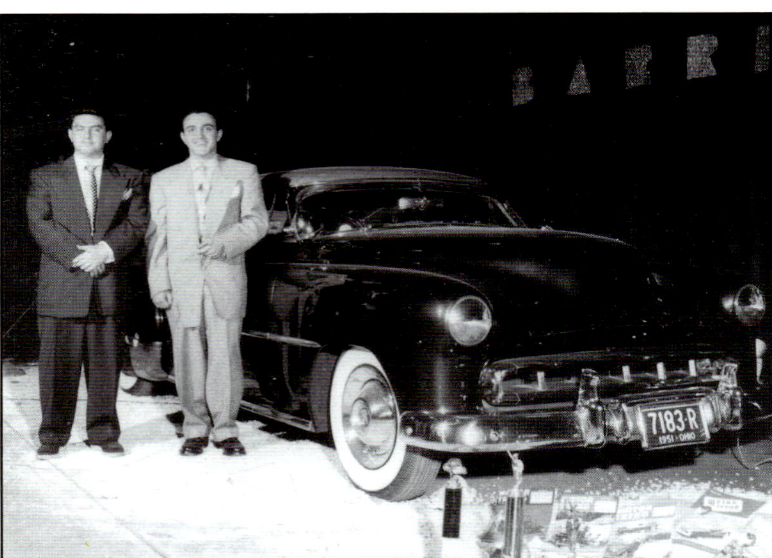

Sam and George Barris with an example of their work at an auto show, 1950. Photo courtesy Greg Sharp.

The art of pinstriping dates back to the Egyptians. The Romans striped their chariots. In the modern world, pinstriping has been used to accent numerous products, ranging from bicycles to safes to sewing machines. On these items the lines formed a static "frame" or followed an obvious contour, such as along the edge of a bicycle fender. Von Dutch was the first person to introduce freestyle, overall, programmatic pinstriping to the hot rod world.

"The whole idea of striping," Dutch once said,

> "is to make a vehicle look better, not to demonstrate the striper's ability. The finished appearance or personalization is what's important. What I did for the custom car was to develop modern pinstriping. Not only was I one of the original guys who were experimenting, but I was the first one to develop a distinctive and original style. My striping was the first modern technique to be really popular. As a matter of fact, there was a time when if you wanted your car custom-striped, you would ask for it to be "Dutched."
>
> My particular style of pinstriping sort of grew out of necessity. I was working for George Barris at the time. He does excellent work. Always has. But there were other customizers

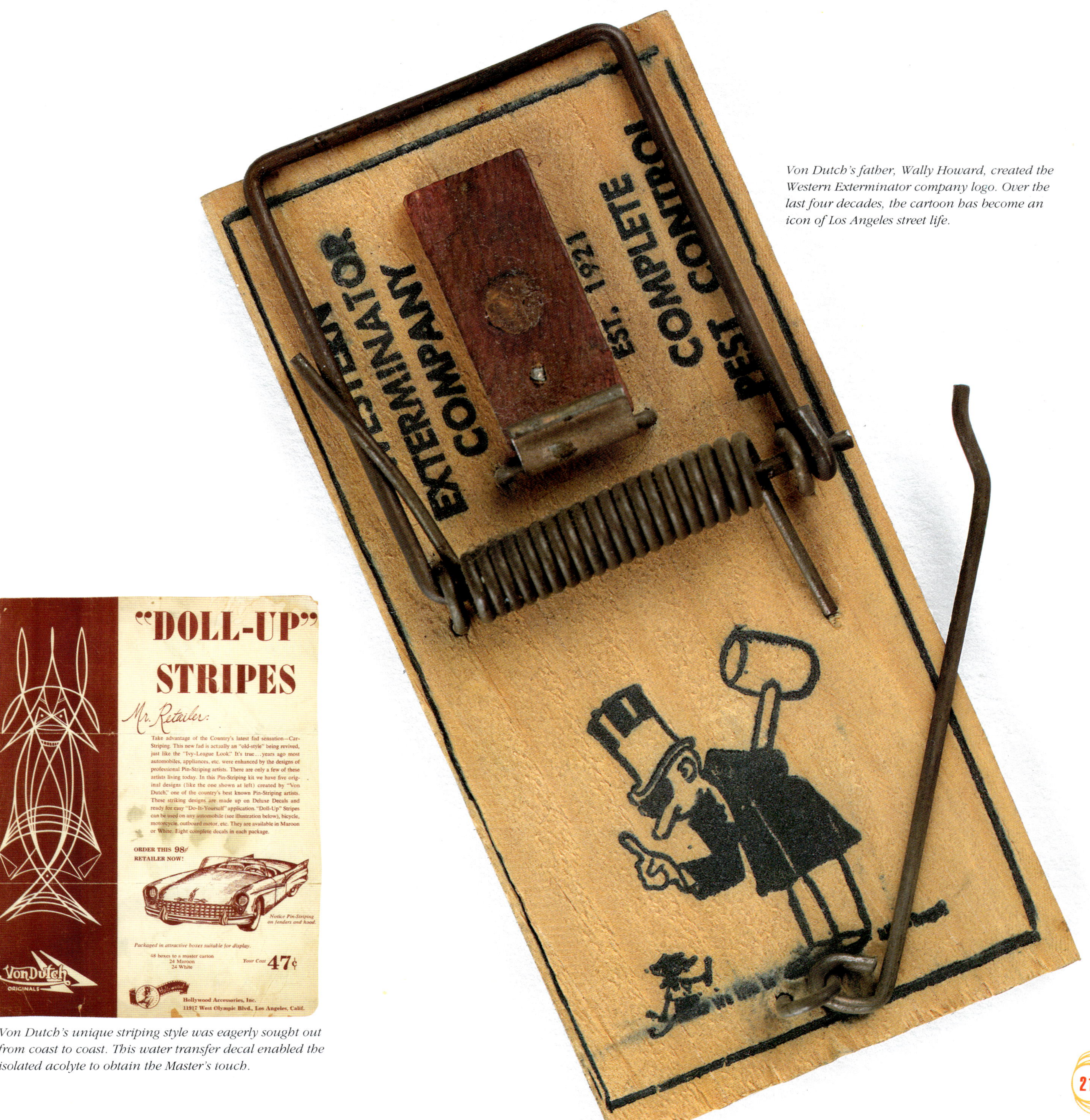

Von Dutch's father, Wally Howard, created the Western Exterminator company logo. Over the last four decades, the cartoon has become an icon of Los Angeles street life.

Von Dutch's unique striping style was eagerly sought out from coast to coast. This water transfer decal enabled the isolated acolyte to obtain the Master's touch.

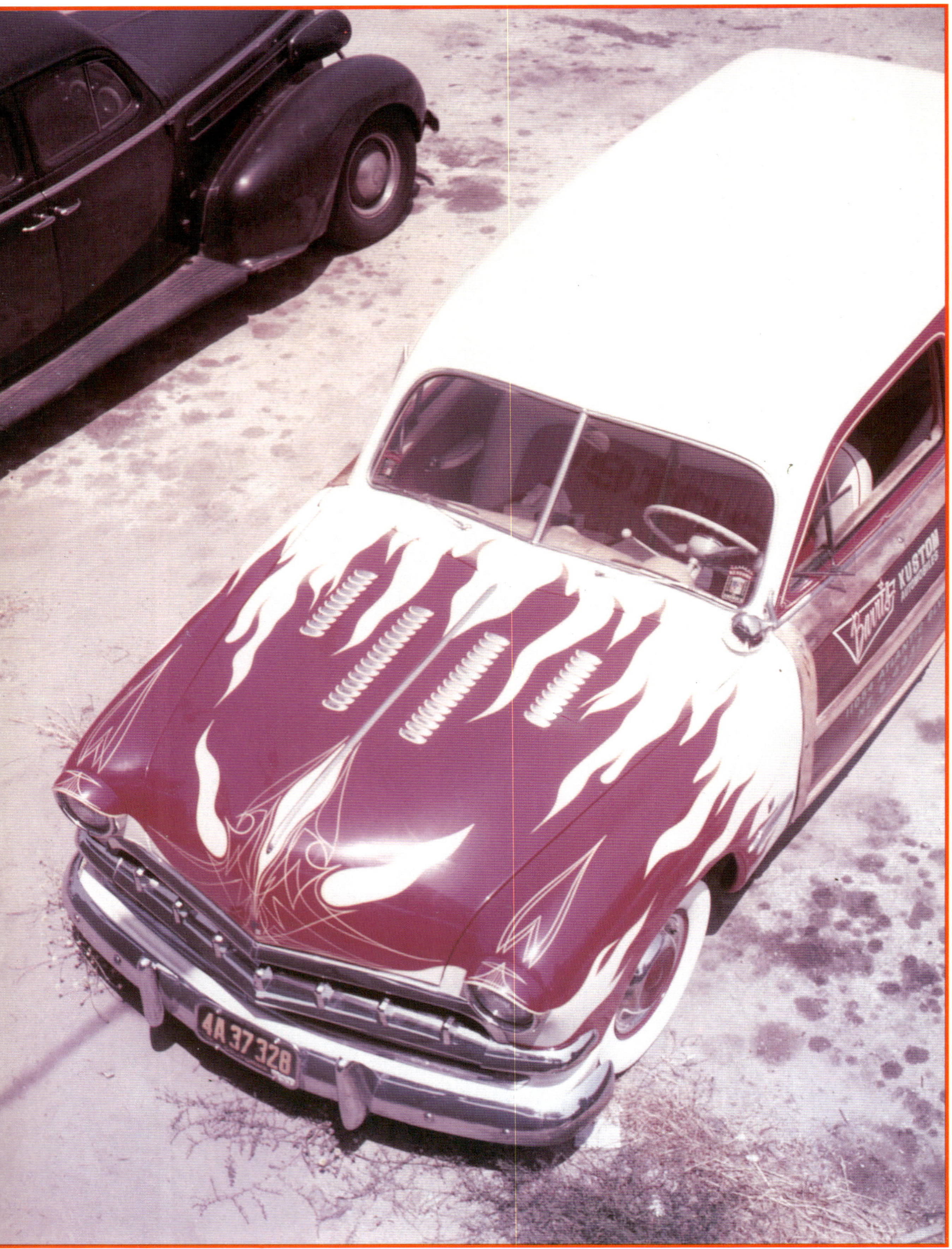

> around the Lynwood area whose work was not so excellent. Guys would bring their newly customized cars to Barris and ask him to fix 'em up. And an easy way to cover up sloppy body work was with paint. That's where I came in.
>
> Once someone brought in a car with grinder marks on the door. What I did was to put a curved stripe over the mark to cover it up. Then I put the same kind of curved line opposite it, where there was no grinder mark. All of a sudden I had a free-form design right in the middle of a large flat space. I liked it, and so did the customer. From there I developed it.

His introduction of caricature into his stripe jobs was another legendary Von Dutch habit. Many times he determined the theme for his elaborate paint jobs by observing the owner of the vehicle. "Sometimes it is the car owner himself who suggests the scene. I don't mean he tells me what to paint, but he reminds me of something. Like maybe the guy looks like a spider. Or maybe he reminds me of a crazy landscape, so I make it surrealistic. Sometimes I slap on an interplanetary scene. Or maybe music around radios. Anything that can't be obtained in any other way."

The stripes also satisfied other needs, and Dutch described the execution of his art in humanistic terms. "Modern automobiles need some human element on them. Without it they look like they've been ground out by a mechanical monster—which they have! I treat striping brushes like a musical instrument and whatever I stripe becomes a melody."

Von Dutch also popularized and greatly expanded the use of painted flames. In the 1940s he began using flames on race cars and motorcycles. His original inspiration, he said, came from pictures of World War I airplanes, which sometimes were decorated with flames in logical places, such as behind an exhaust manifold. Similarly, when flames first appeared on autos, their placement was usually near a vent pipe or wheel opening.

The day LA nightclub owner Earl Bruce showed up with a car to paint, Dutch changed all that.

"One day this guy brought in his car, and it had some bad spots in the paint job. He tells me, 'Flame this thing to cover up the bad spots,' and I say, 'But they're all over the car.' Now the catch is that the car was a 300 SL Mercedes Gull Wing, which was a heavy number even at that time. We ate up about two cases of beer, a few jugs of wine and about 20-odd rolls of masking tape. After I turned this thing loose on the world, it caused accidents. People couldn't accept a flamed 300 SL Gull Wing back then. They thought it was desecrating a shrine."

As the pressure of his increasing fame became a distraction, Von Dutch looked for ways to divert attention from his considerable talent. The persona of the dangerously eccentric Dutchman, he later admitted to intimates, was a calculated ruse. He would often relate humorous explanations of his erratic behavior. His ever-present can of beer led to rumors of his frequent incarceration in mental institutions for alcohol-based dementia. Von Dutch allowed such misinformation to spread because he felt it helped stem the unwanted intrusion of outsiders. The truth of the matter was that he would tire of his striping chores and simply choose to cut out. Months later he would pop up again and reemerge as a leader of the rod scene. To accommodate this gypsy work/lifestyle, he outfitted a surplus 1954 public transportation bus with a complete machine shop, a sleeping berth and a toilet. The tools he installed were antique castoffs, which he had painstakingly reconditioned. From this mobile base, Von Dutch was free to travel wherever he pleased. He would support himself on these wanderings by fixing machinery, painting signs, bartering guns and knives of his own manufacture and striping.

His comings and goings in this rolling workshop only served to increase his mystique. "I don't want to be known as a personality," Dutch said, but the interest surrounding him increased to mania. Von Dutch became a man trapped in a myth. If he played the crowd, it only got worse; if he went into seclusion, then the legend also expanded. The longer he stayed away from the media, the more preposterous the stories about him became. When eventually the hysteria over his absence led to widespread rumors of his death, he began wearing a T-shirt emblazoned with the statement, "Von Dutch is still alive." As he put it at the time, "It saves answering a whole lot of questions."

An accomplished machinist and designer, Dutch continually amazed people with his resourceful fabrications. He could build complicated mechanisms out of scrap materials. For example, he could easily create, and often did, a working gun of his own design entirely from scratch. As a machinist he had few equals and he never bothered to measure parts, feeling that "if it looks right, then it will fit right."

Ed Roth recalls, "Dutch could just sight something up and figure out the dimensions in his mind. He'd never do the same project

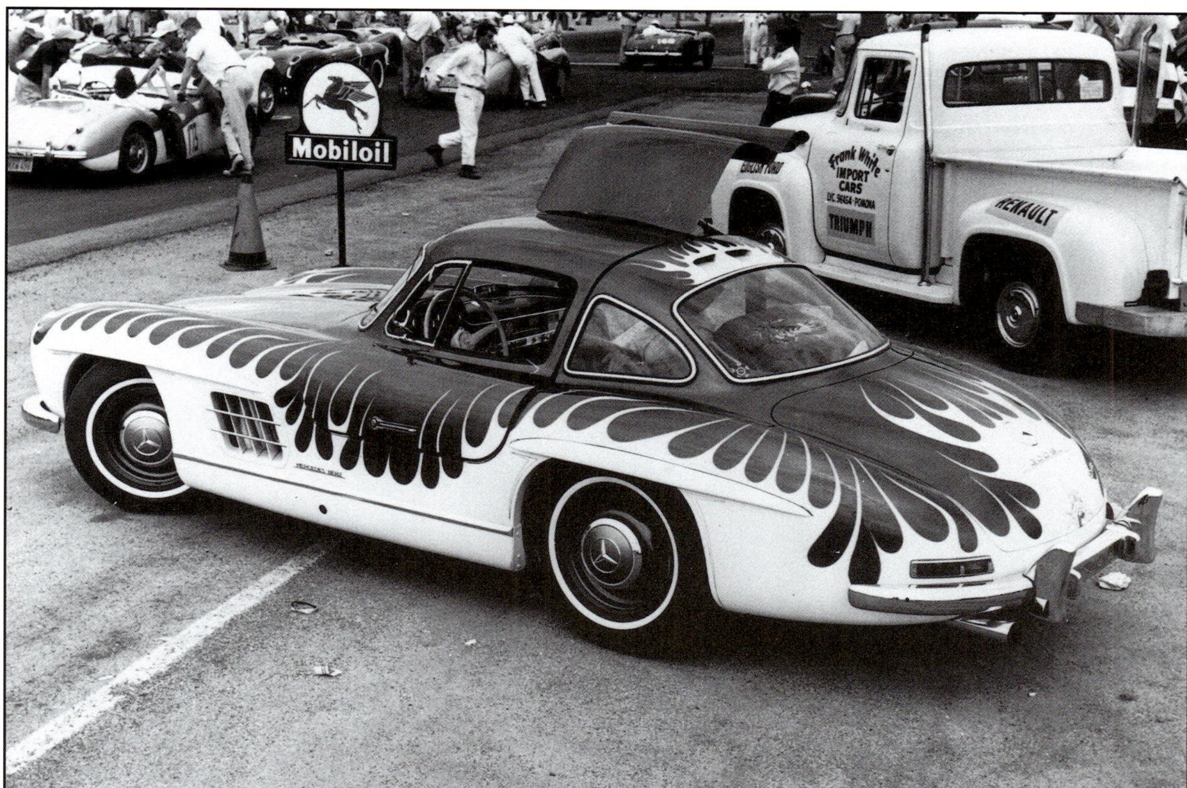

(Above) Earl Bruce's 300 SL Mercedes sported Dutch's most infamous flame job. Photo courtesy Pat Ganahl. (Opposite) The Barris Kustom Industries shop car. This wagon received one of Von Dutch's more elaborate treatments. Photo courtesy Greg Sharp.

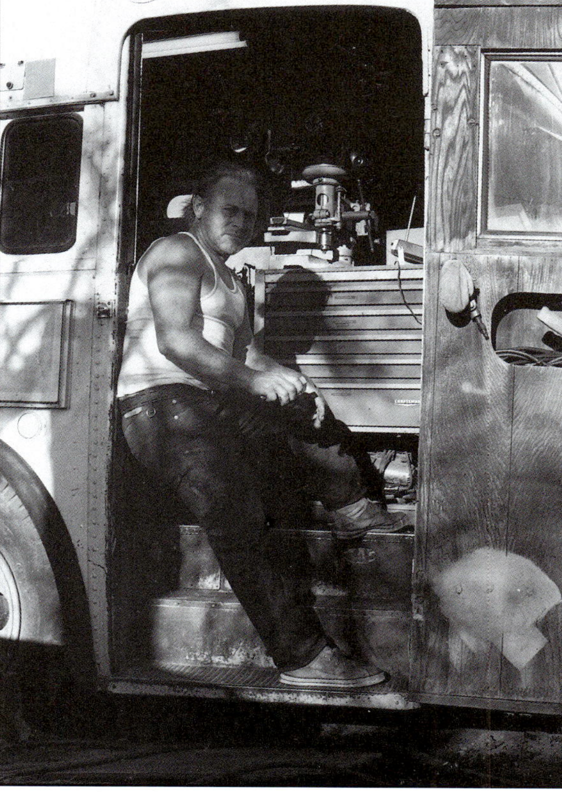
Von Dutch in the door of his mobile workshop and home. Photo by Temma Kramer.

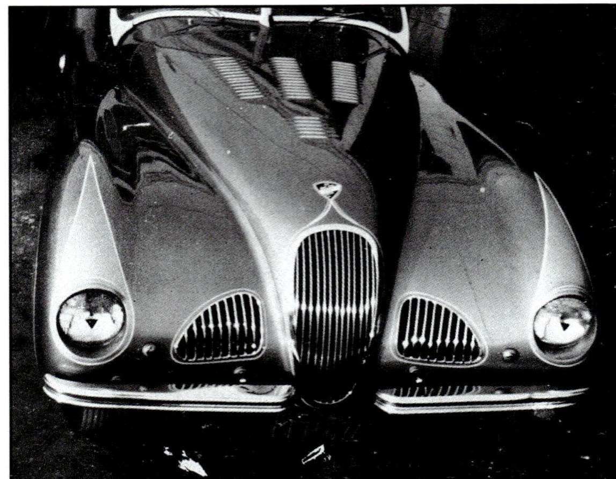

The front view of Dutch's personal Jag displays extensive body modifications and paint work. Photo by Von Dutch.

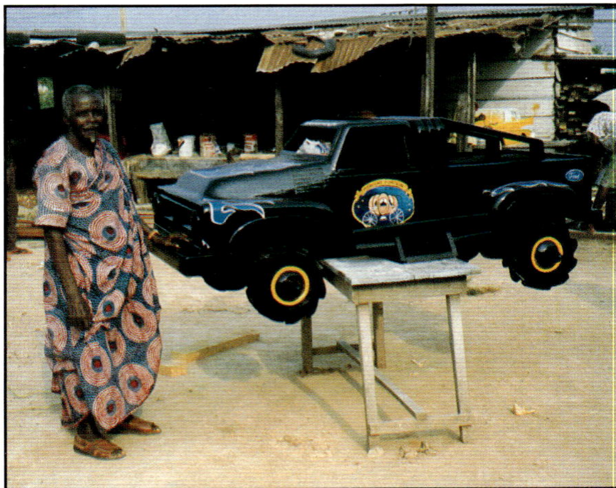

Kane Kwei and his "Von Dutched" creation CINDY'S PUMPKIN, *Ghana, Africa, 1991. Photo by Ernie Wolfe III.*

(Opposite) Von Dutch, Rancho Sespe, 1992.

twice because that would be boring. Look at his knives—they're each distinctively different from each other."

For Von Dutch the elementary act of machining had real meaning. He observed that "the nut and bolt are the summation of generations' worth of effort to conquer metal technology, and we should all be aware of their significance." The vehicles built by Von Dutch were predictably idiosyncratic. Unfortunately, his best early custom, a 1950s Jaguar XK120 with an extremely reworked front end, was destroyed in a tragic crash.

Other than his bus, Dutch's best known personal vehicle was his "Kenford" truck, a stylistically functionalized Ford crossed with a Kenworth. This effort featured extensive engine-turned metal adornment on its interior and numerous mechanical mods on the outside. Dutch scratch-built the Winton Flyer, a spoke-wheeled horseless carriage, for the Steve McQueen film *The Reivers* in 1968. His personal involvement with McQueen led to the artist being hired to work on some of the racing cars for the movie *Le Mans*. For this film, Von Dutch would repaint the cars at the end of a day's shooting so that they could appear on camera as a different racer on the next day.

The pyrotechnic skills of Von Dutch enabled him to hire out as a powder man on Hollywood productions. Industry insiders still recall the amazing marksmanship of the man. Others remember better his private demonstrations with self-built weaponry. The "pirate's naval cannon" that he used to shoot off Catalina Island and his shop "air rifle," which was capable of delivering a ball bearing payload through a quarter-inch thick piece of plate steel, were particular favorites.

Von Dutch was an inveterate tinkerer, always creating some sort of machine. His coin-operated guillotine, he once remarked, "should be in front of every courthouse in the land." The experiments of Nikola Tesla fascinated him and he often quoted from the scientist's writings. He kept a giant, high voltage Tesla coil in the shop, which he often turned on as a visual aid. No one who witnessed Dutch being assaulted by the machine's lightning field ever forgot the point of the lecture.

In the final analysis, people will probably remember Von Dutch as much for the folklore as for his true accomplishments. The irony of this was not lost on the man. "People remember what they want. Everybody can handle somebody else being full of shit. The problem comes when they have to admit that they're full of crap too."

Von Dutch felt his cynical attitude had been forged during childhood. "The first big lie they tell you is Santa Claus. For me, I knew the world was a lie when I was a kid. Because my dad painted signs I was always real interested in letters and words. We lived on Beach Street. Now the catch was that all of the surrounding streets were named after trees, like Fir Street, Elm Street and so on. Now on the street I lived, some developer had decided instead of spelling it BEECH as in the tree, to spell it BEACH. I guess he thought it would sell more houses if people felt they could live by the ocean."

Von Dutch never suffered fools gladly. Instead he preferred to either avoid their presence or drive them off with humorous barbs and displays of calculated eccentricity. Yet his favorite aphorism was "Logic is the law of the universe."

The researcher Ernie Wolfe III told me that in July 1991 he approached craftsman Kane Kwei at his workshop outside of the rural village of Accra, Ghana. Kwei was painting a fantasy coffin that he had sculpted from a tree trunk into the shape of a customized '56 Ford pickup truck. It was a functional sculpture Kwei called "Cindy's Pumpkin." Wolfe, a veteran of thirty-eight trips to Africa, was astounded to discover that the painted flame treatment on the coffin was so familiar "it could have been on any car in East LA." Asked about it, Kane Kwei referred to the technique as "Von Dutching." As memorials go, that's not too bad.

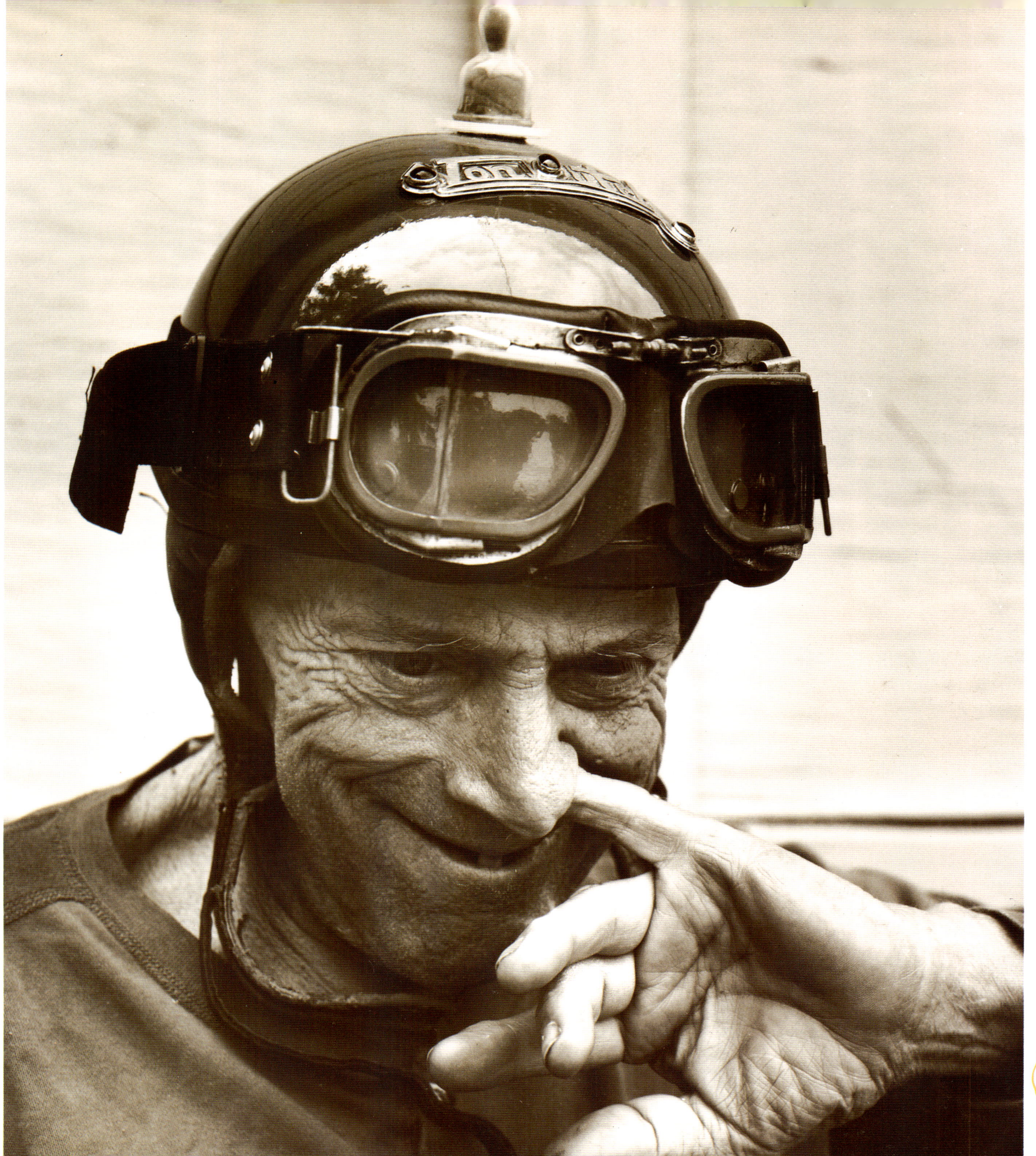

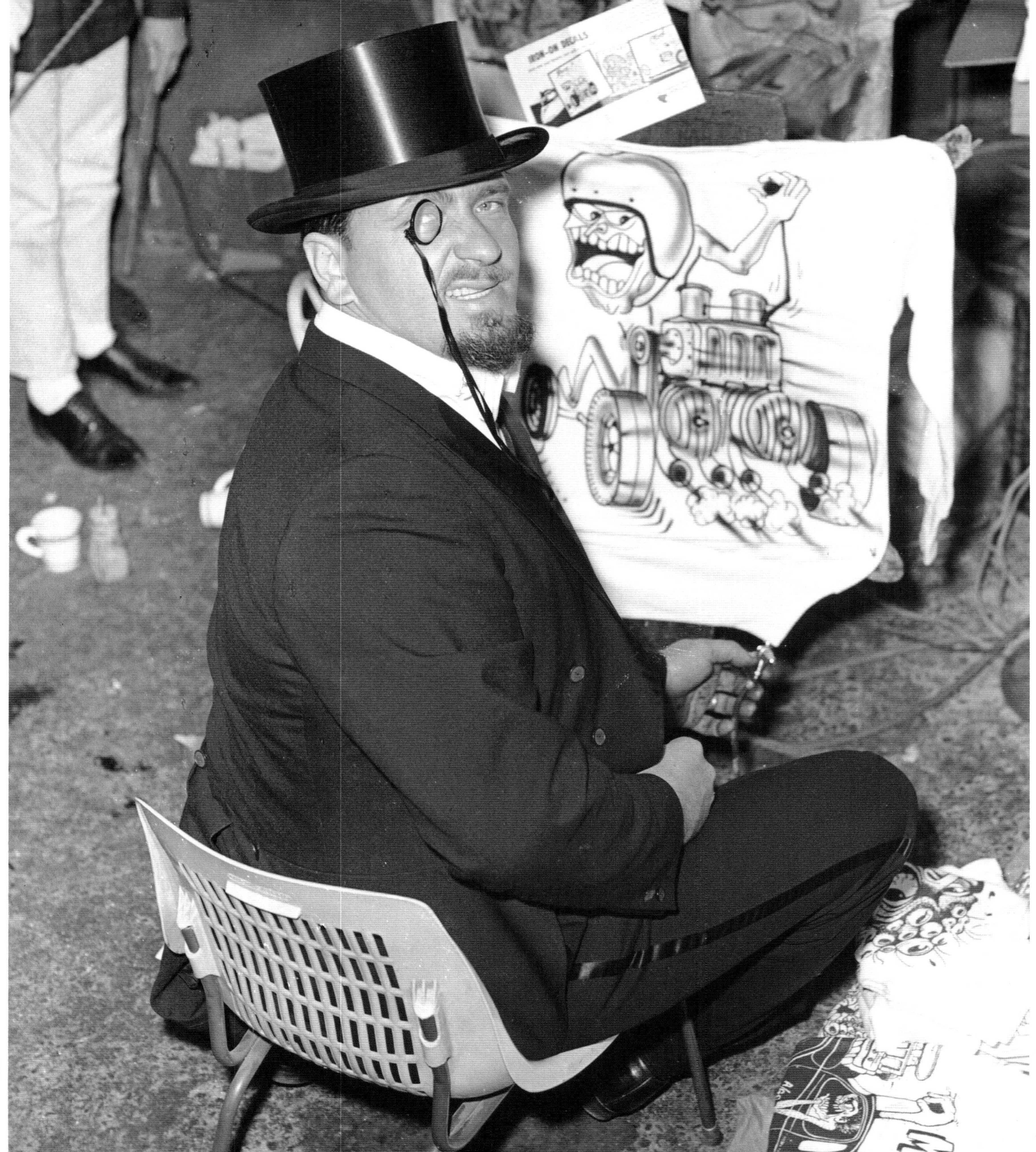
IRON-ON DECALS

Ed "Big Daddy" Roth

Ed Roth grew up on the avenues of the city of Bell, your basic speed-and style-addicted guy. He could sketch and he could wrench. What else was there? The cars he crafted, such as his leaded-in 1939 Chevy (done in '47), or his 1956 piece the Little Jewel, were impeccable masterpieces.

In 1951, the United States Air Force plucked Roth from his utopian rod existence and transplanted him to North Africa. Once there, he says, he worked as a senior cartographer and adjunct to a high security mission to document UFOs. Ed spent much of his spare time there cutting hair, painting signs and drawing caricatures for the amusement of his fellow soldiers. But mostly, he spent the months theorizing about the wild cars he would create upon his return. The Little Jewel was his first gesture after re-entry into civilian life. Ed enthusiastically followed Dutch's work, but was personally schooled in the basics of the art by The Baron, another well-known painter. His mentor, who had been employed in the Studebaker assembly plant, was a master executor of the traditional striping style.

Later, Big Daddy combined his talent for caricature with the tools of custom car painting, like the sword brush and the air brush. This combination resulted in a plethora of uniquely painted monster shirts. The original impetus for the monster vibe is attributed by Roth to Von Dutch's incorporation of fantastical beings into his striping jobs. Dutch had also airbrushed several shirts (primarily for his own amusement), thus innovating another major trend, the personalized T-shirt.

BDR's genius was in putting the package together and taking it out on the road to car shows. He eventually painted thousands of original-design shirts while his customers watched at car shows across the country. Ed then discovered the process of photographic silkscreening and adapted it to his work. This new process allowed Big Daddy to replicate his images quickly and accurately. His first design, Rat Fink, was photocopied directly from a drawing he'd made on the studio's refrigerator door. Now his designs could be produced in large numbers. T-shirts were on

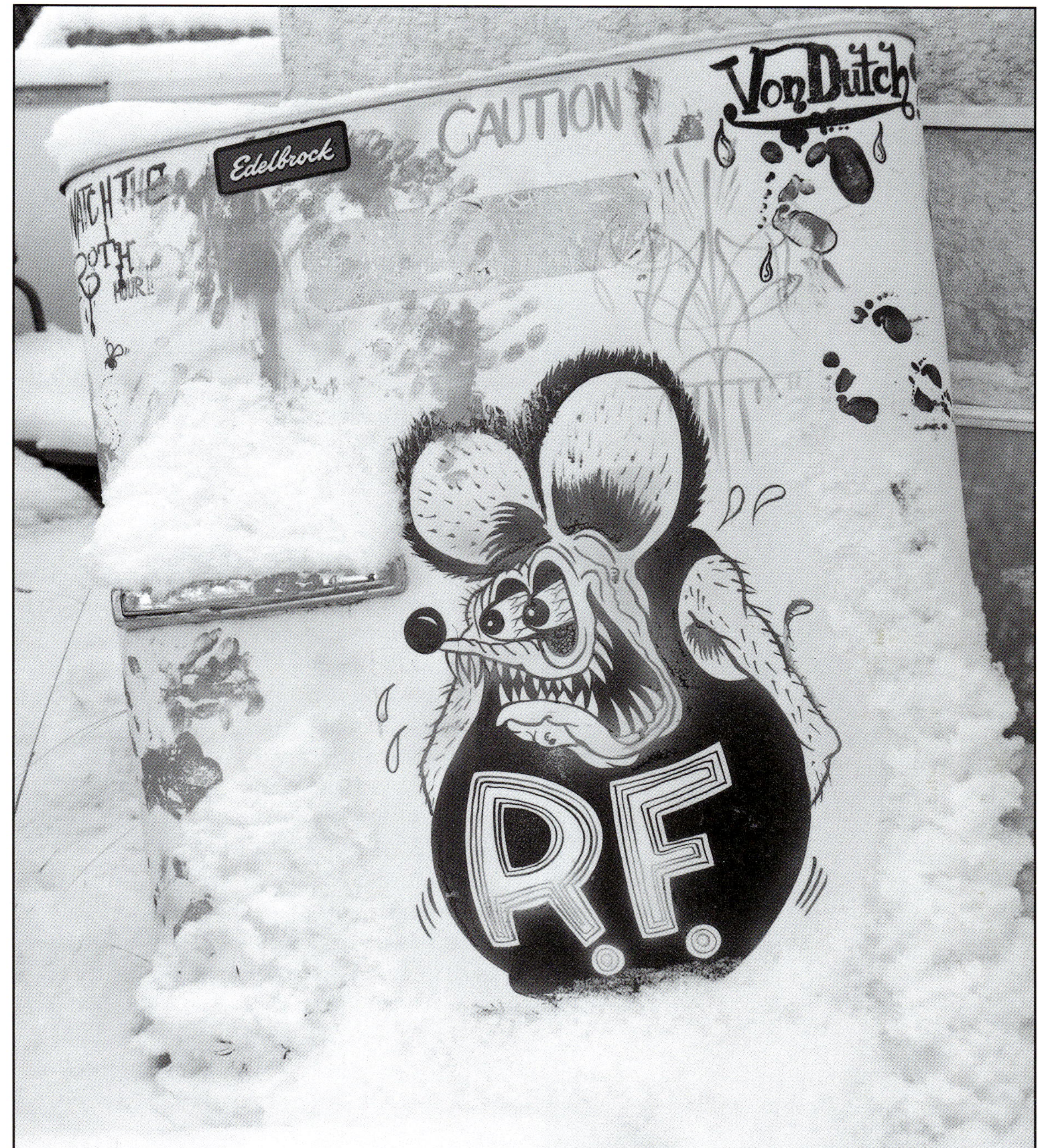

✠ *Ed "Big Daddy" Roth,* Rat Fink Refrigerator Door *(paint on metal, 72 x 48 in.; collection of the artist). Roth made the original Rat Fink drawing on a refrigerator door in his studio in Maywood, California, in 1962; here viewed in the snow in Manti, Utah, 1992, is a slightly later version.*

(Opposite) Ed Roth at work at a car show in the early 1960s. Photo courtesy Ed Roth.

their way to becoming instruments of self expression: Roth sold his shirts at car shows throughout the land.

The autos BDR created to be seen at these venues were also revolutionary. Rather than restyling the pre-existing forms of Detroit cars, as his contemporaries did, Ed sculpted unique new shapes from plaster and then molded them in fiberglass. His 1959 Outlaw (originally called Excaliber), broke major ground in the auto world. Suddenly cars were being built from scratch in a garage by a single person rather than by crews of hundreds in industrial complexes. Roth went headup and toe to toe with the Detroit hordes and beat them, using low buck, backyard methods. Following upon the success of the Outlaw, a car that was utterly unlike any car before or since, Roth began producing one uninhibited design custom rod each year. Some of the best remembered ones include the Beatnik Bandit (1960); the Road Agent (1961), the Orbitron (1964), Rotar (a remote-controlled, air-cushioned hovercraft, built in 1962), the Surfite (an off-road beach vehicle featuring a built-in Gordie surfboard, 1962), the asymmetrical Megacycle bike/truck, and the twin V8-powered Mysterion (1963).

The Revell Corporation, makers of plastic scale-model assembly kits, came out with a line of Roth designs. Kids in all corners of the globe eagerly built

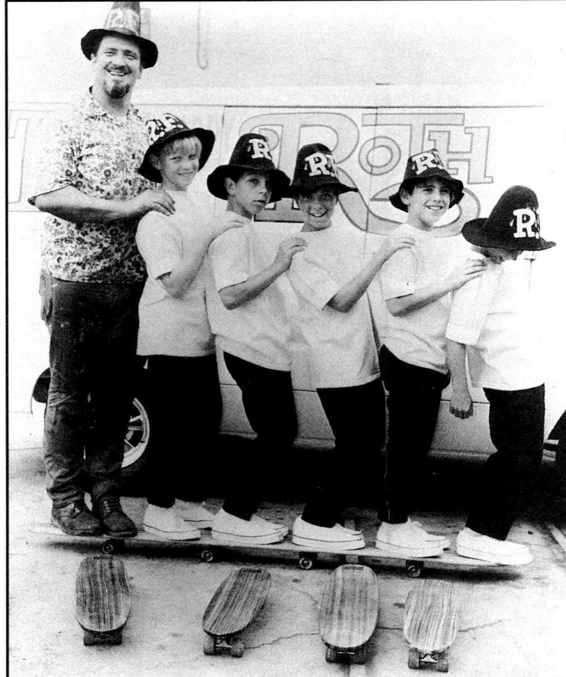

The Rat Fink skateboard crew, 1965. Photo courtesy Ed Roth.

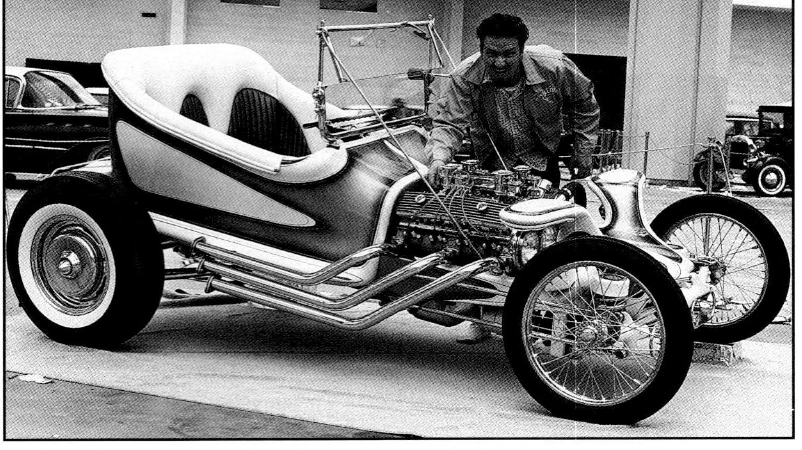

Roth and the OUTLAW, *1959. Photo courtesy Ed Roth.*

✠ *Ed "Big Daddy" Roth,* BEATNIK BANDIT, *1960 (fiberglass, plexiglass, steel, lacquer and enamel paint, 43 x 135 x 70½ in.; collection of the National Automobile Museum, Reno, Nevada). Photos courtesy Ed Roth.*

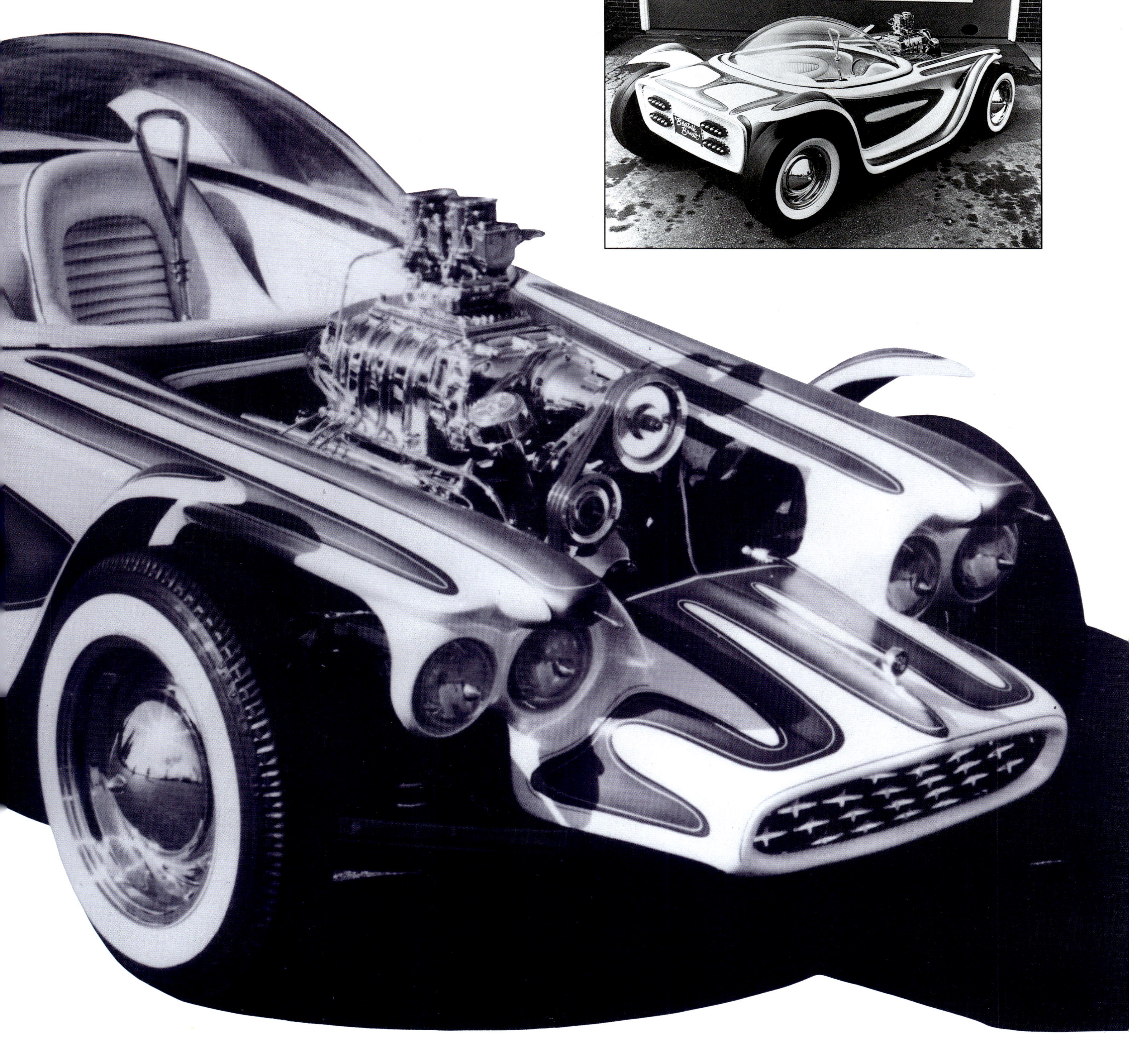
Beatnik Bandit

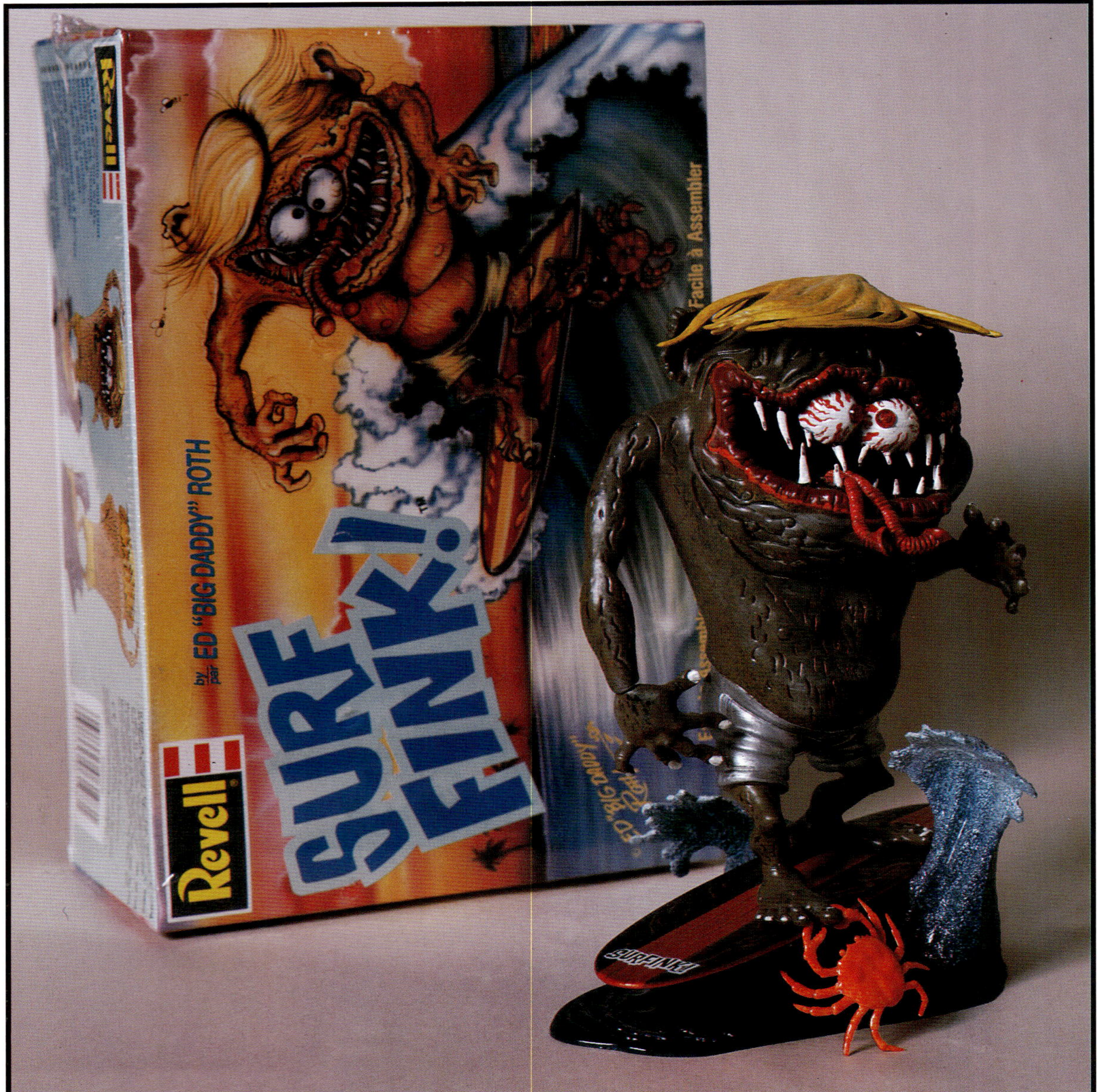

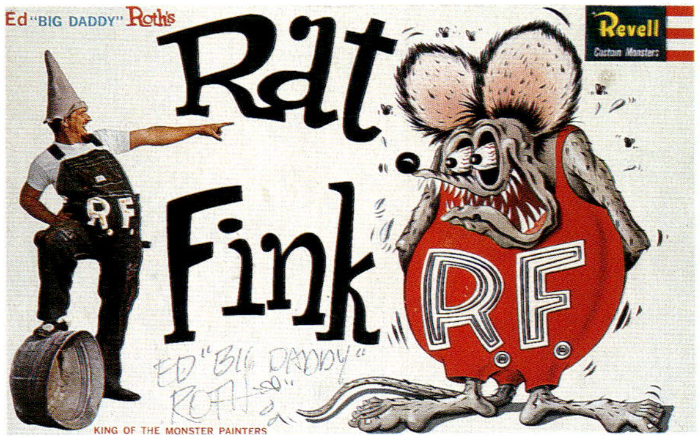

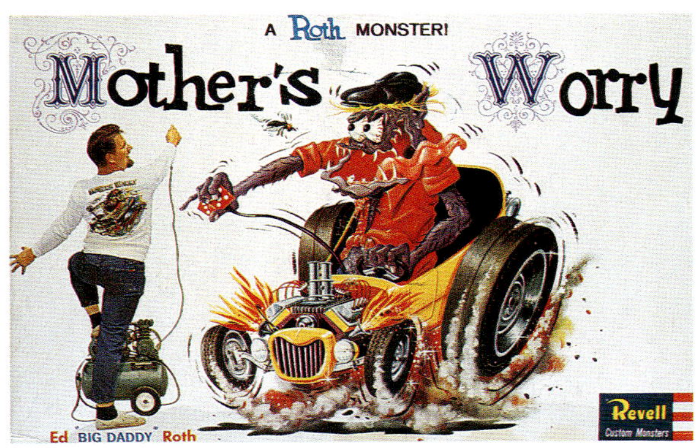

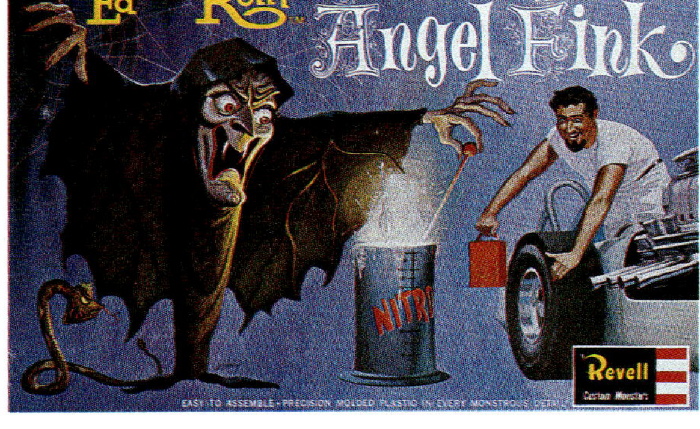

✠ *Ed "Big Daddy" Roth,* Revell™ Roth Monster Kits, *1960s (plastic models in display boxes, 3 x 5 x 7 in. each; collection of Long Gone John).* Surf Fink!, *above, is a recent re-issue.*

(Opposite, lower right) Roth's fully operational Rat Fink vehicle. Photo courtesy Jim and Dan Brucker.

Big Daddy's weirdo monsters and replicas of his show cars. The sales of these kits generated millions of dollars for the corporation, and they put Roth's work into the homes of people from all walks of life in places like Japan, Europe, Australia and Scandinavia, as well as the US.

Big Daddy Roth had become a counterculture idol. *Time* magazine portrayed him as the "supply sergeant to the Hells Angels." *Surfer* magazine decried his manufacturing of German wermacht helmets and his promotion of negative surf images. Roth's direction as a designer headed further and further afield from the more conventional work of his contemporaries. His vehicles radically pushed the functions and standards of the rod and custom field. The Rat Fink, Peace Fink and Electric Rat each were driveable sculpture, vehicular versions of Roth monsters. The 1967 Druid Princess was a baroque masterpiece crafted around an Old West hearse. (The Princess, originally created for *The Addams Family* television show, was released onto the car show circuit after the series had been unexpectedly canceled.

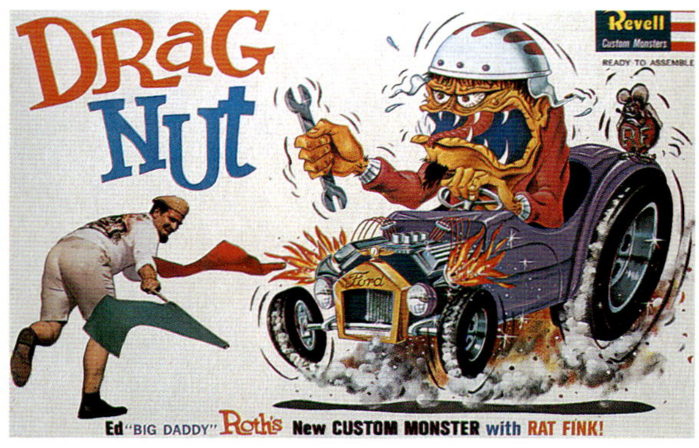

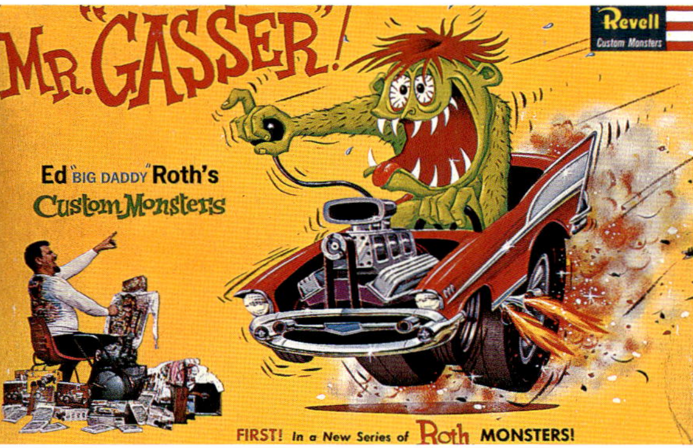

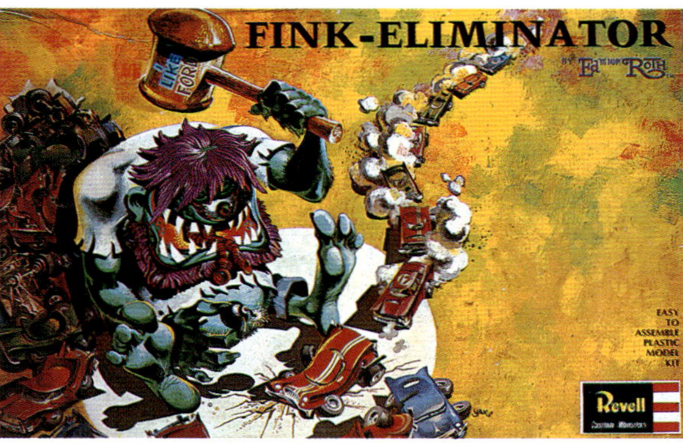

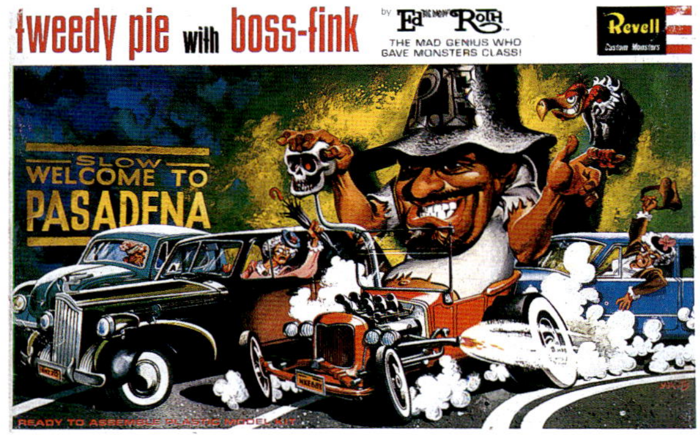

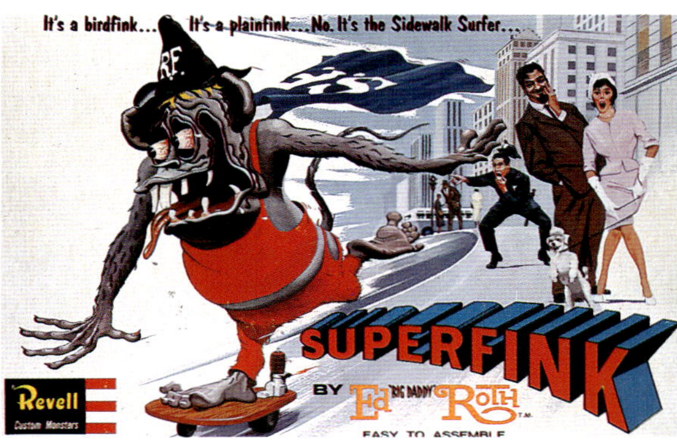

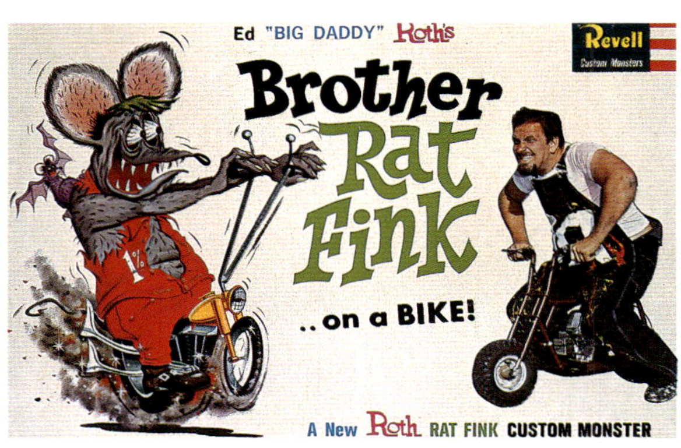

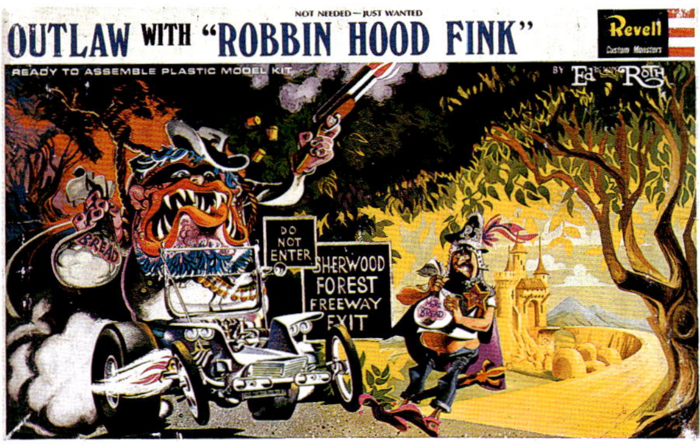

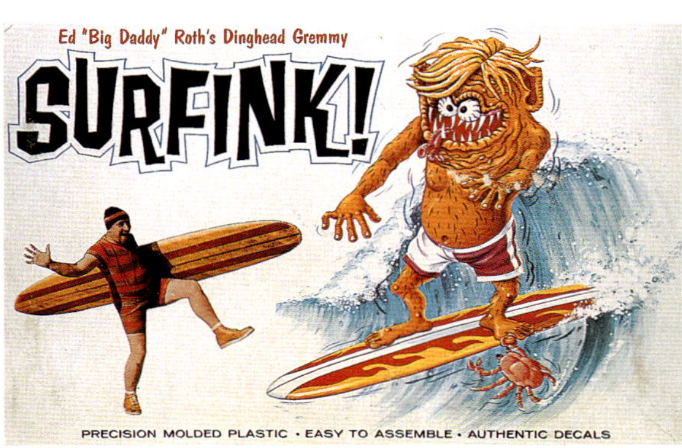

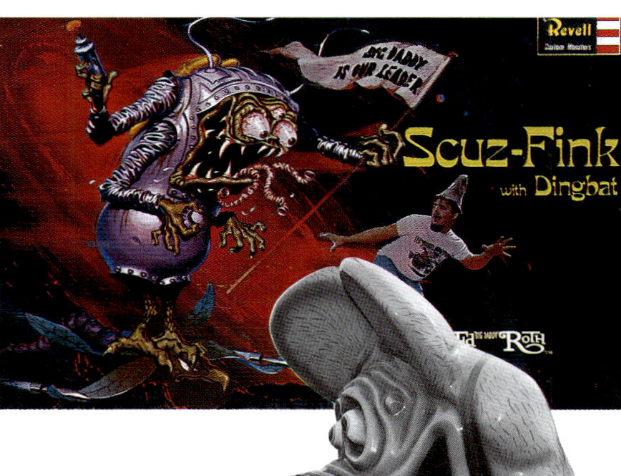

"Without the promotional tie-in of the series backing it, the average guy at a show was mystified," Roth later laughed.)

Big Daddy's revolutionary V8-powered California Cruiser trike (1966) explored the netherworld between cars and motorcycles. Roth further investigated this realm with the Tree Viper (1967), the Mail Box (1968), the Panzer Trike (1969), the Great Speckled Bird (1978), the Asphalt Angel (1984) and the Globe Hopper (1989). By 1969 BDR's building of these free-styled trikes had effectively alienated him from much of the hot rod establishment. The vehicles were summarily outlawed from participating in many shows and events. Roth welcomed the controversy, asking at the time, "If they aren't cars and they aren't bikes, what are they? Isn't the point to do something different?" One of the major reasons Big Daddy created these hybrids was because he thought that "the future required smaller, lighter, more fuel-efficient vehicles. My cars were always smaller and lighter than everyone else's. Look at the Bandit: it was really a downsized, futurized, traditional roadster."

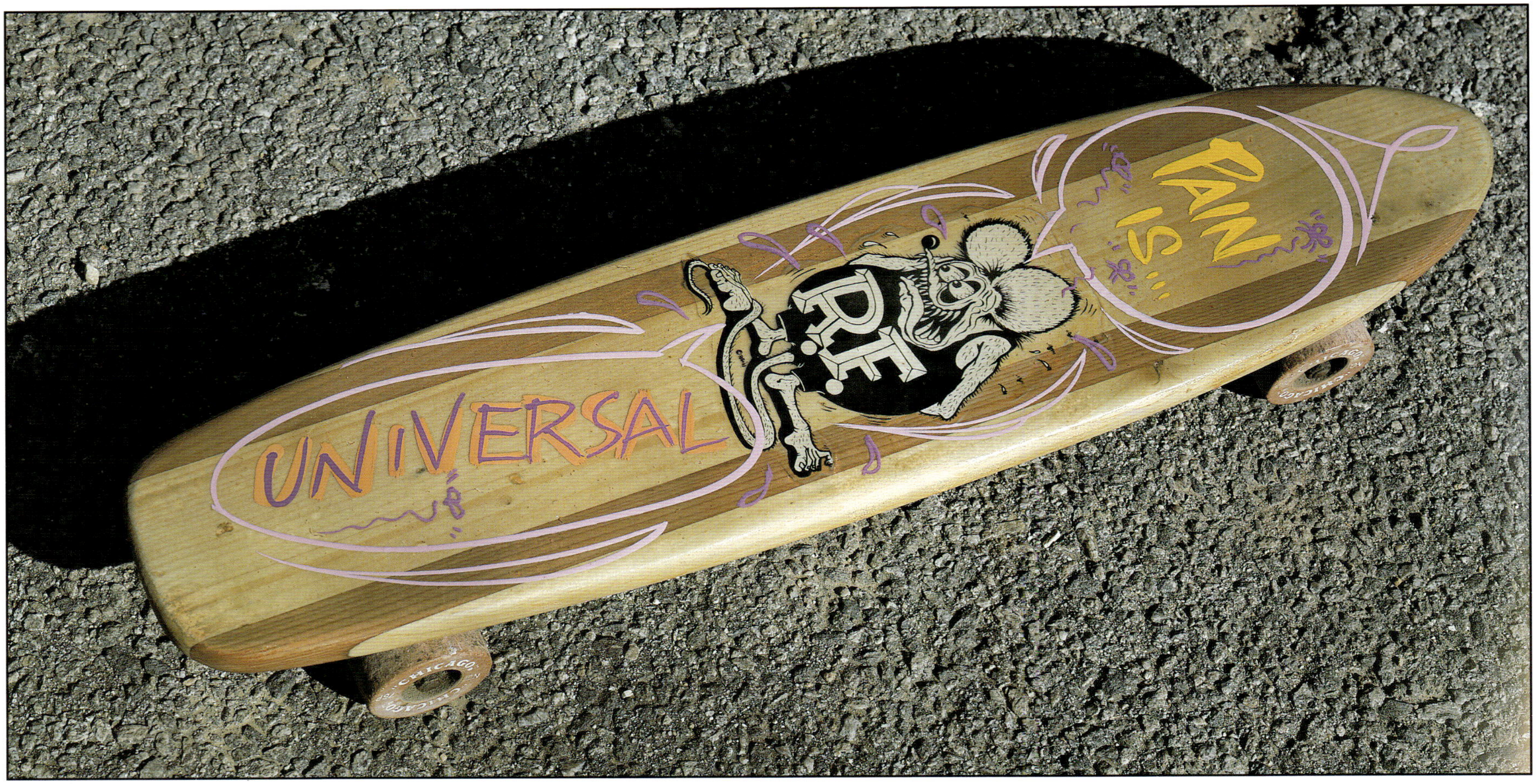

✠ *Ed "Big Daddy" Roth,* Rat Fink Skateboard, *1965 (laminated wood, composition clay wheels and metal trucks, 6 x 27 x 1 in.; collection of Skip Engblom).*

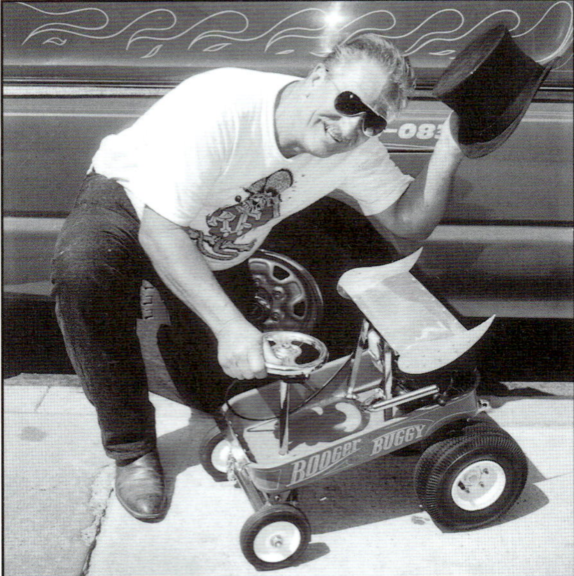

B.D.R. and Booger Buggy, *1992.*

(Opposite) Roth wields the stripers' "dagger brush," Manti, Utah, 1992.

These days BDR dwells in Manti, Utah, where he is an involved member of the Mormon religion. Current Roth designs center on solar power. "I'm out to build a 200-miles-per-gallon rod," he says. "I came close with the Globe Hopper which I drove to Alaska and back on my shake-down cruise." Other BDR projects are typified by The Conestoga Star. The child's wagon, which won the 1992 Best Wagon Award at the Oakland Roadster Show, is powered by a hopped-up lawn mower engine. It also sports a hand-fabricated linkage steering and drive system.

Why does a man spend months of time on such a strange project, one with absolutely no potential for profit? Big Daddy's answer is simple: "It's about fun."

Back in 1962, when author Tom Wolfe arrived, to Roth "he was just another guy in a pink suit with an expense account." Wolfe's comparison of BDR's car work to work by fine artists like Salvador Dali was "flattering but way off the mark." In Ed's words, "I was just a guy trying whatever wild thought popped into my mind. I never spent any time thinking about art, I just did things. I would go with any concept I understood, based on what was going on around me. The monster stuff was a reflection of the people I knew. Making vehicles out of old cars never appealed to me. It was too restrictive. I really got off on the idea of making ones exactly like I wanted them. Honesty has always been a big thing with me. If something's honest to itself then people will respond to it. If you're lying, the people can always tell."

On art matters, Roth is also forthright: "In the old cave man days, artists hadda be good mechanics. Nowadays, creeps do stuff in the name of art that totally stinks. As far as I'm concerned, blobs of paint just plopped onto a canvas or sculptures of broken soda bottles are just pure trash. In these twisted times ya don't need talent to be an 'artist,' just a good line and some connections."

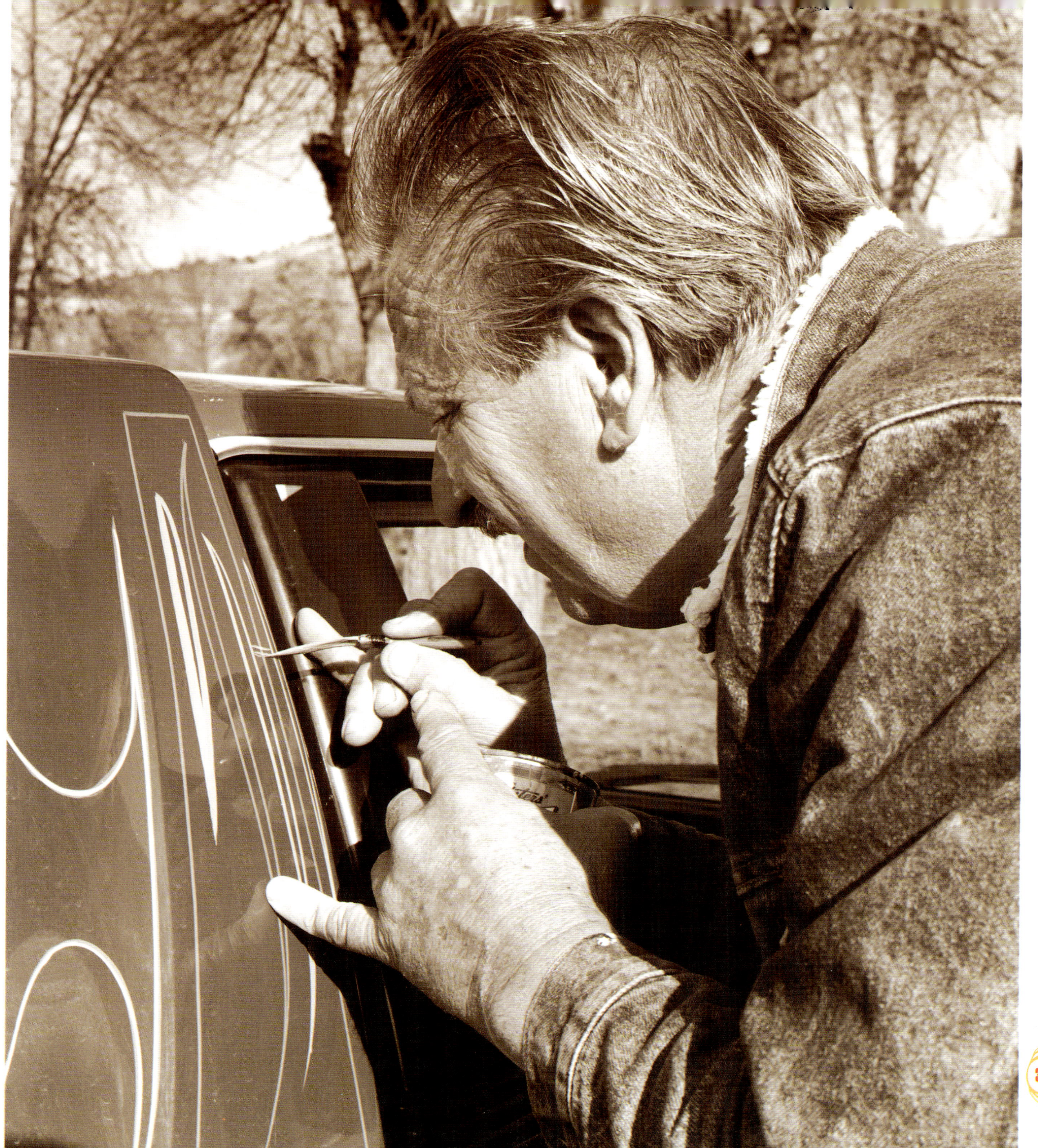

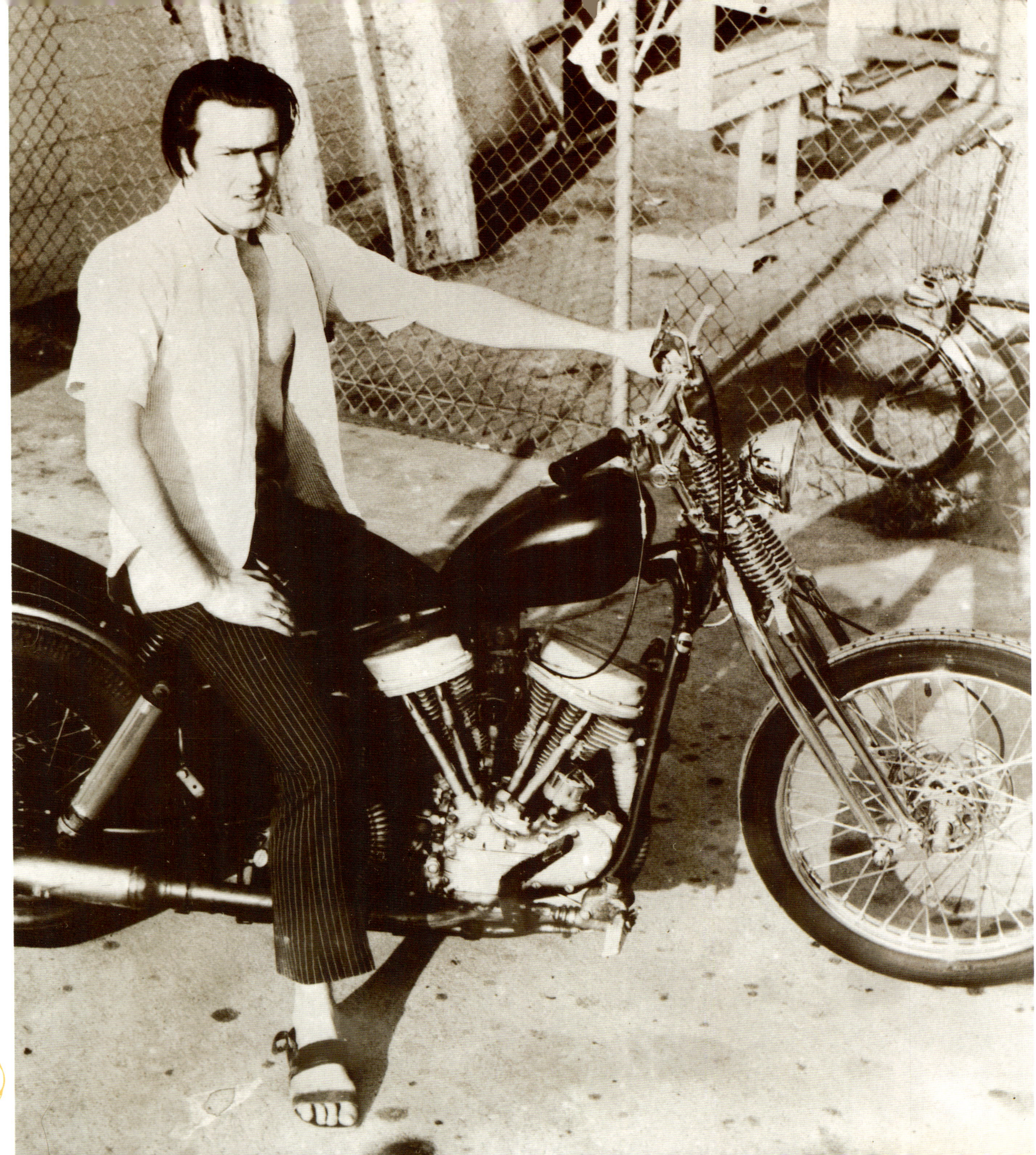

ROBT. WILLIAMS

Robert Williams first came across the works of Von Dutch and Roth through printed accounts in the car periodicals of the period.

I was living in the South and mags like *Hop Up, Hot Rod, Honk, Rod and Custom* and *Car Craft* were like my bible. I never really fit in at school and mechanical things were all I understood or cared about. Dutch and Roth were like these gods. As soon as I saw their work I knew I had to go check them out. Von Dutch was extremely brilliant and I can't overemphasize the influence he had on young, blue-collar America. He was like a spiritual god—he seemed to add a soul to nuts and bolts, a spirit to machinery, as it were, that no mere engineer could do. Sheet metal—well, it gave the vehicle a karma all its own; it came alive. Ed Roth was to the youth of America in the nineteen sixties what P.T. Barnum was to the average farm boy in the eighteen sixties. Roth invoked the hot rod spirit of the future with overtones of beatnik style.

By the time he was twelve, Williams had a 1934 Ford five-window coupe and was obsessed with the motoring life. Inevitably he ended up in Los Angeles.

After attending junior college, Williams went to the Chouinard Art School for a brief period but "felt very out of place. I guess I wasn't Disney material." His first paying job was as an art director for *Black Belt* magazine, where he "did a little cut and paste." Next followed a nerve-wracking coat-and-tie gig as a container designer for the Weyerhauser Corporation. As he recalls, "It was such a clash, it didn't take them long to realize that I was just not executive stock."

He eventually wound up at an employment agency. There, he says, he was told, "For an artist, we don't have much—other than this one job. Nobody we send there will take it, it's too grimy. There's a guy down in Maywood, Ed Roth, looking for an art director." Williams landed the job, being the most qualified applicant imaginable. He easily fit into the ferment of Studio Roth, circa '63. His skills allowed him full participation in the various creative enterprises going on in the atelier-like environment, and he worked on everything from advertisements to actual cars. The time with Roth was a happy one for Williams, in a chaotic, collaborative environment full of kindred spirits. The loosely structured art factory also afforded him the opportunity to be around Von Dutch. Several of the products that Williams was exposed to at Roth's would have a particularly strong influence on his later work. The sardonic tone of the illustrated ads that Ed and Robert would brainstorm together would show up in Williams's later underground comic work.

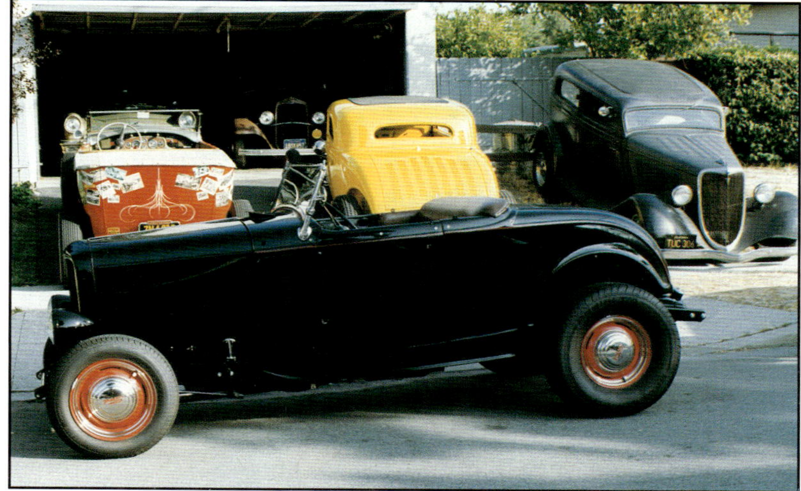

Sunday traffic jam at the Williams house, 1992.

Narrative art projects that the Roth Studio was involved in during the same period, like BDR's "stuff catalogues," *Petersen's Cartoons, Big Daddy Roth Comics* and *Pete Millar's Drag Toons*, were prototypical of latter day underground comics. Rick Griffin, who became a close friend when he worked on Roth's comics, later was linked with Williams at the highly influential *Zap Comix* braintrust.

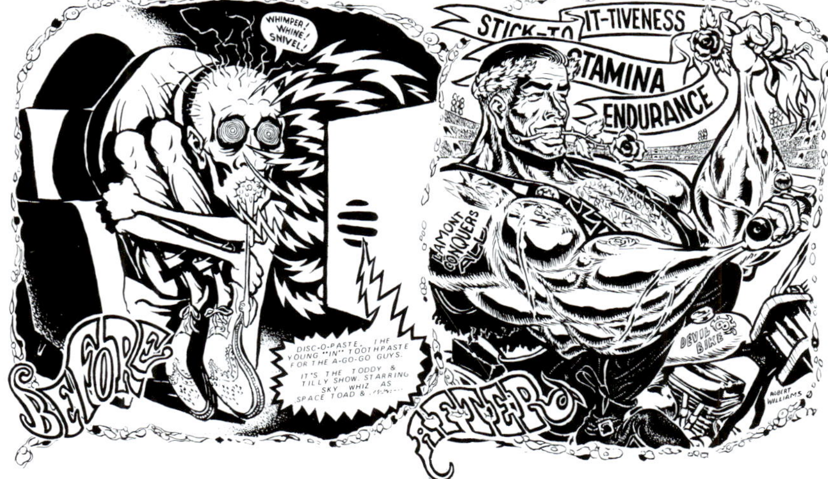

✠ *Roth advertisement by Robert Williams,* Before and After, *1967 (ink on paper, 4½ x 7½ in.; collection of Jim and Dan Brucker).*

(Opposite) Robert Williams at Roth Studio, 1967. Photo courtesy Robert Williams.

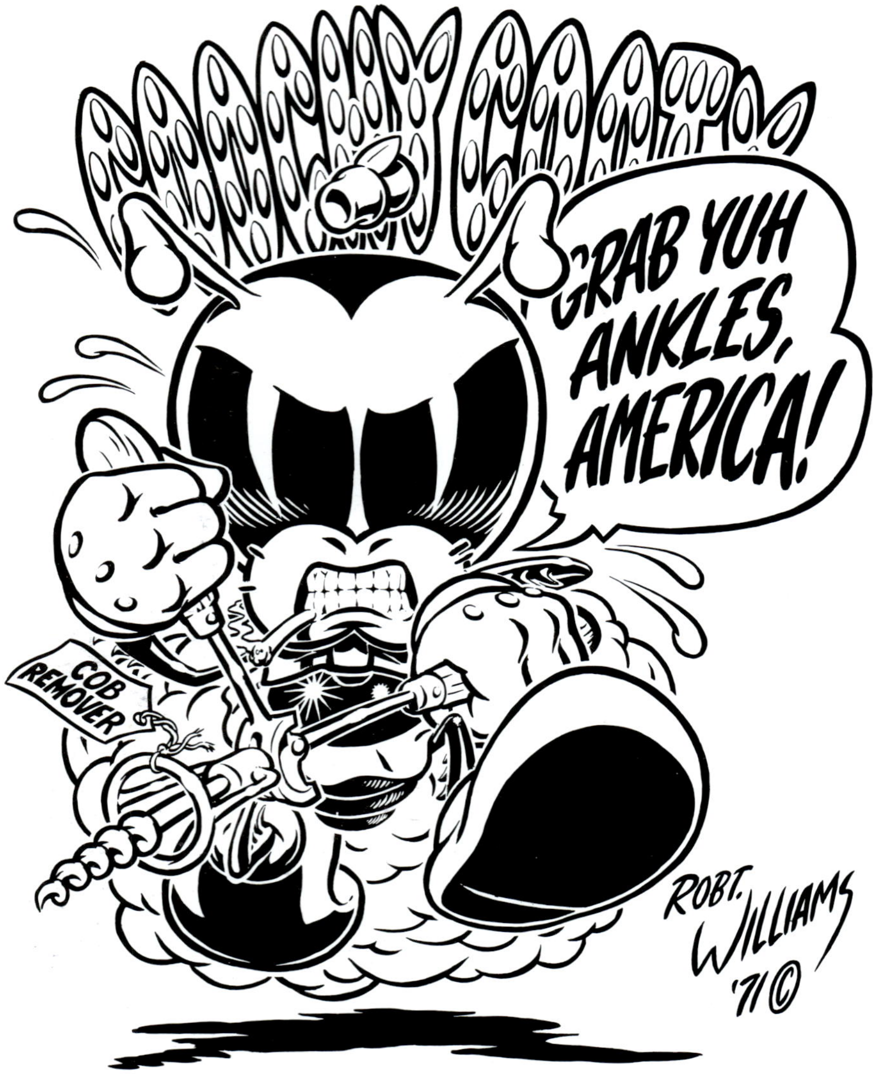

It was in the unexpurgated realm of underground books like *Zap*, *Coochy Cooty Men's Comics* and *Griffin's Tales from the Tube* that Williams's talent for visionary vulgarity really came to the fore. The content of these underground publications was unregulated, the style unformatted. The best books really pushed the limits of both the artist and audience. Williams's initial influence on the art world was through his prominence in the underground comic field.

In fact, society today operates under obscenity law interpretation and law enforcement practices that Williams and his *Zap* cohorts helped to determine. *Zap's* fourth issue premiered in August 1969. Williams recalls that the *Zap* collective "decided to severely test the norm with this issue and to actually try to produce the most extremely disgusting periodical imaginable. We really wanted to push people's buttons." Immediately upon its release it was removed from circulation on both the East and the West Coasts as the result of a series of busts. In New York City, the charges were pursued with vigor, resulting in a now-legendary trial.

The *Zap #4* case differs from recent censorship in an important way: the powers that be moved to prevent the distribution of the art in the first place, keeping the public from seeing *Zap #4* and making a choice on their own.

The case came to trial in the Criminal Court of the City of New York. Judge Joel Tyler, a morality crusader who several years before had suppressed the film *Deep Throat*, eventually decided that

> In the final analysis, the Court must be the expert in assessing what is the dominant theme, prurient interest, community standards, any redeeming social value, and the like...Merely because the magazine in question does not appeal to the prurient interest of the sophisticated or other small group of intellectuals does not remove it from the prohibition [against obscenity]. To do so would permit the substitution of the opinions of defendants' sophisticated and intellectual experts for those of the average person in the contemporary community...The cartoon is ugly, cheap and degrading. Its purpose—to stimulate erotic responses, and does not, as claimed, deal with basic realities of life. It is grossly shocking, demeaning the sexual experience by perverting it...It is a part of the underworld [sic] press—the growing world of deceit in sex, and it is not reality or honesty, as they often claim it to be. It represents an emotional incapacity to view sex as a basis for establishing genuine human relationships, or as a normal part of human condition.

The Association of American Publishers and the New York Civil Liberties Union both filed *amicus curiae* briefs in support of the appeal over this decision. In March 1973 the Court of Appeals rejected those briefs and the appeal itself, affirming the original obscenity conviction by a vote of 4 to 3. No other major case like the one involving *Zap #4* arose, even after the Supreme Court returned extra power to determine obscenity to local communities. The lack of further cases, despite the proliferation of similar comics, has led many to conclude that the New York *Zap* trial was a *de facto* counterculture bust, rather than an obscenity trial.

Williams later offered comment on such legalistic manipulations when he had printed on the cover of his *Coochy Cooty Men's Comics*, "Any persons found in the act of masturbation with this material in their possession must be considered subject to fetish as this material is hardly prurient."

✠ *Robert Williams,* Grab Yuh Ankles, America!, *1971 (ink on board, 16 x 13 in.; collection of Jim and Dan Brucker). The comic escapades of Williams's Coochy Cooty forever eclipsed such panty-waisted super heroes as Captain America.*

(Opposite, left to right) Zap cartoonists in Santa Monica: S. Clay Wilson, Stanley Mouse, Victor Moscoso, Robert Crumb, Rick Griffin, Robert Williams, Kim Deitch, Spain Rodriguez. Photo © Bob Seidemann, 1985.

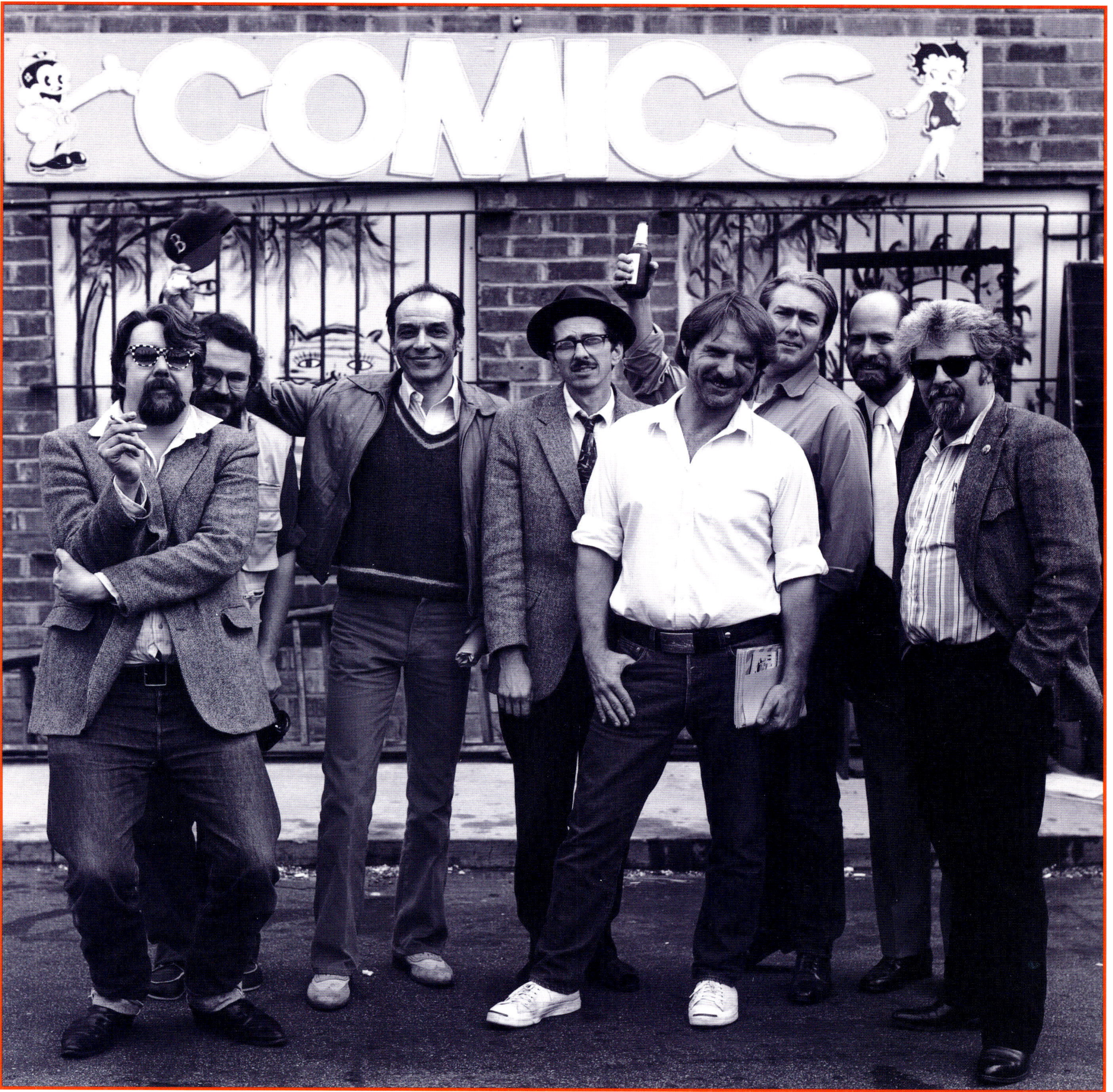
COMICS

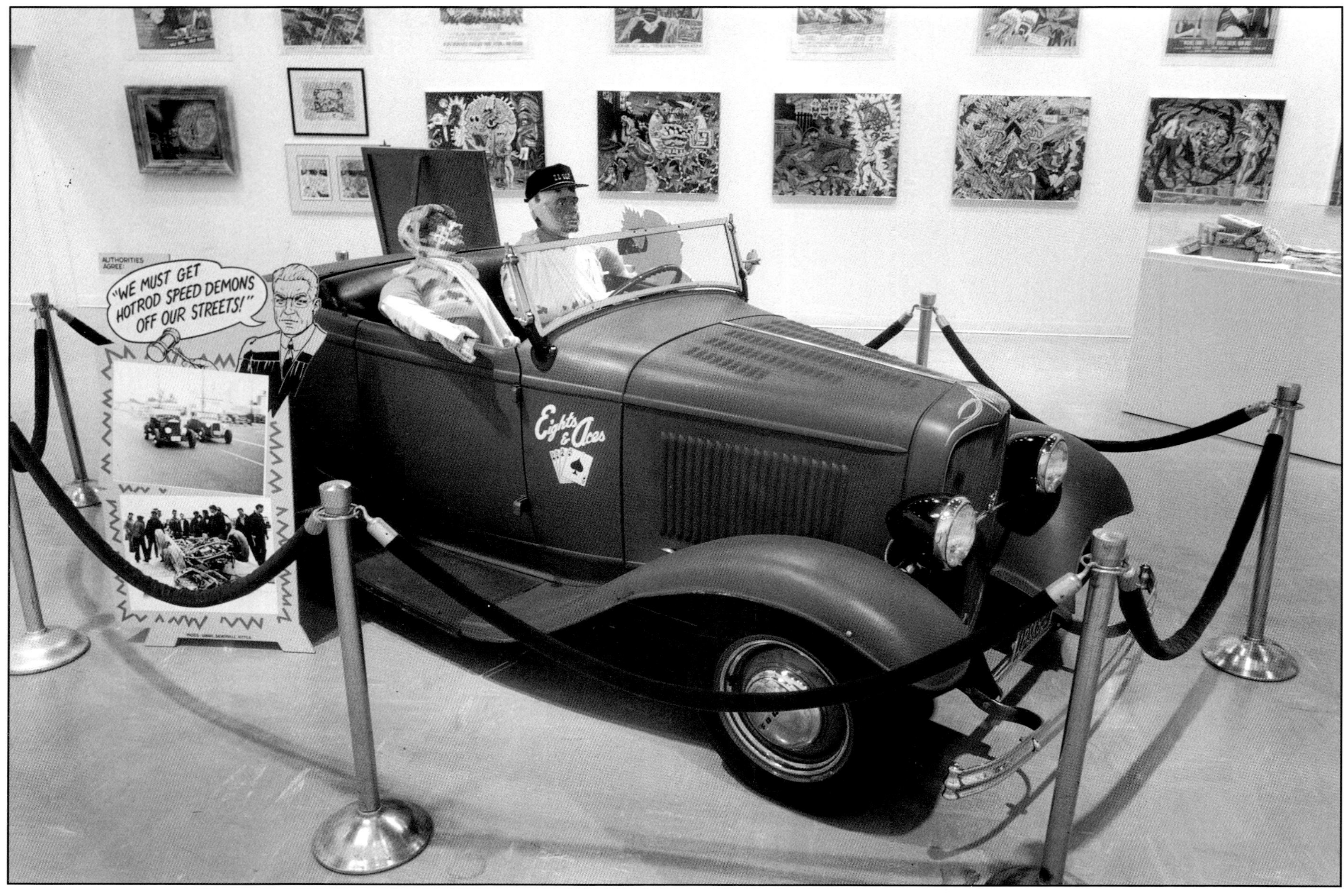

✠ *Robert Williams,* Eights and Aces, *1987 (1932 Model B Ford Roadster/tableau; collection of the artist and Bob Larivee, Sr.). Photo by Pat Ganahl, courtesy* Rod and Custom.

The selection of "inappropriate" or otherwise overlooked subject matter and themes, common in the work of all three artists, can be traced to their involvement in hot rod culture. Racers aren't a sentimental lot. "If it doesn't make it go, it's gone" is an old racers' axiom. In the words of Von Dutch, "Speed is an absolute. Something is either fast or not." Roth says, "When racers are working on their cars it's the real thing. There are no laws, no brainwashing, no everlasting truths and no thought restrictions. The world of the garage is their sanctuary of artistic control. Imagination is the limit and speed is the need. Everything else is irrelevant." Williams's analysis is that "hot rodding is an integral part of the mind set of the American male. Ask the Germans why they got beat in World War II. They were up against the typical American boy who could fix anything mechanical with spit and baling wire. The GIs took that hot rod attitude and they stopped the axis juggernaut with their Jeeps. The superior technology of the Panzer tank was defeated by the mobility of the Jeep and the adaptability of the GIs. The jeep was a government issue hot rod in olive drab paint."

With regard to the art world, Robert Williams displays a calculated distrust similar to that of his associates Von Dutch and Roth. As he puts it,

> Art in the past 60 years has avoided the obvious appeal to the eye in favor of a more cultivated lean towards intellectual appreciation of texture, volume and size. Art has become bigger, blander and more distant from simple pleasure. The theory of concept overrules art as an object and tends to deny anything that resembles craftsmanship or technical proficiency. We live in an age of cold domineering art that screams of profundity, but says nothing. Anyone who can produce something big, obtrusive, rough and impractical has fulfilled all the requirements needed to become a master artist; consequently, a large segment of the society with little or no skills has joined the ranks of the art world. In the art school of defecation we are all Rembrandts.

The Roth Studio eventually disbanded in 1970 due to a combination of factors. Ed had become disenchanted with the custom car world when shows and auto enthusiast magazines refused to display his trike works. And the magazines in which he advertised began to censor heavily the content of the Williams-penned ads. (In response, Ed had founded his own magazine in 1966. *Choppers* was the first title to cater exclusively to the modified motorcycle enthusiast. Quite logically, one of the first articles he ran was called "The Phenomenon of Von Dutch: The Legend Continues.") Roth eventually tired of business entirely and liquidated his assets.

Additionally, the hard tenor of the late '60s and its increasingly angry rhetoric didn't set well with the Big Daddy. "I didn't dig the politics, I didn't dig the drugs," he says, "so I went out in the desert and rode bikes and got crazy. I was hanging with the outlaw bikers and had a real gas. We rode and had fun and everyone pretty much steered clear of us." During this period Roth's biking and futuristic hedonism caused the Revell Corporation to terminate their involvement with him. BDR was now a phantom on the wind, a persona non-grata in the temple of auto worship he had helped to build.

James Brucker was a local boy from the fertile ranching land immediately northwest of Los Angeles. Like most California youth he was passionately involved with the automobile. Unlike most others, Brucker, along with his father and brother Daniel, had the awareness and financial resources to aggressively pursue this interest.

To classify the Bruckers as collectors would be a supreme understatement. The scale and scope of their operations put them in another class. Furthermore, the prescience of their selections was astounding. For example, they once acquired several thousand original motion picture scripts when they were discarded by MGM studios. Years later, museums and historians would vie for this historical treasure trove, which included such gems as Clark Gable's personally annotated script for *Gone with the Wind.* Other notable Brucker holdings include a

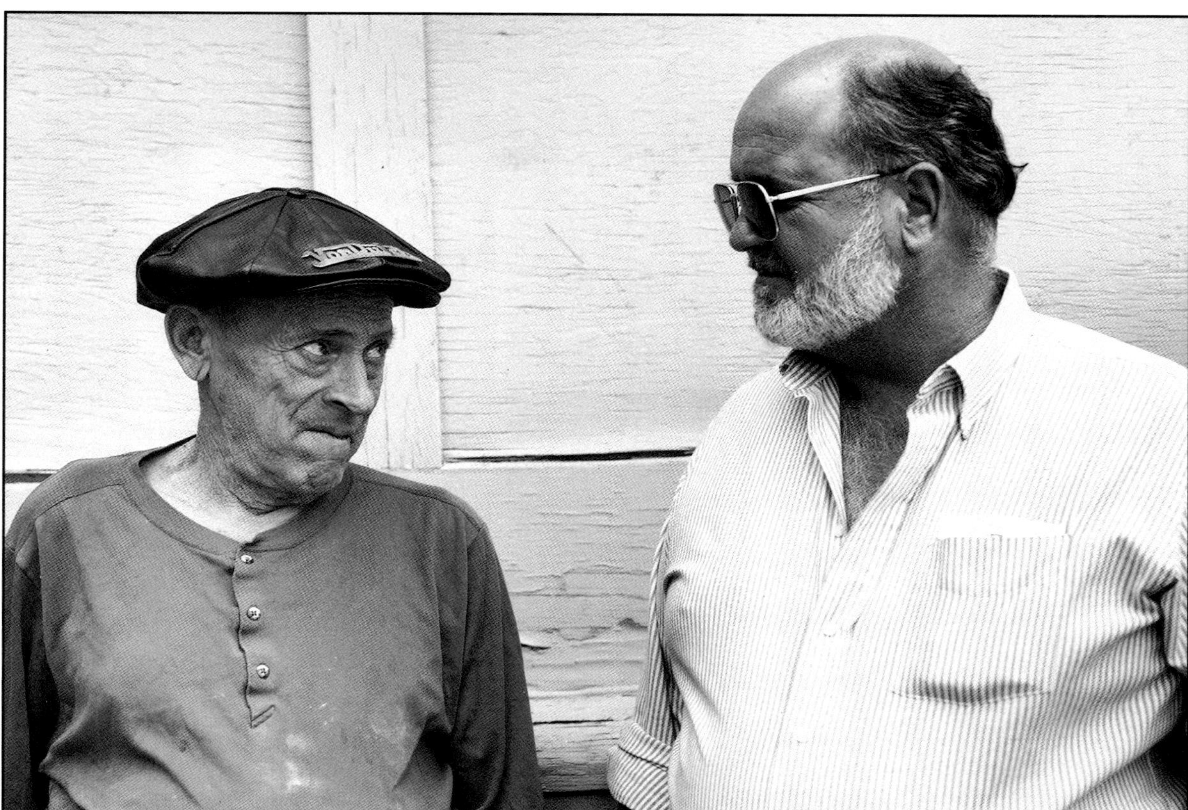

Von Dutch and his patron, Jim Brucker, 1992.

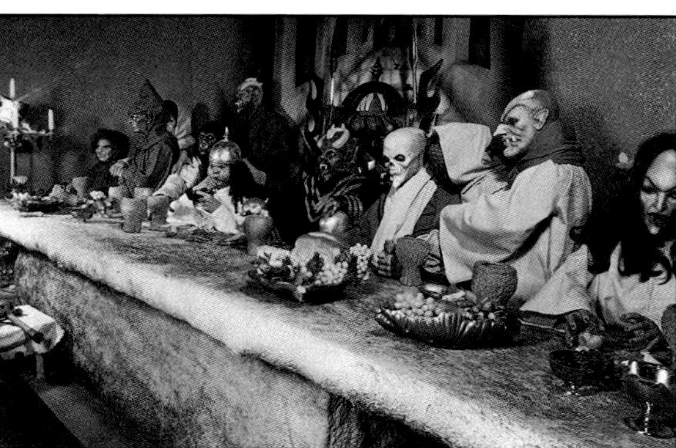

THE LAST SUPPER *at the Bruckers' Movieworld Cars of the Stars and Planes of Fame in Orange County, 1976. Von Dutch collaborated on this tableau for the Brucker family. Photo courtesy of Jim and Dan Brucker.*

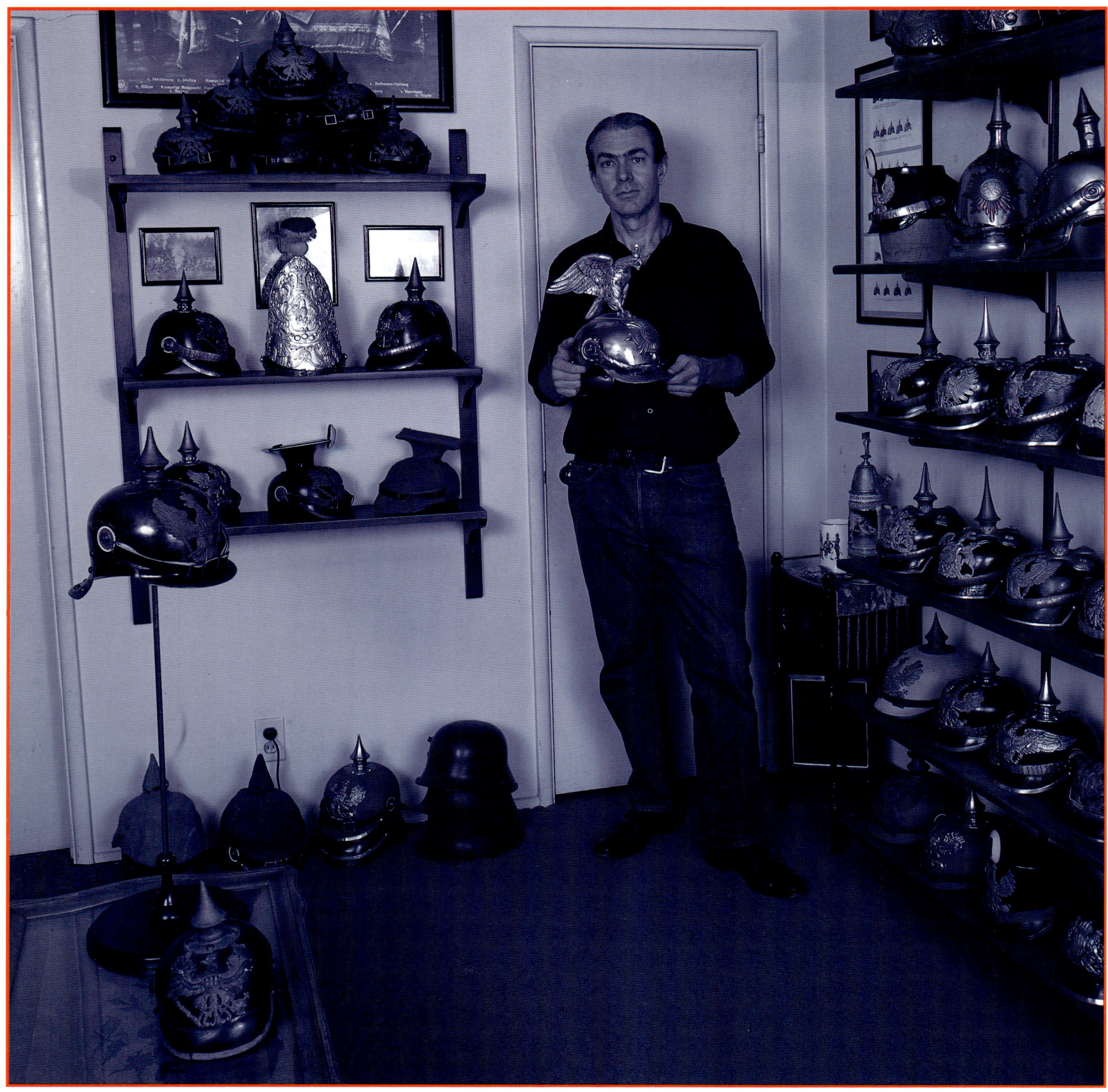

sombrero collection that is considered the world's finest, a well-regarded library of early California literature, a museum-quality American Indian artifact grouping and a selection of real estate featuring sites of archaeological and paleontological importance.

Other family assemblages of interest include selections of automotive art, illustration art, original comic strip art, weaponry, tools, an example of every technologically significant television set in the history of the medium, panoramic photography, armor, early California art, orange crate labels and newspapers.

Of all of the Bruckers' diverse holdings, it is the automobile, airplane and motorcycle collection that has always garnered the most attention. Comprising over 1,000 specialty and modified vehicles, the Bruckers' collection was at one time the world's largest. It also was the first collection to be interested in hot rods and customs in addition to the traditionally prestigious marques. The automobile collection evolved into a business as the Bruckers provided historical stunt vehicles and aircraft to motion picture productions.

Realizing the significance of his car holdings in 1970, Jim Brucker built a museum to present them to the public. In addition to many of Ed Roth's customs, which Brucker had purchased outright, there were pieces on display done by Winfield, Barris and Westerqard. Other historically viable attractions at "Movieworld Cars of the Stars and Planes of Fame" included Fatty Arbuckle's touring car, Countess di Frasso's Darrin Rolls Royce, Eva Braun's Horch special roadster and Dr. Ferry Porsche's Adler prototype, a 1929 Murphy bodied Mercedes Benz race car, as well as Cords, Duesenbergs, Pierce-Arrows, '32 Maybeck Zeppelins, Stanley Steamers, James Dean's Merc from *Rebel without a Cause*, etc. The museum was a popular Orange County attraction until 1979, when Brucker disbanded it to pursue other interests.

During this period Jim Brucker functioned as Robert Williams's primary patron. Ed Roth worked at the museum for several years doing exhibition design and graphic signage. Von Dutch re-entered the scene when he dropped in unexpectedly. (As Brucker recalls, "Dutch showed up one day and said `let me park my bus behind the museum and I'll hang out.'" This began a close relationship between the two men, which lasted until the artist's death. It also rekindled the interaction with Roth and Williams.)

There are other concerns in Los Angeles narrative art styles that correspond to the elemental distillation of themes in the work of Von Dutch, Roth and Williams. Call it a preoccupation with the downbeat. Analyze the output of LA chroniclers all across the spectrum, from novelist Raymond Chandler to the rapper Ice Cube: the attitude is coarse, edgy and hard, obsessed with a clinical examination of the underbelly of human existence. This trait can be observed in the first instances of culture imported into the region. Richard Henry Dana's *Two Years before the Mast*, the essential narrative of the clash between native culture and interlopers of the Spanish hide trade, examines in detail the commonality of everyday experience. Novels such as Fitzgerald's *The Last Tycoon*, Nathanael West's *Day of the Locust*, and James M. Cain's *The Postman Always Rings Twice* portray the offbeat as the surreal ordinary.

More recent works of popular culture also revel in this unadorned joie de misère. The works of actor producer Jack Webb, such as the television series *Dragnet*, *Adam 12* and *Emergency,* are cases in point. Listen to Webb's dispassionate world-weary staccato speeches as Sergeant Joe Friday in *Dragnet*. Now cue up Ice T's epic rap cut *Midnight*. The themes are pure Angeleno and the presentations are hard-ass narratives straight out of the *con safos* school of Chingadero culture. Other proponents of the style include Little Willie G, Jim Thompson, John Fante, Ruben Guevara, Charles Bukowski, Kid Frost, Dashiell Hammett, Henry Rollins, Frank

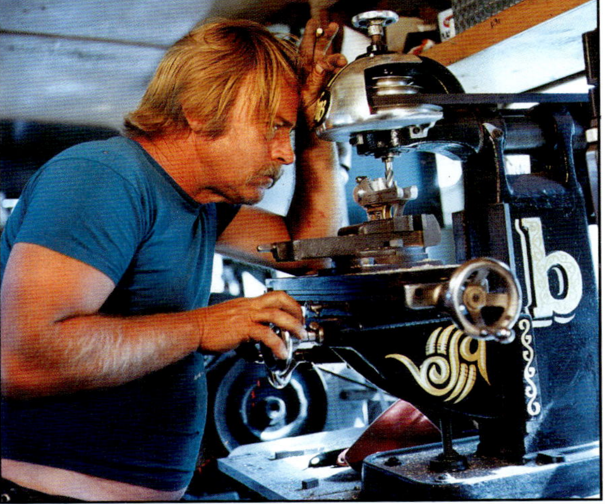

Von Dutch at work in his bus, 1975. Photo by Temma Kramer.

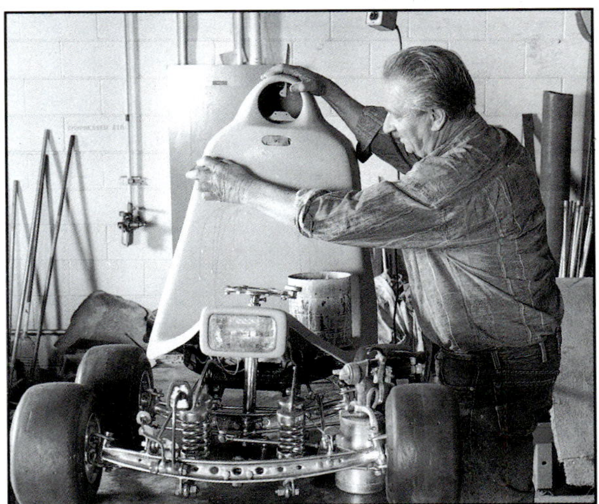

Roth sanding the Yankee Blitz*, 1992.*

(Opposite) Robert Williams with a portion of his German Empire helmet collection, 1987.

Zappa, Robert Towne, John Doe, Exene Cervenka, NWA (Niggas With Attitude), Don Van Vliet (Captain Beefheart), and Jim Morrison.

The multicultural complexity of Los Angeles also has been an influence. Stanton MacDonald-Wright's body of LA work drew heavily upon local topography and Pan-Asian imagery. Considering that Wright was among America's preeminent artists (what other US artist had founded a recognized European theoretical movement?), the profound changes in his work after settling in Los Angeles are extremely provocative. It is clear that his attraction to this new environment moved his work away from formal Synchromism towards a more personalized multiculturalism.

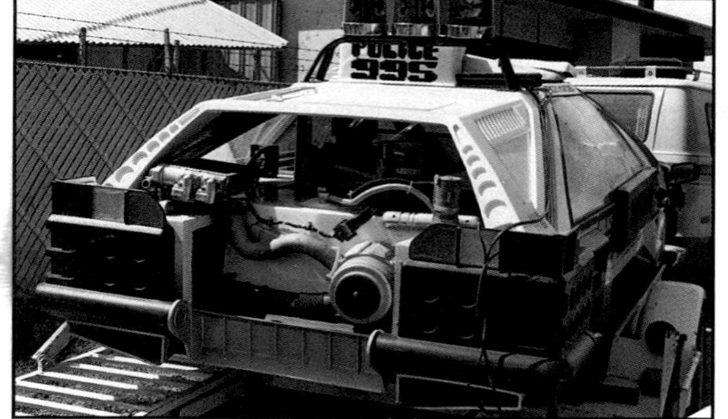

Robert Benchley's musings during his *Garden of Allah* period are celebrations of an unpredictable environment in constant flux. The artistic output of Basil Wolverton was a fatalistic, futuristic version of LA years in advance of Ridley Scott's *Bladerunner.* The efforts of artists like Edward Kienholz, H.C. Westermann, Ron Cobb, Michael C. McMillen and Betye Saar have all been focused somewhat on the aberrations of Angeleno life. Von Dutch's stripped-down satirical sketches can be equated to Bukowski's poetry. Both are unapologetically aimed at your jugular vein. Compare Roth's 1967 tragicomic *Cong Killer* to John Wayne at his most rabid, pro-American best in *The Green Berets.* Only bold, provincial upstarts such as these would have dared to be so politically incorrect.

Two cars from Ridley Scott's LA retro-future fantasy film, Blade Runner*: (top) police cruiser at Gene Winfield's shop; (above) police patrol unit, photographed at George Barris's shop.*

Forget content: Williams' titles alone were enough to inspire a major demonstration over his inclusion in the Museum of Contemporary Art's *Helter Skelter* exhibition. The painting *Oscar Wilde in Leadville, Colorado, April 13th, 1882*, was singled out as an example of Williams's alleged homophobia. The piece, which is the result of exhaustive historical research, depicts an actual incident where the culture-craving citizens of a boom mining town invited Wilde to speak. Oscar was enthusiastically received and was reported to have greatly enjoyed his time in the rough and ready town. Other protesters at MOCA referred to Williams's purported "exploitation of women" in his work.

Both of these claims are based on rather cursory examinations of the work. The Oscar Wilde painting merely presents history. Williams is just as aware of the persecution of the author Wilde in his time as he is of the *de facto* second-class treatment women receive in this society. The artist offers up slices of evidence many would like to avoid. To point out society's misogynistic practices does not necessarily make one a woman hater. How likely is it that a man raised by a lesbian couple, as Williams was, would be either homophobic or anti- female? Does an artist who has been hounded and harassed by government operatives and threatened with incarceration due to the content of his art turn out work that is opposed to other people's right of free speech?

To reflect on the negative aspects of the society in which we live has become increasingly unpopular. Just as Roth was once assaulted for the alleged promotion of the Nazi and Williams has drawn fire for portraying unpopular themes such as incest, others working in the LA *noir vérité* style have been singled out. The Body Count *Cop Killer* outrage followed controversies over NWA's *Dopeman*, a frank tale of the crack cocaine trade in South Central and Ice Cube's commentary on many blacks' distrust of the Korean community. These three songs have been blamed for everything from inciting national riots to encouraging prostitution and police homicide. In the tradition of ancient Sparta, it now appears we kill the messenger for the crime of bringing us the message.

(Opposite) Robert Williams, 1993.

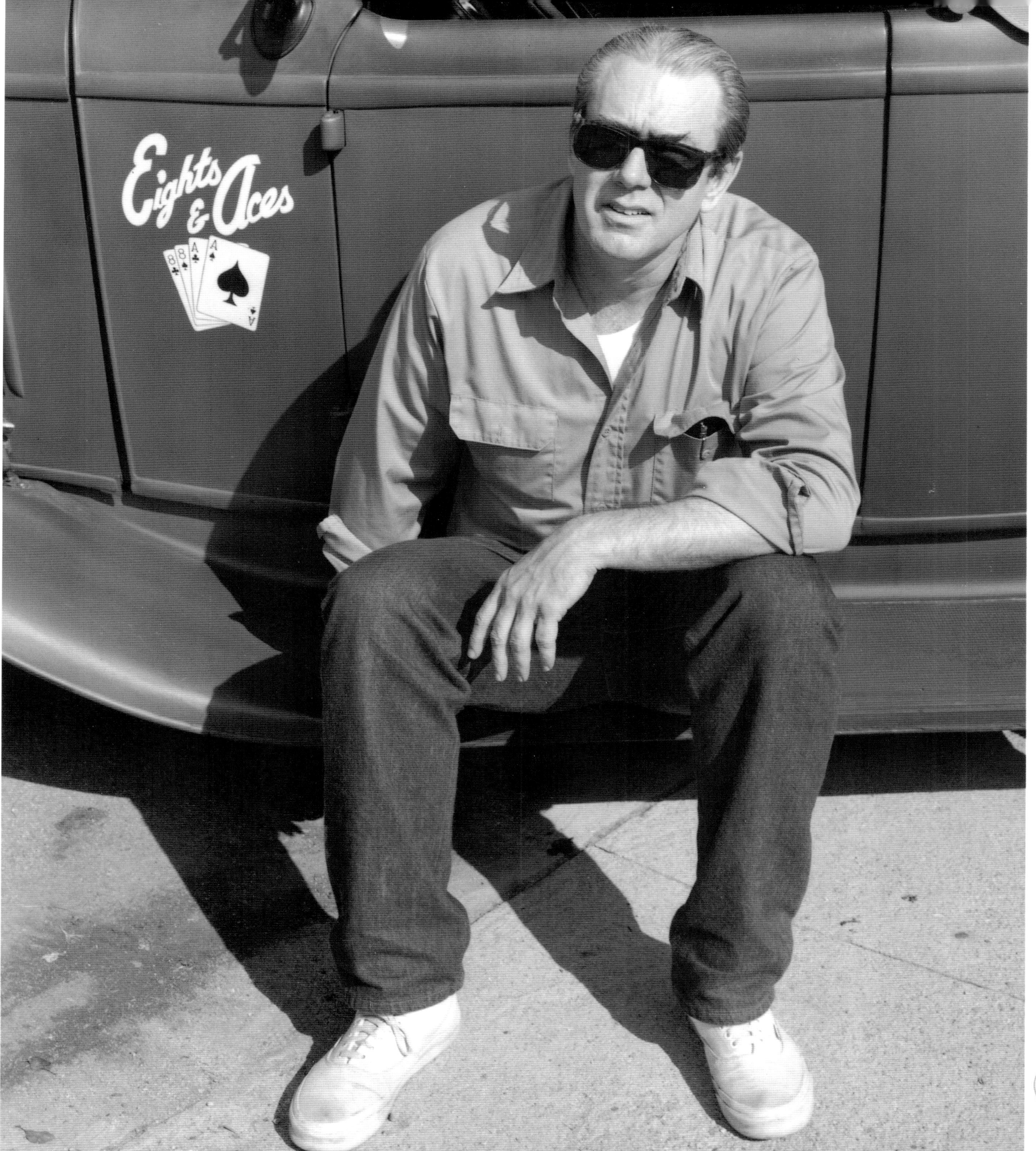
Eights & Aces

Von Dutch

RITES OF PASSAGE—CUSTOMIZED

Temma Kramer

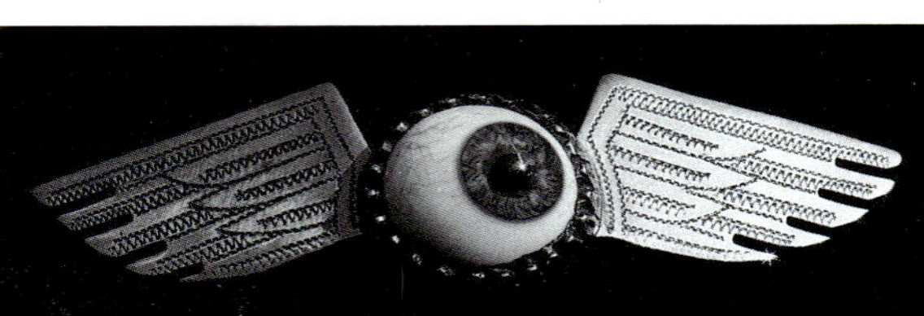

Temma Kramer is Professor of Film at California State University, Northridge, and a friend of Von Dutch.

The Golden Era of the Custom Car began in the late 1940s. After the end of World War II, ration books were discarded and an abundance of steel, fuel and rubber sparked the American dream of mobility. Government and oil interests spun a web of highways to connect the forty-eight states into one marketplace, indivisible in the name of commerce.

Not only does technology have a propensity for change, but change has become increasingly rapid in modern times. Meanwhile, social and cultural institutions have been hard put to evolve at this accelerated rate. The human condition is not as readily re-tooled as is a factory. The result is a culture gap where social institutions relate less and less meaningfully to the physical reality of the environment

It took 350 years to achieve the mechanical press (1814) after the invention of the Gutenberg press (1455). Society had centuries to get ready for the mass distribution of information and knowledge.

There was a gap of 100 years between the invention of the steam engine (1720) and the advent of the railroad (1825). A span of at least four generations was available to prepare for the social impact of mass transit.

In the twentieth century, the pace of technological development has accelerated almost to the point of instant change, leaving no meaningful time for society or culture to accommodate to that change.

Only thirty-six years separated Kitty Hawk (1903) from jet propulsion (1939), and only twelve years separates Sputnik (1957) from the moon landing (1969).

Is it any wonder that the Women's Movement and the Men's Movement decry the arbitrary and antiquated gender identities that are imposed on us—identities that were devised to accommodate a society and culture that no longer exists?

Long before Robert Bly formulated his ideas about *Iron John*, young men, in search of male bonding and rites of passage, filled the culture gap by developing a culture around the Custom Car.

These young men became iron johns, small i, small j, who worshiped their Goddess, the Custom Car. This mechanical icon— the automobile—embodies both male and female principles as defined by the prevailing culture.

The automobile is a synthesis of the Power and the Beauty metaphors of gender identification that post-industrial American culture has embraced. Worshiping her—the automobile—confirms manhood on the acolyte.

The sanctuary for the Custom Car Goddess is the garage. The garage serves the spiritual and communal function of the long house or sweat house, where elder males pass on their knowledge and manhood to the young.

The young acolyte learns from the elder priest about tools and attitudes that will identify the acolyte as one of the elect.

The ritual chant is a litany of cubic inches, fuel efficiency, gear ratios, horsepower and revolutions per minute. Sacramental Beer is drunk in the garage sanctuary, and tribal customs are passed on and reaffirmed.

The bible is a compendium of magazines such as Hot Rod and repair manuals. The Goddess herself is washed and polished and buffed and paraded for others to admire.

The customizing of a car is like a ritual circumcision, where the machine stands in for the human initiate and is forever marked as being unique. The transformation of a mass-produced object into a personalized icon of power and beauty is a way of claiming individuality in a mass-produced world.

The power principle—the engine—is identified as masculine and adult. Paradoxically, the power is contained within and protected by the fluid sculptural body of the goddess— representing the principle of beauty. She is adorned with paint and chrome and glass. Thus, rather than an icon that separates the genders, the customized car is a synthesis of gender. The icon has been co-opted by men and used as a sacred object in a ritual rite of passage, but the metaphor is available to everyone.

As society makes the transformation from the Machine Age to the Electronic Age, process-integration and multi-tasking will become the imperatives of progress and success. Perhaps the cultural phenomenon of the Custom Car holds symbolic clues for this transformation.

Von Dutch understood the mystical value of the Custom Car. For painting flames on a Mercedes Gull Wing back in the 1950s, he said, "Everyone got mad at me. They thought I had desecrated a shrine!" Von Dutch knew what he had really done.

Von Dutch was at once the embodiment of all that was Custom Car culture, and at the same time he was such an individual that he was typical of no one but himself.

During interviews in the 1970s, he waxed eloquent about his love of the machine. The idea of building an engine fascinated him. The idea of fabricating something that could generate heat and light and power moved him to ecstacy.

One of the happiest periods of Von Dutch's life was during the years that he worked with Bud Ekins restoring antique motorcycles. Dutch often spoke of the pleasure he derived from being able to create something that was both beautiful and met the functional challenges of mechanics and physics. The social satisfaction for Dutch and Bud was the unspoken knowledge they shared and their synchronicity of purpose. Often, when Bud would see that he needed a particular tool, Dutch would anticipate the need and was at his side handing the tool to Bud without being asked.

Hours might pass without a word being spoken as both men worked in harmony toward a common purpose. Their work was a meditation.

Love of machinery and the ability to work with one's hands is a sign of identity that traverses class lines. While working on the motion picture Le Mans, Von Dutch was introduced to a man identified as being of English nobility. Dutch recalled that his first impression of the man was that he was "some candy-assed, stuck-up aristocrat—utterly worthless."

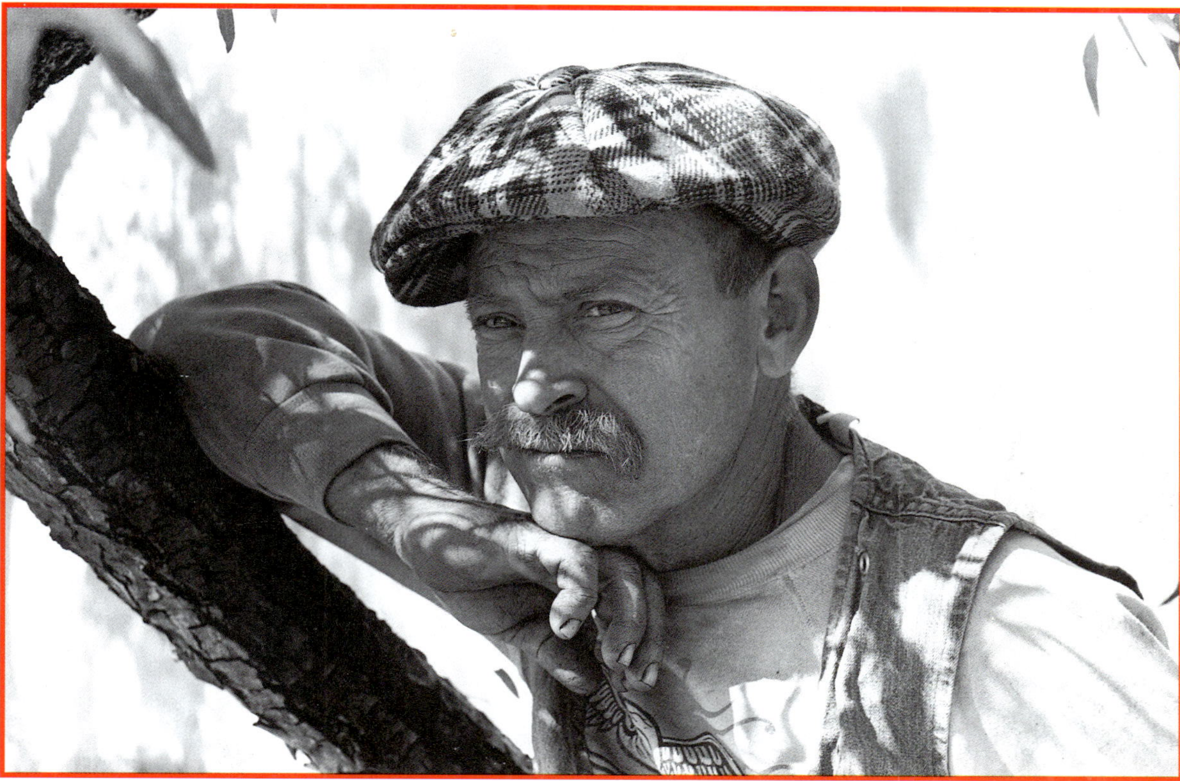

Kenneth Howard, aka Von Dutch, 1974. Photo by Temma Kramer.

✠ *(Opposite) Von Dutch,* FLYING EYEBALL, *c. 1975 (etched brass with inlaid eye, 1 ¼ x 4 x ¼ in.; collection of Jim and Dan Brucker).*

Then they shook hands. The man's hands were calloused from working with tools and his cuticles were stained with engine oil. Dutch's attitude did a 180-degree turn. The aristocrat was a car buff who worked on his own vehicles. These two men, worlds apart in social class, shared a more significant cultural identity—the automobile.

Von Dutch was at once the high priest of the Custom Car world and its renegade iconoclast. He was a truth-sayer, to the point of madness. Von Dutch was the first to criticize what he saw as the heretical aspects of the car culture. For example, he decried the idea that "cubic money" was taking over from "cubic inches" as the divining standard of an engine's worth. Yet, Von Dutch was the most sincere worshipper of the culture, because machines let him down a lot less often than people did.

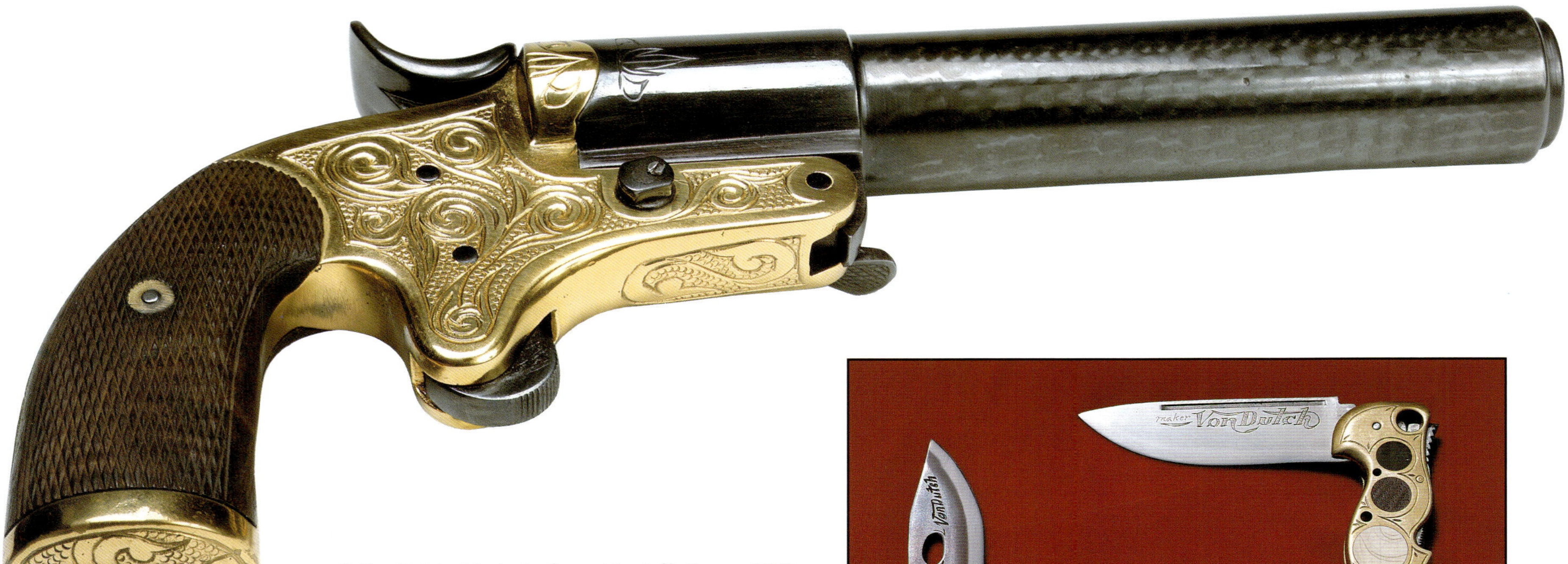

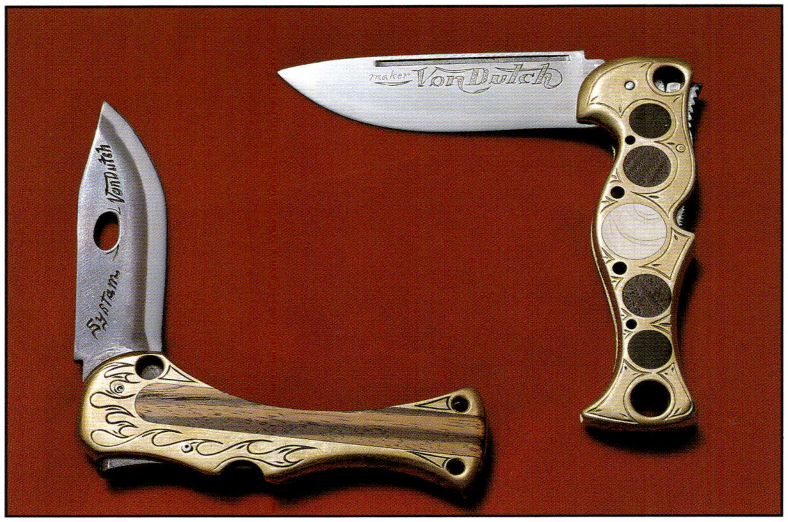

✠ *Von Dutch, (clockwise from upper left)* GUN, *c. 1975 (metal and brass, 5½ x 11½ x 1¼ in.);* STARRETT WORKING STAHL *and* THE GYPSY, *c. 1975 (metal with wood and ivory inlay, 1½ x 9 x ¼ in. each);* ELGIN NAVAL CUTLASS, *1970 (metal and wood, 6½ x 18 x 1¼ in.);* COFFIN KNIFE, *c. 1975 (brass, metal and wood, 1¾ x 6 x 2½ in.) All collection of Jim and Dan Brucker.*

✠ *(Opposite) Von Dutch,* SELF-PORTRAIT, *1965 (oil on board, 30 x 24¼ in.; collection of Jim and Dan Brucker).*

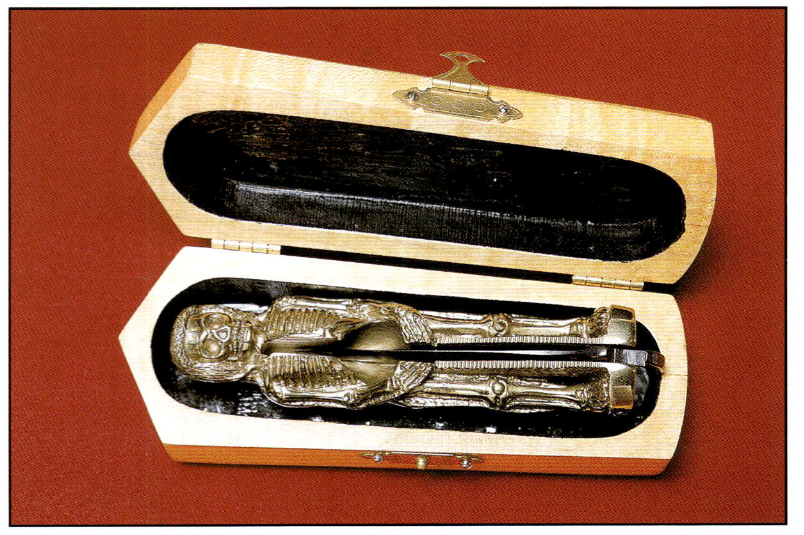

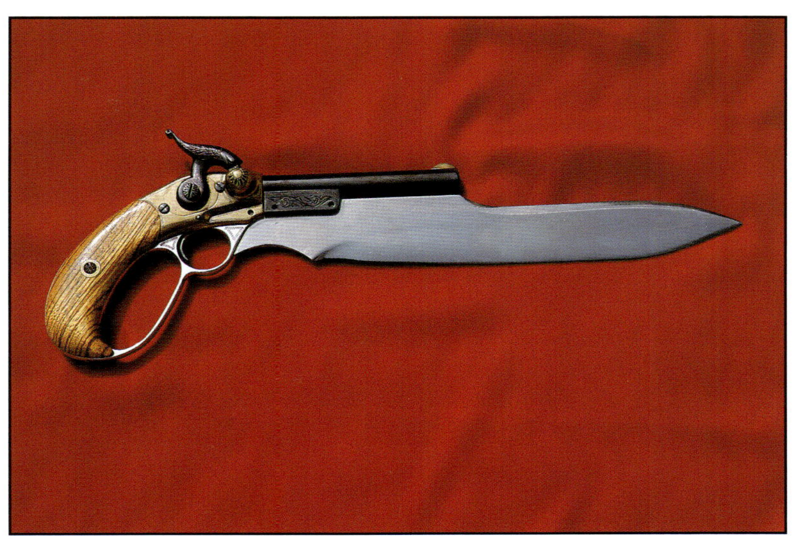

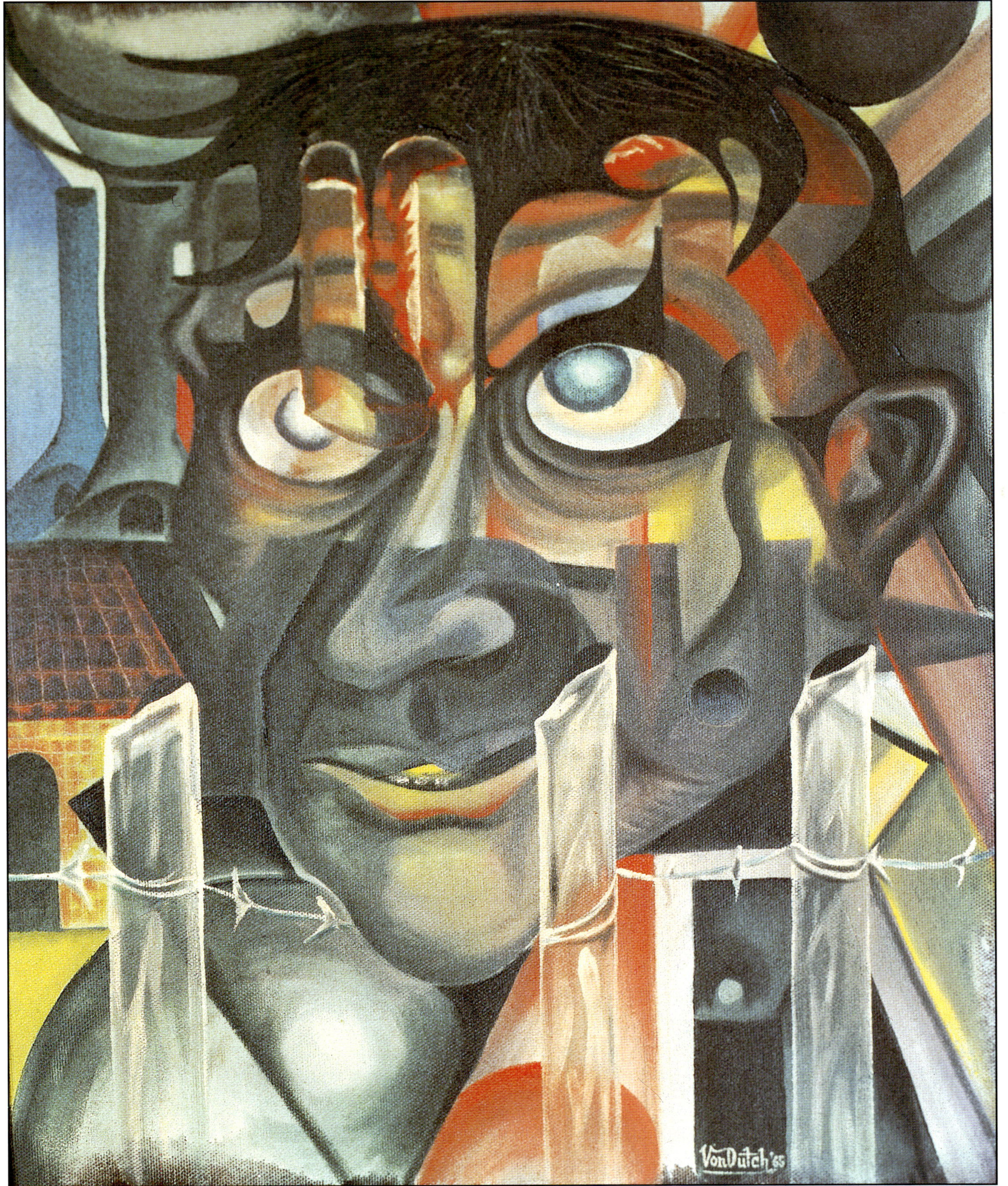
VonDutch '65

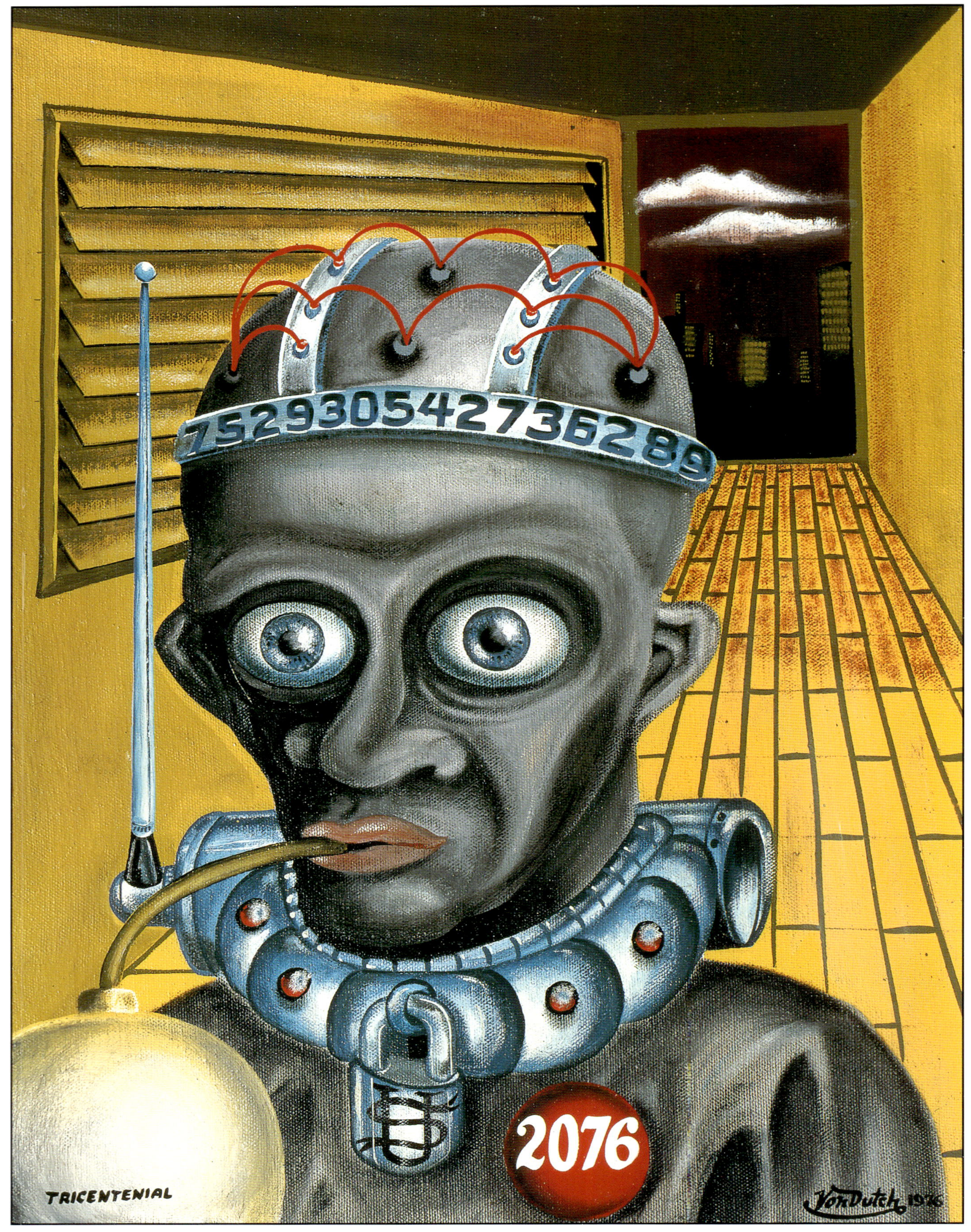
2076
TRICENTENIAL
Von Dutch

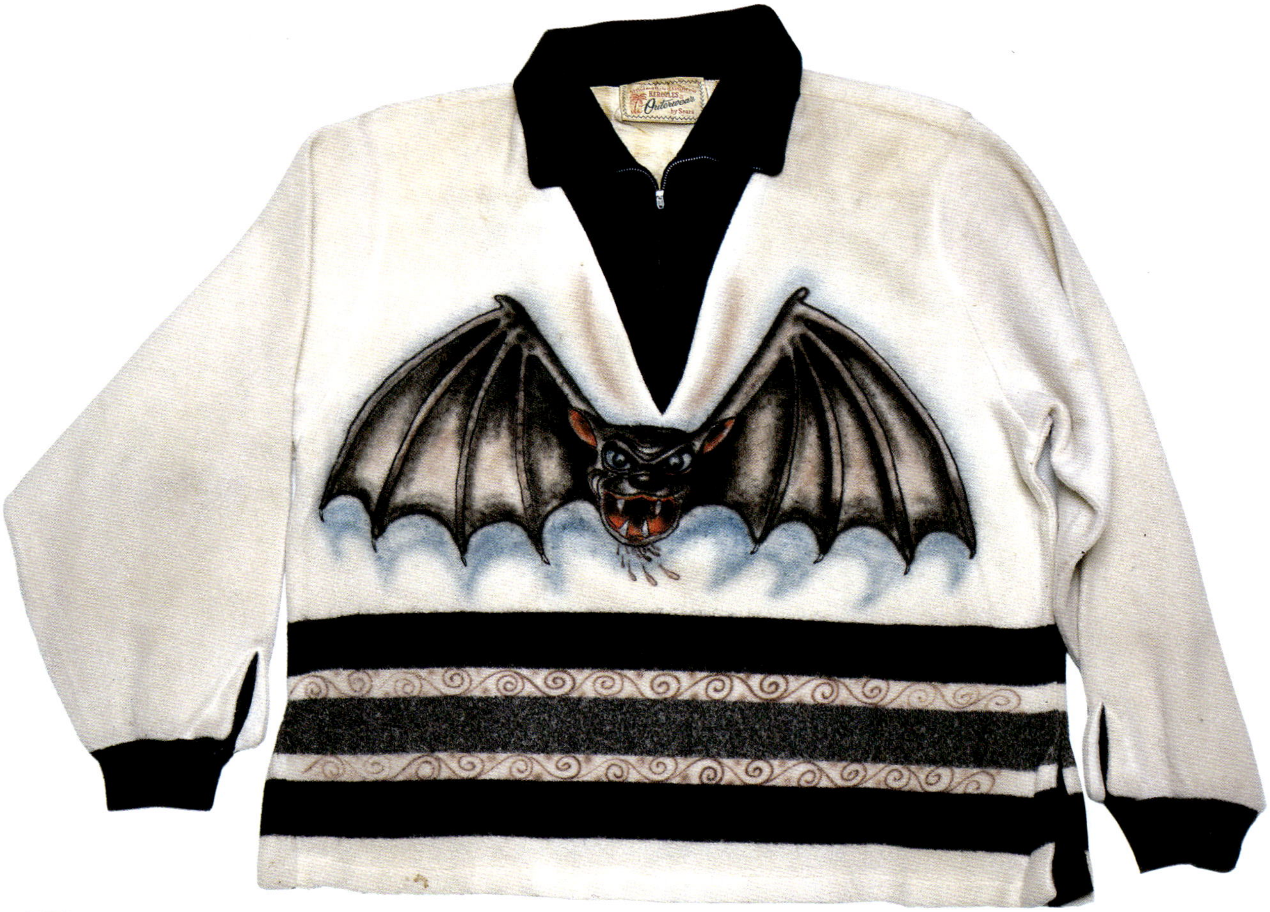

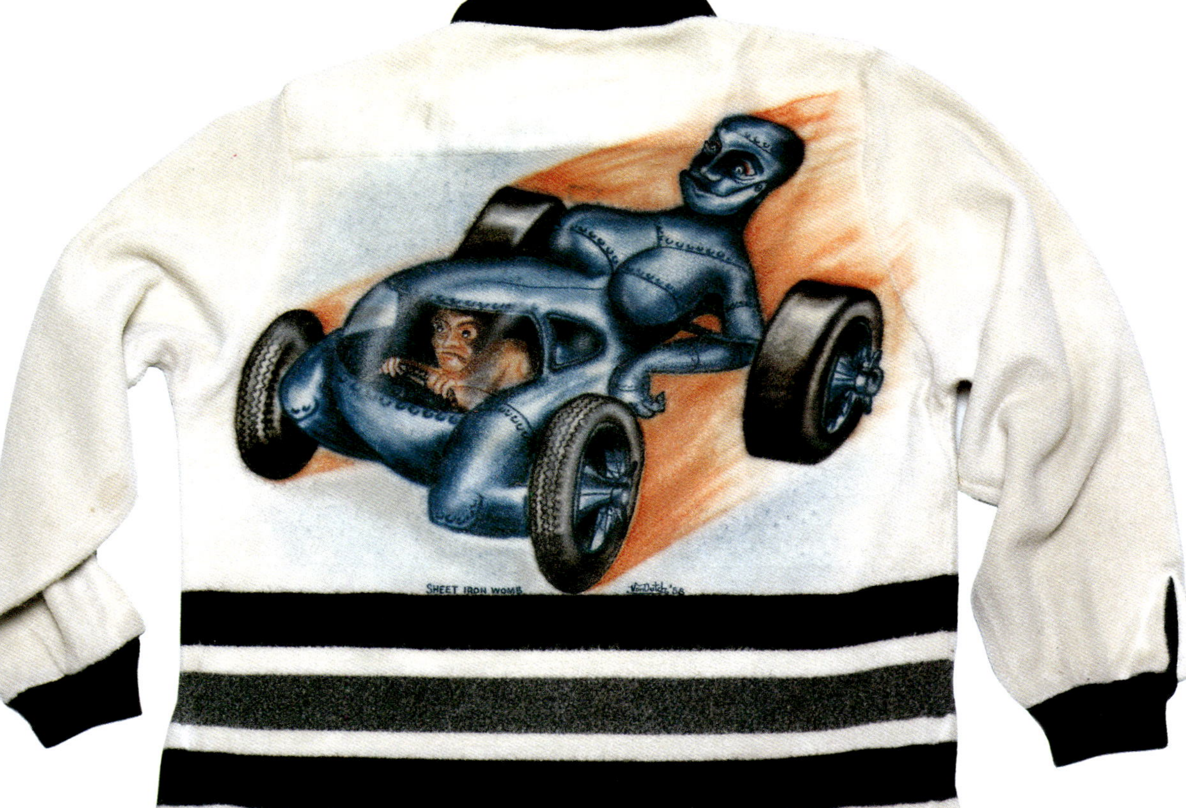

✠ *Von Dutch,* STEEL-IRON WOMB/BAT/SIGNATURE, *1958 (spray-painted, two-sided sweater, 23 x 18 in.; collection of Edward Moberg).*

✠ *(Opposite) Von Dutch,* TRICENTENNIAL 2076, *1976 (enamel on board, 18 x 14 in.; collection of Jim and Dan Brucker).*

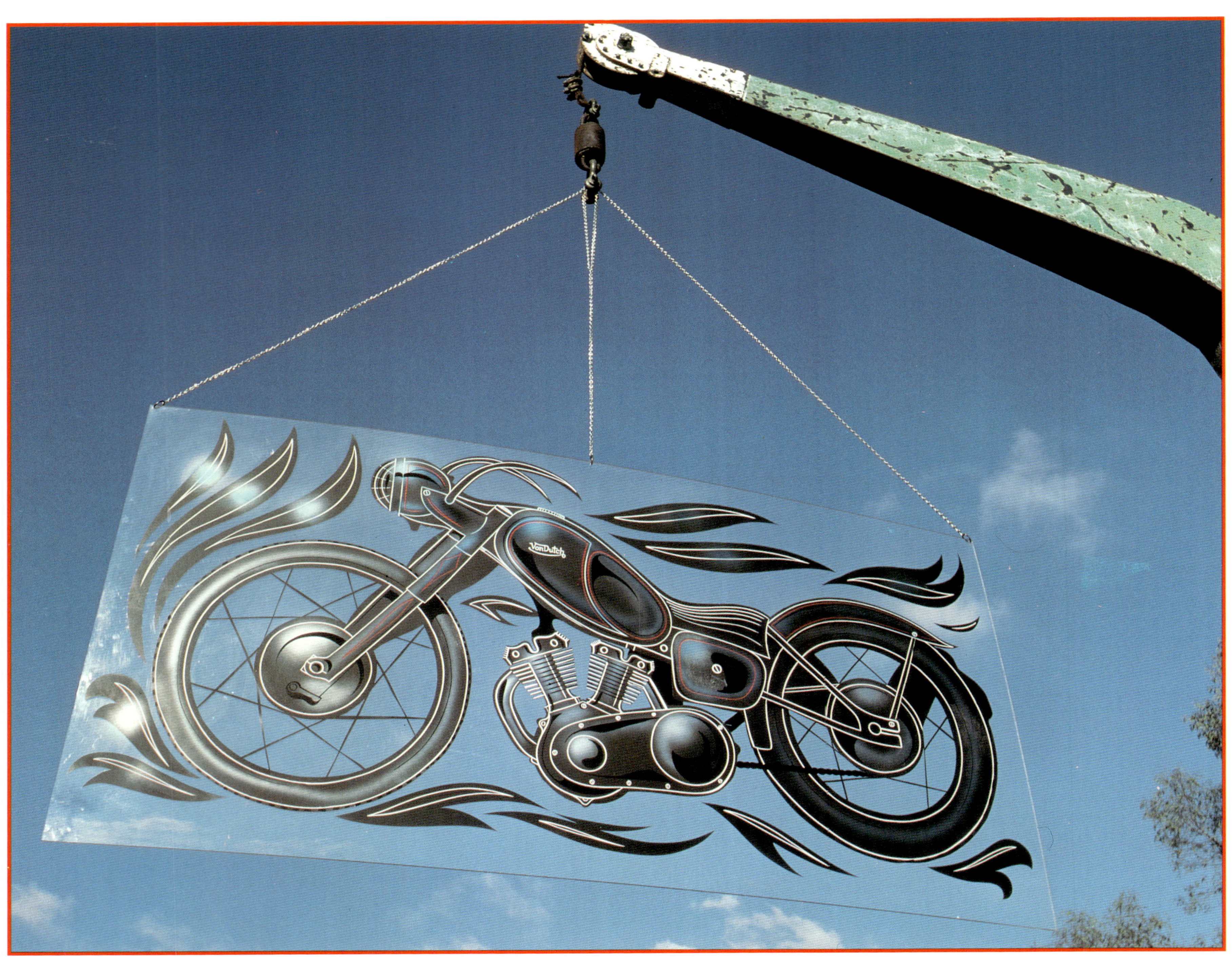
VonDutch

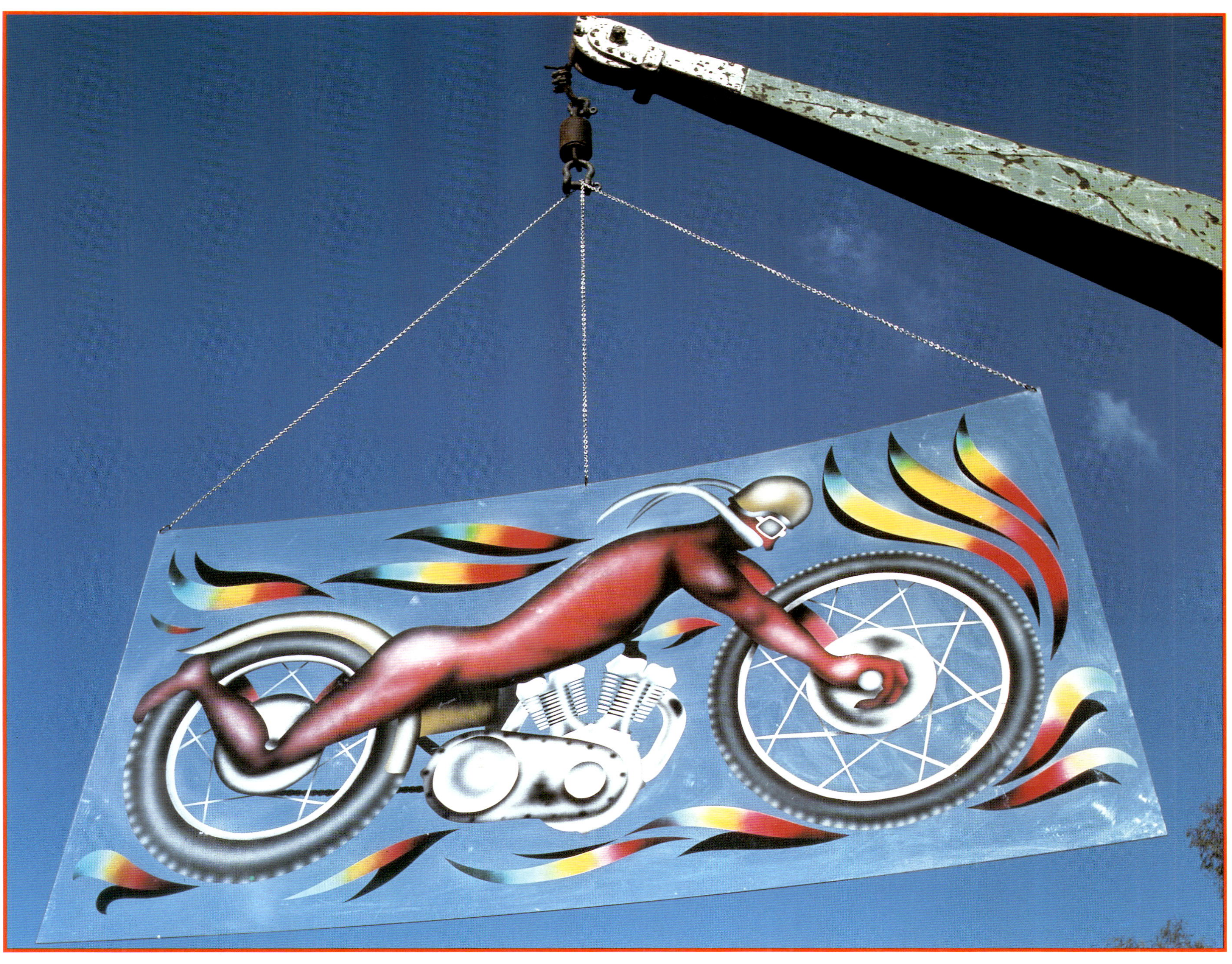

✠ *Front and back views of Von Dutch's two-sided motorcycle painting on plexiglass,* METAMORPHOSIS, *c. 1970. Photo courtesy Jim and Dan Brucker.*

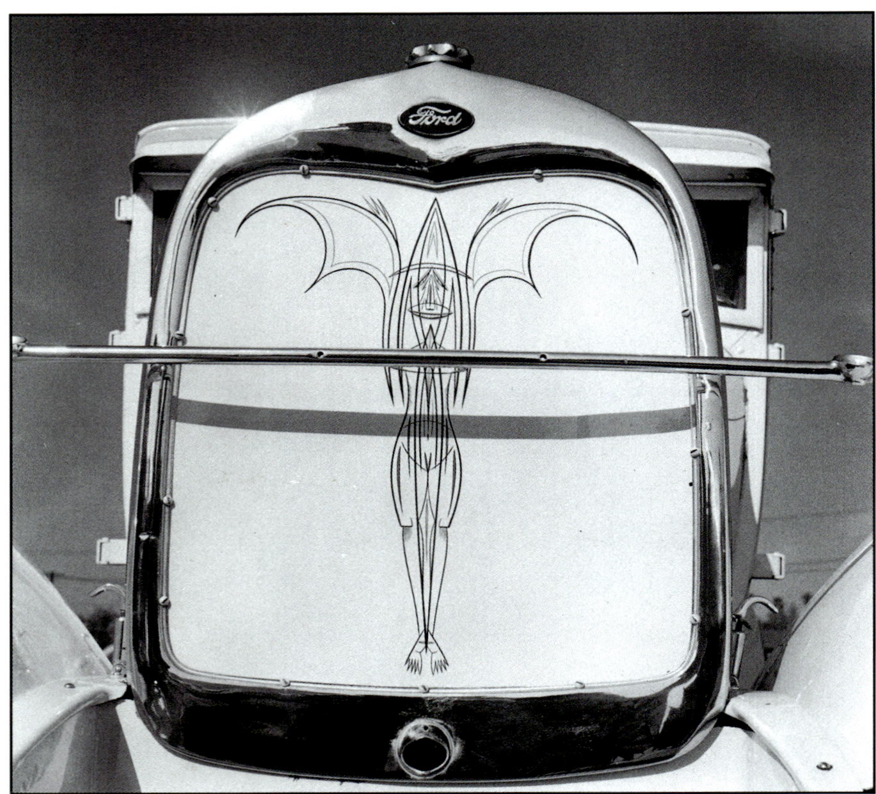

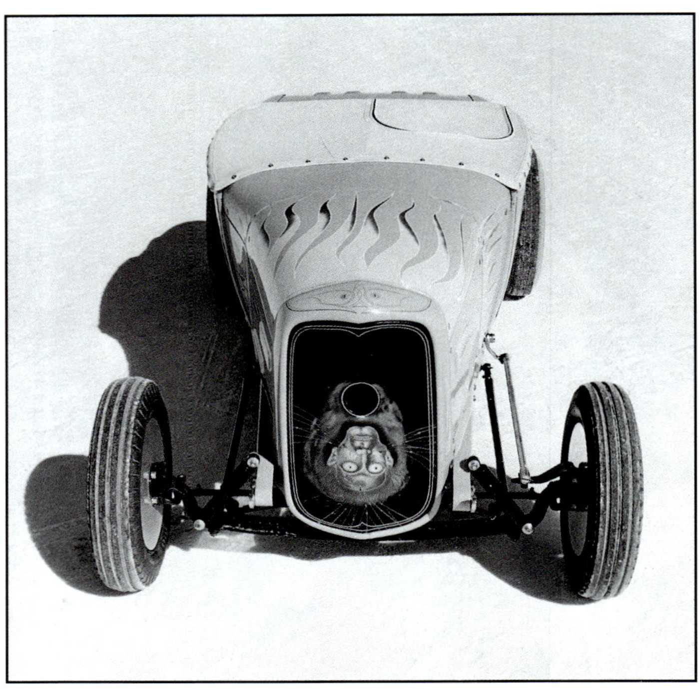

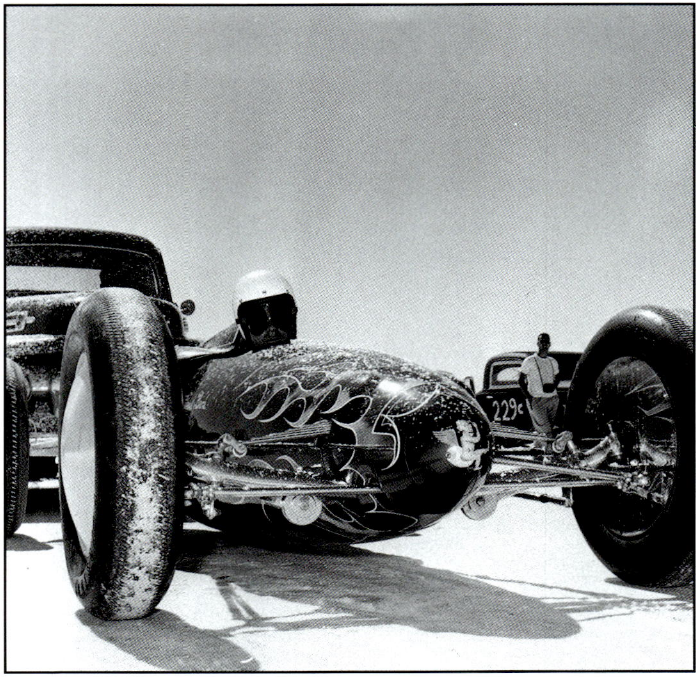

Three examples of Von Dutch's art on racing vehicles in the California dry lakes region. Photos courtesy Rod and Custom.

✠ *(Opposite) Von Dutch,* GOOD-BYE CRUEL WORLD, *1968 (oil on canvas, 24 x 20 in.; collection of Jim and Dan Brucker).*

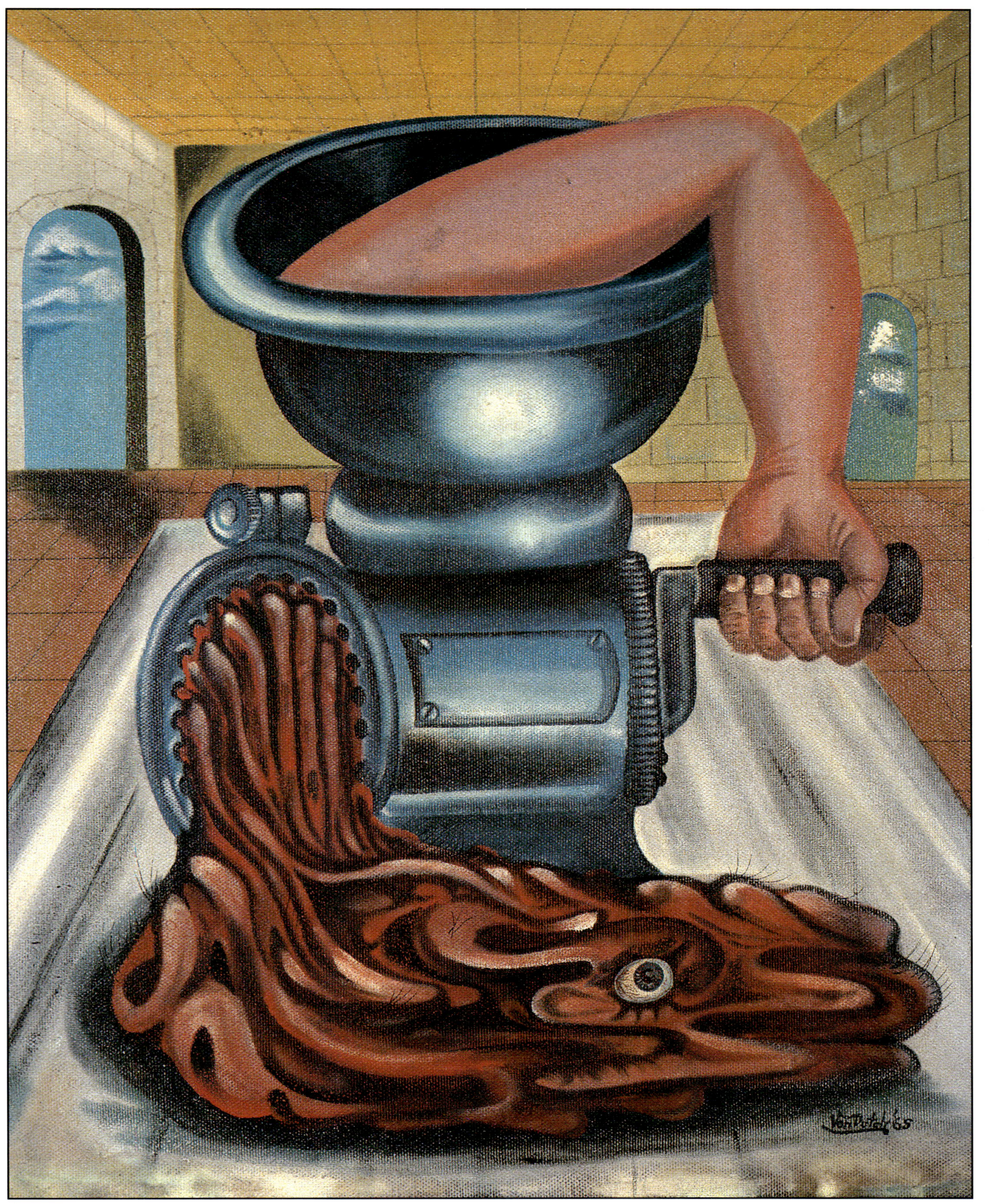

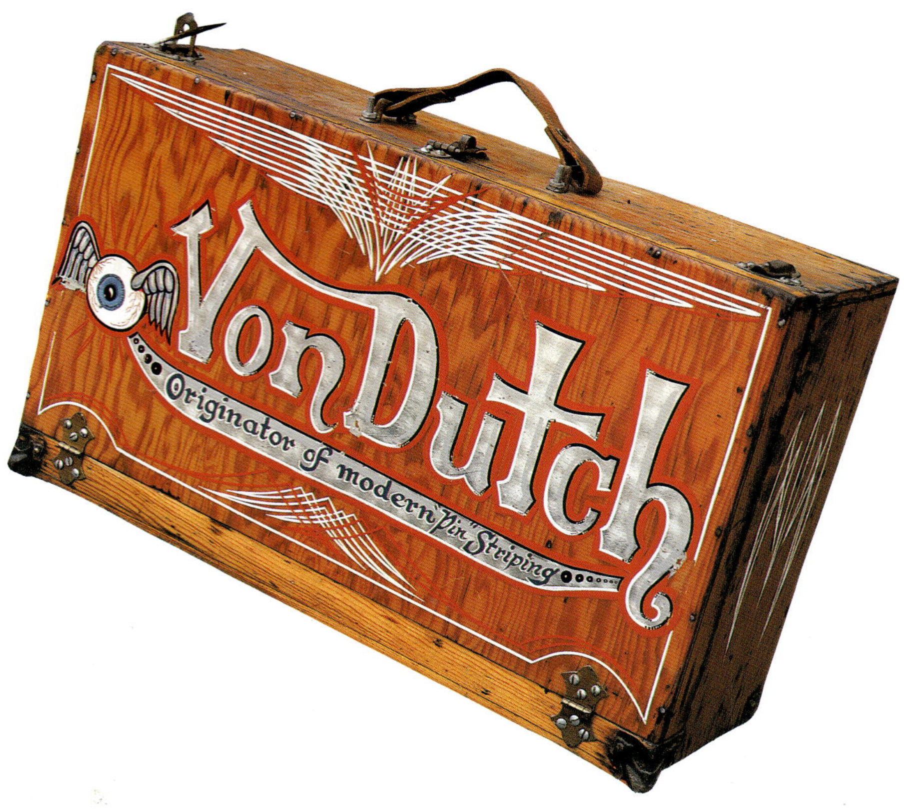

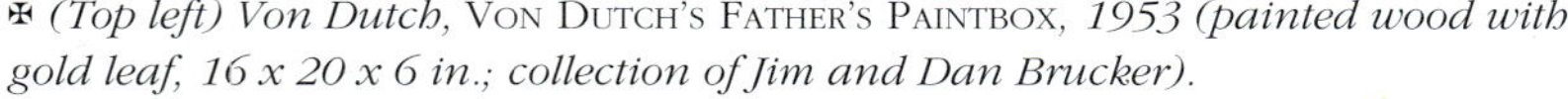

✠ *(Top left) Von Dutch,* Von Dutch's Father's Paintbox, *1953 (painted wood with gold leaf, 16 x 20 x 6 in.; collection of Jim and Dan Brucker).*

✠ *(Bottom left) Von Dutch,* I Am a Rabbit Too, *1956 (pinstripe and airbrush on board, 20 x 24 in.; collection of Jimmie Duffy, III).*

✠ *(Top and bottom right) Von Dutch,* Tool Box, *1985 (enamel on metal, 50 x 27 x 24 in.; collection of Jim and Dan Brucker).*

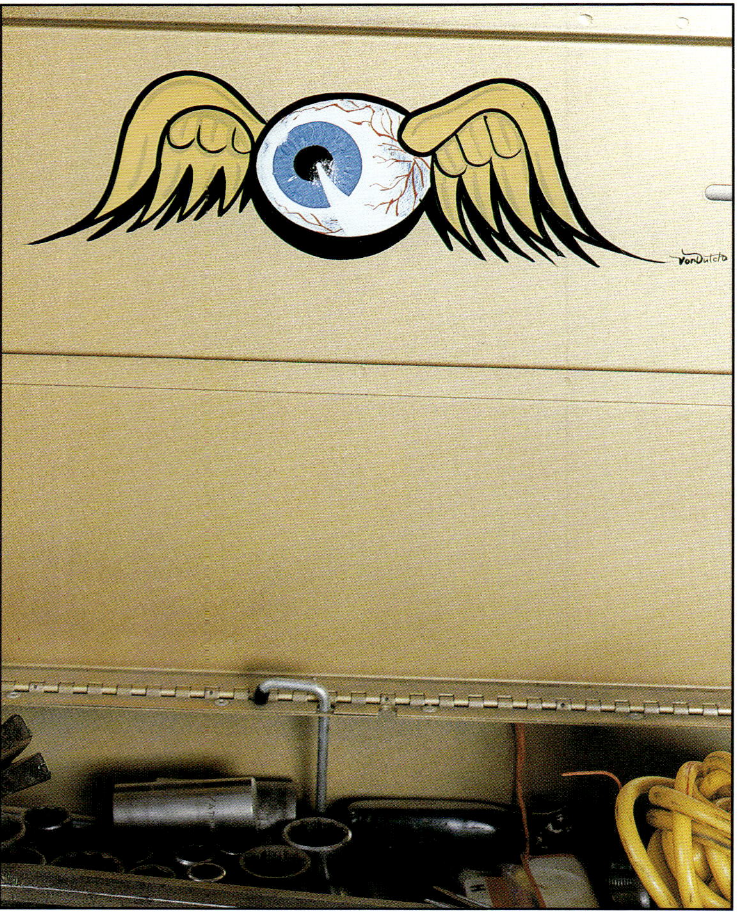

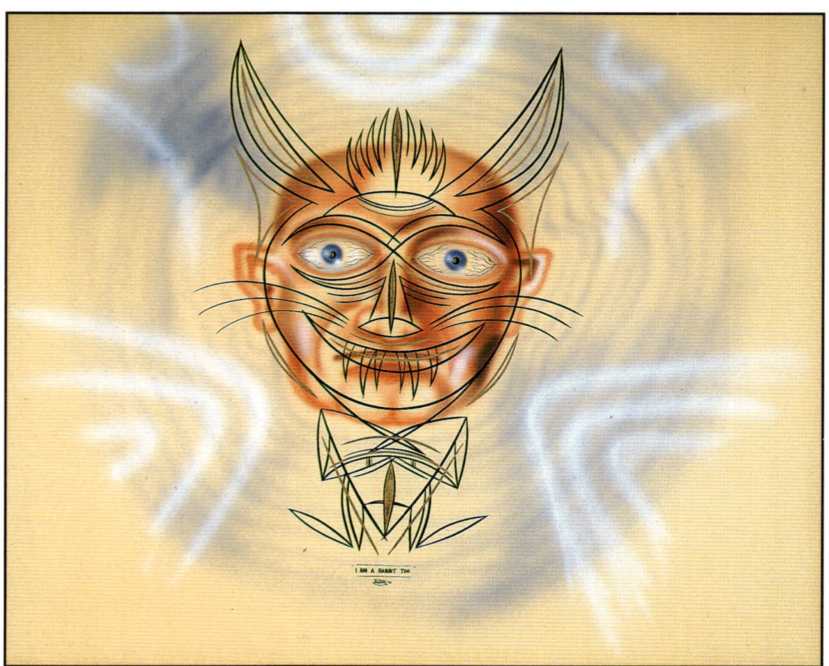

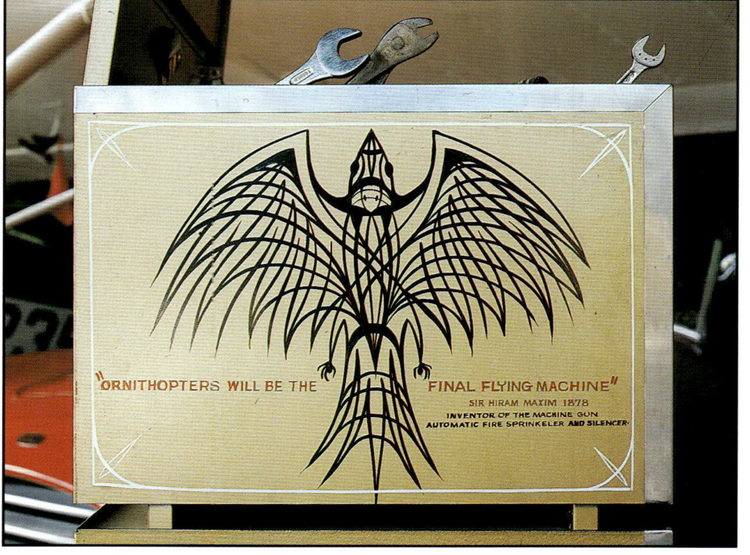

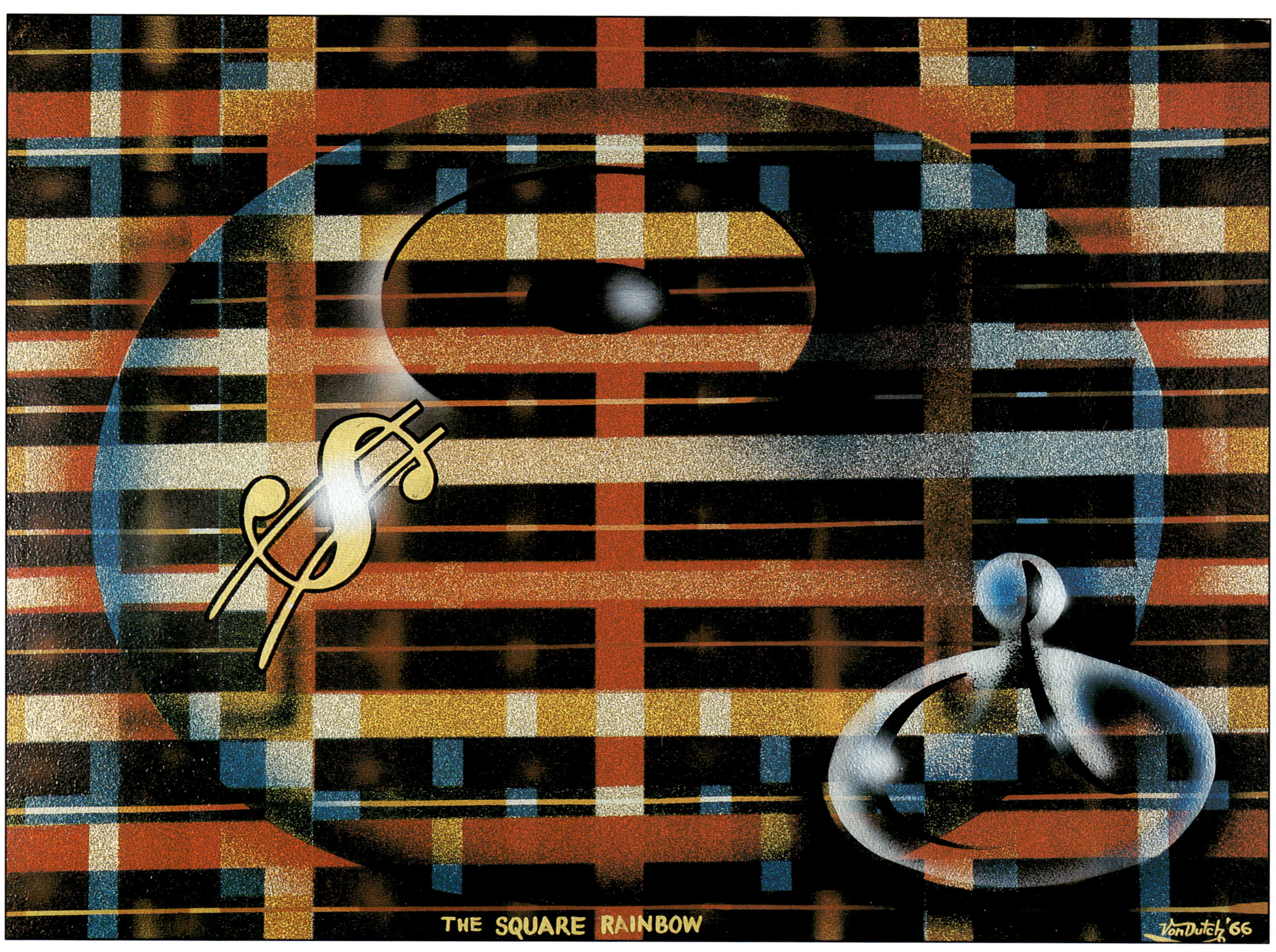

✠ *Von Dutch,* The Square Rainbow, *1966 (enamel on board, 24 x 30 in.; collection of Jim and Dan Brucker).*

THE KANDY-KOLORED TANGERINE-FLAKE STREAMLINE BABY

Tom Wolfe

I've mentioned Ed Roth several times in the course of this without really telling you about him. And I want to, because he, more than any other of the customizers, has kept alive the spirit of alienation and rebellion that is so important to the teen-age ethos that customizing grew up in. He's also the most colorful, and the most intellectual, and the most capricious. Also the most cynical. He's the Salvador Dali of the movement—a surrealist in his designs, a showman by temperament, a prankster. Roth is really too bright to stay within the ethos, but he stays in it with a spirit of luxurious obstinacy. Any style of life is going to produce its celebrities if it sticks to its rigid standards, but in the East a talented guy would most likely be drawn into the Establishment in one way or another. That's not so inevitable in California.

I had been told that Roth was a surly guy who never bathed and was hard to get along with, but from the moment I first talked to him on the telephone he was an easy guy and very articulate. His studio—and he calls it a studio, by the way—is out in Maywood, on the other side of the city from North Hollywood, in what looked to me like a much older and more run-down section. When I walked up, Roth was out on the apron of his place doing complicated drawings and lettering on somebody's ice-cream truck with an airbrush. I knew right away it was Roth from pictures I had seen of him; he has a beatnik-style beard. "Ed Roth?" I said. He said yeah and we started talking and so forth. A little while later we were sitting in a diner having a couple of sandwiches and Roth, who was wearing a short-sleeved T-shirt, pointed to this huge tattoo on his left arm that says "Roth" in the lettering style with big serifs that he uses as his signature. "I had that done a few years ago because guys keep coming up to me saying, 'Are you Ed Roth?'"

Roth is a big, powerful guy, about six feet four, two hundred seventy pounds, thirty-one years old. He has a constant sort of court attendant named Dirty Doug, a skinny little guy who blew in from out of nowhere, sort of like Ronny Camp over at Barris'. Dirty Doug has a job sweeping up in a steel mill, but what he obviously lives for is the work he does around Roth's. Roth seems to have a lot of sympathy for the Ronny Camp-Dirty Doug syndrome and keeps him around as a permanent fixture. At Roth's behest, apparently, Dirty Doug has dropped his last name, Kinney, altogether, and refers to himself as Dirty Doug—not Doug. The relationship between Roth and Dirty Doug—which is sort of Quixote and Sancho Panza, Holmes and Watson, Lone Ranger and Tonto, Raffles and Bunny—is part of the folklore of the hot-rod and custom-car kids. It even crops up in the hot-rod comic books, which are an interesting phenomenon in themselves. Dirty Doug, in this folklore, is every rejected outcast little kid in the alien netherworld, and Roth is the understanding, if rather overly prankster-ish, protective giant or Robin Hood—you know, a good-bad giant, not part of the Establishment.

Dirty Doug drove up in one of his two Cadillacs one Saturday afternoon while I was at Roth's, and he had just gone through another experience of rejection. The police had hounded him out of Newport. He has two Cadillacs, he said, because one is always in the shop. Dirty Doug's cars, like most customizers', are always in the process of becoming. The streaks of "primer" paint on the Cadillac he was driving at the time had led to his rejection in Newport. He had driven to Newport for the weekend. "All the cops have to do is see paint like that and already you're 'one of those hot-rodders,'" he said. "They practically followed me down the street and gave me a ticket every twenty- five feet. I was going to stay the whole weekend, but I came on back."

Excerpted from *The Kandy-Kolored Tangerine-Flake Streamline Baby* by Tom Wolfe

(New York: Farrar, Straus and Giroux, 1965).

Reprinted by permission of the publisher.

At custom-car shows, kids are always asking Roth, "Where's Dirty Doug?", and if Dirty Doug couldn't make it for some reason, Roth will recruit any kid around who knows the pitch and install him as Dirty Doug, just to keep the fans happy.

Thus Roth protects the image of Dirty Doug even when the guy's not around, and I think it becomes a very important piece of mythology. The thing is, Roth is not buying the act of the National Hot Rod Association, which for its own reasons, not necessarily the kids' reasons, is trying to assimilate the hot- rod ethos into conventional America. It wants to make all the kids look like candidates for the Peace Corps or something.

The heart of the contretemps between the NHRA Establishment and Roth can be illustrated in their slightly different approach to drag racing on the streets. The Establishment tries to eliminate the practice altogether and restricts drag racing to certified drag strips and, furthermore, lets the people know about that. They encourage the hot-rod clubs to help out little old ladies whose cars are stuck in the snow and then hand them a card reading something like, "You have just been assisted by a member of the Blue Bolt Hot Rod Club, an organization of car enthusiasts dedicated to promoting safety on our highways."

Roth's motto is: "Hell, if a guy wants to go, let him go."

Roth's designs are utterly baroque. His air car—the Rotar—is not nearly as good a piece of design as Barris', but his beatnik Bandit is one of the great *objets* of customizing. It's a very Rabelaisian *tour de force*—a twenty-first century version of a '32 Ford hot-rod roadster. And Roth's new car, the Mysterion, which he was working on when I was out there, is another *tour de force*, this time in the hottest new concept in customizing, asymmetrical design. Asymmetrical design, I gather, has grown out of the fact that the driver sits on one side of the car, not in the middle, thereby giving a car an eccentric motif to begin with. In Roth's Mysterion—a bubbletop coupe powered by two 406 horsepower Thunderbird motors—a thick metal arm sweeps up to the left from the front bumper level, as from the six to the three on a clock, and at the top of it is an elliptical shape housing a bank of three headlights. No headlights on the right side at all; just a small clearance light to orient the oncoming driver. This big arm, by the way, comes up in a spherical geometrical arc, not a flat plane. Balancing this, as far as the design goes, is an arm that comes up over the back of the bubbletop on the right side, like from the nine to the twelve on a clock, also in a spherical arc, if you can picture all this. Anyway, this car

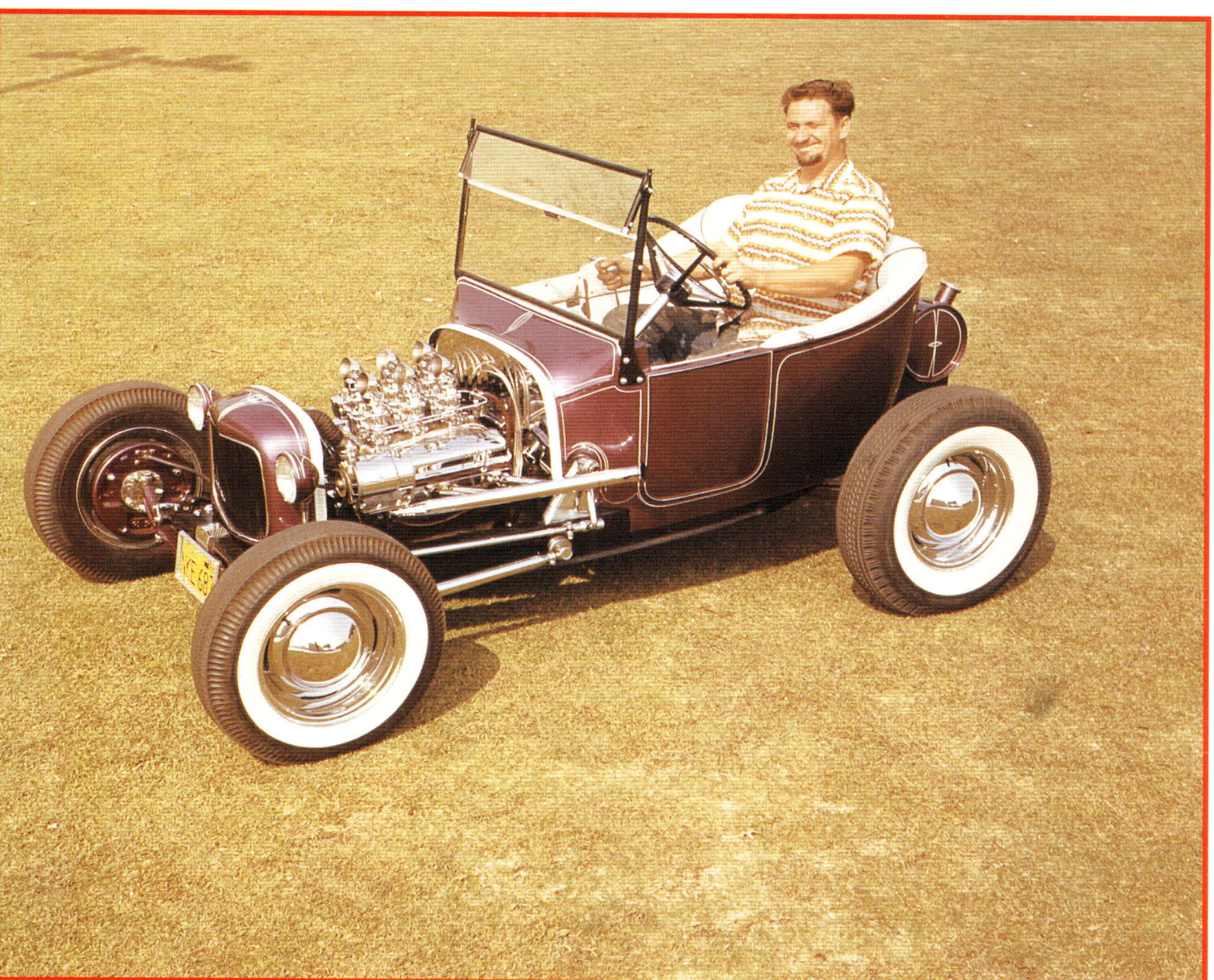

Ed Roth and Tweety Pie. *Photo courtesy Pat Ganahl.*

takes the streamline and the abstract curve and baroque curvilinear one step further, and I wouldn't be surprised to see it inspiring Detroit designs in the years to come.

Roth is a brilliant designer, but as I was saying, his conduct and his attitude dilutes the Halazone with which the Establishment is trying to transfuse the whole field. For one thing, Roth, a rather thorough-going bohemian, kept turning up at the car shows in a T-shirt. That was what he wore at the big National Show at the New York Coliseum, for example. Roth also insists on sleeping in a car or station wagon while on the road, even though he is making a lot of money now and could travel first class. Things came to a head early this year when Roth was out in Terre Haute, Indiana, for a show. At night Roth would just drive his car out in a cornfield, lie back on the front seat, stick his feet out the window and go to sleep. One morning some kid came by and saw him and took a picture while Roth was still sleeping and sent it to the model company Roth has a contract with, Revel, with a note saying, "Dear Sirs: Here is a picture of the man you say on your boxes is the King of the Customizers." The way Roth tells it, it must have been an extraordinarily good camera, because he says, with considerable pride, "There were a bunch of flies flying around my feet, and this picture showed all of them."

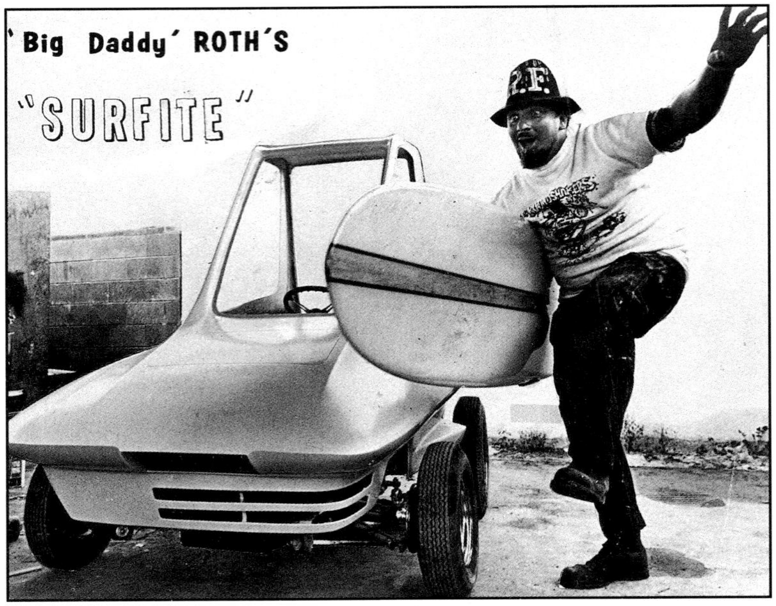

THE SURFITE, *built in 1962, was a lightweight, all-terrain, fuel-efficient, functional surf vehicle. Photo courtesy Lynn E. Coleman.*

Revel asked Roth if he wouldn't sort of spruce up a little bit for the image and all that, and so Roth entered into a kind of reverse rebellion. He bought a full set of tails, silk hat, boiled shirt, cuff links, studs, the whole apparatus, for $215, also a monocle, and now he comes to all the shows like that. "I bow and kiss all the girls' hands," he told me. "The guys get pretty teed off about that, but what can they do? I'm being a perfect gentleman."

To keep things going at the shows, where he gets $1,000 to $2,000 per appearance—he's that much of a drawing card—Roth creates and builds one new car a year. This is the Dali pattern, too. Dali usually turns out one huge and (if that's possible any more) shocking painting each year or so and ships it on over to New York, where they install it in Carstairs or hire a hall if the thing is too big, and Dali books in at the St. Regis and appears on television wearing a rhinoceros horn on his forehead. The new car each year also keeps Roth's model-car deal going. But most of Roth's income right now is the heavy business he does in Weirdo and Monster shirts. Roth is very handy with the airbrush—has a very sure hand—and one day at a car show he got the idea of drawing a grotesque cartoon on some guy's shirt with the airbrush, and that started the Weirdo shirts. The typical Weirdo shirt is in a vein of draftsmanship you might call Mad Magazine Bosch, very slickly done for something so grotesque, and will show a guy who looks like Frankenstein, the big square steam-shovel jaw and all, only he has a wacky leer on his face, at the wheel of a hot-rod roadster, and usually he has a round object up in the air in his right hand that looks like it is attached to the dashboard by a cord. This, it turns out, is the gearshift. It doesn't look like a gearshift to me, but every kid knows immediately what it is.

"Kids *love* dragging a car," Roth told me. "I mean they really love it. And what they love the most is when they shift from low to second. They get so they can practically *feel* the r.p.m.'s. They can shift without hardly hitting the clutch at all."

These shirts always have a big caption, and usually something rebellious or at least alienated, something like "MOTHER IS WRONG" or "BORN TO LOSE."

"A teen-ager always has resentment to adult authority," Roth told me. "These shirts are like a tattoo, only it's a tattoo they can take off if they want to."

I gather Roth doesn't look back on his own childhood with any great relish.

Apparently his father was pretty strict and never took any abiding interest in Roth's creative flights, which were mostly in the direction of cars, like Barris'.

"You've got to be real careful when you raise a kid, " Roth told me several times. "You've got to spend time with him. If he's working on something, building something, you've got to work with him." Roth's early career was almost exactly like Barris', the hot rods, the drive-ins, the drag racing, the college (East Los Angeles Junior College and UCLA), taking mechanical drawing, the chopped and channeled '32 Ford (a big favorite with all the hot-rodders), purple paint, finally the first custom shop, one stall in a ten-stall body shop.

"They threw me out of there," Roth said, "because I painted a can of Lucky Lager beer on the wall with an airbrush. I mean, it was a perfect can of Lucky Lager beer, all the details, the highlights, the seals, the small print, the whole thing. Somehow this can of Lucky Lager beer really bugged the guy who owned the place. Here was this can of Lucky Lager beer on *his* wall."

The Establishment can't take this side of Roth, just as no Establishment could accommodate Dadaists for very long. Beatniks more easily than Dadaists. The trick has always been to absorb them somehow. So far Roth has resisted absorption.

"We were the real gangsters of the hot-rod field," Roth said. "They keep telling us we have a rotten attitude. We have a different attitude, but that doesn't make us rotten."

Several times, though, Roth would chuckle over something, usually some particularly good gesture he had made, like the Lucky Lager, and say, "I am a real rotten guy."

Roth pointed out, with some insight, I think, that the kids have a revealing vocabulary. They use the works "rotten," "bad" and "tough" in a very fey, ironic way. Often a particularly baroque and sleek custom car will be called a "big, bad Merc" (for Mercury) or something like that. In this case "bad" means "good," but it also retains some of the original meaning of the "bad." The kids know that to adults, like their own parents, this car is going to look sinister and somehow like an assault on their style of life. Which it is. It's rebellion, which the parents don't go for—"bad," which the kids do go for, "bad" meaning "good."

Roth said that Detroit is beginning to understand that there are just a hell of a lot of these bad kids in the United States and that they are growing up. "And they want a better car. They don't want an old man's car."

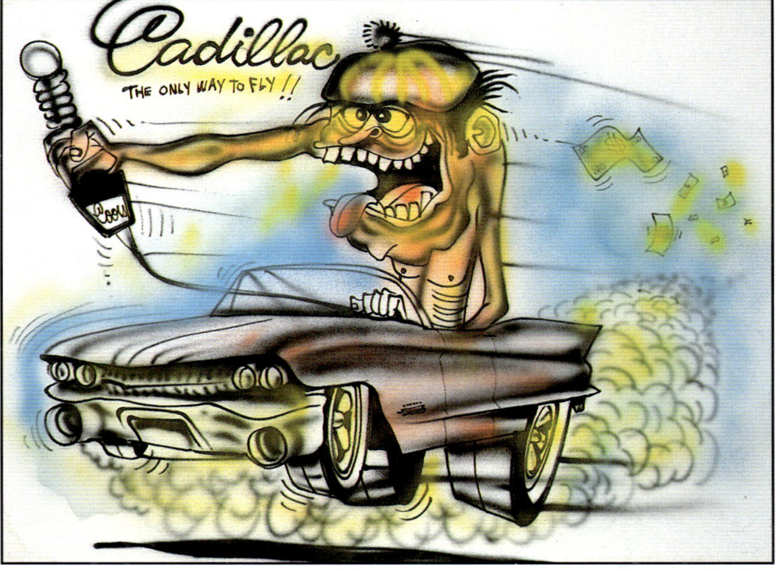

✠ *Ed "Big Daddy" Roth,* CADILLAC, THE ONLY WAY TO FLY!!!, *1962 (airbrush on illustration board, 26 x 35 in.; collection of Jimmie Duffy, III).*

Roth has had pretty much the same experience as Barris with the motor companies. He has been taken to Detroit and feted and offered a job as a designer and a consultant. But he never took it seriously.

"I met a lot of the young designers," said Roth. "They were nice guys and they know a lot about design, but none of them has actually done a car. They're just up there working away on those clay models."

I think this was more than the craftsman's scorn of the designer who never actually does the work, like some of the conventional sculptors today who have never chiseled a piece of stone or cast anything. I think it was more that the young Detroit stylists came to the automobile strictly from art school and the abstract world of design—rather than via the teen-age mystique of the automobile and the teen-age ethos of rebellion. This status-group feeling is very important to Roth, and to Barris, for that matter, because it was only because of the existence of this status group—and this style of life—that custom-car sculpture developed at all.

With the Custom Car Caravan on the road—it has already reached Freedomland—the manufacturers may be well on the way to routinizing the charisma, as Max Weber used to say, which is to say, bringing the whole field into a nice, safe, vinyl-glamorous marketable ball of polyethylene. It's probably already happening. The customizers will end up like those poor bastards in Haiti, the artists, who got too much, too soon, from Selden Rodman and the other folk-doters on the subject of primitive genius, so they're all down there at this moment carving African masks out of mahogany—what I mean is, they never *had* an African mask in Haiti before Selden Rodman got there.

I think Roth has a premonition that something like that is liable to happen, although it will happen to him last, if at all. I couldn't help but get a kick out of what Roth told me about his new house. We had been talking about how much money he was making, and he told me how his taxable income was only about $6200 in 1959, but might hit $15,000 this year, maybe more, and he mentioned he was building a new house for his wife and five kids down at Newport, near the beach. I immediately asked him for details, hoping to hear about an utterly baroque piece of streamlined architecture.

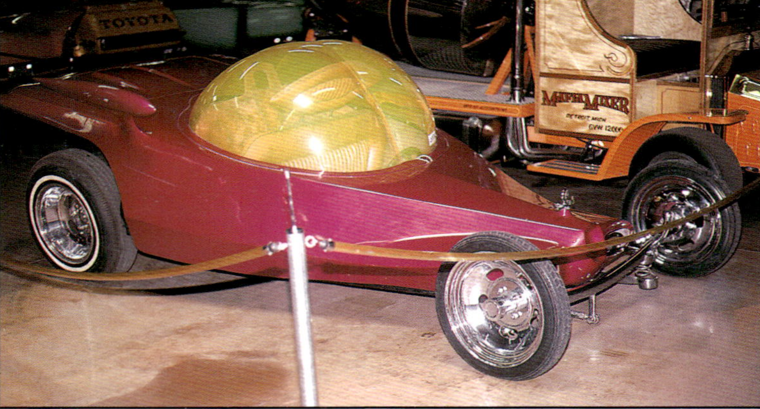

(Top) Revell™'s 1960s model kit of Roth's Road Agent.
(Bottom) Roth's Road Agent, *1961, at the Brucker's museum, Movieworld Car's of the Stars and Planes of Fame.*

(Opposite) Roth's Orbitron, *1964.*
Photo courtesy Pat Ganahl.

"No, this is going to be my wife's house, the way she wants it, nothing way out; I mean, she has to do the home scene." He has also given her a huge white Cadillac, by the way, unadorned except for his signature—"Roth"—with those big serifs, on the side. I saw the thing, it's huge, and in the back seat were his children, very sweet-looking kids, all drawing away on drawing pads.

But I think Roth was a little embarrassed that he had disappointed me on the house, because he told me his idea of the perfect house—which turned out to be a kind of ironic parable:

"This house would have this big, round living room with a dome over it, you know? Right in the middle of the living room would be a huge television set on a swivel so you could turn it and see it from wherever you are in the room. And you have this huge easy chair for yourself, you know the kind that you can lean back to about ninety-three different positions and it vibrates and massages your back and all that, and this chair is on tracks, like a railroad yard.

"You can take one track into the kitchen, which just shoots off one side of the living room, and you can ride backward if you want to and watch the television all the time, and of course in the meantime you've pressed a lot of buttons so your TV dinner is cooking in the kitchen and all you have to do is go and take it out of the oven.

"Then you can roll right back into the living room, and if somebody rings the doorbell you don't move at all. You just press a button on this big automatic console you have by your chair and the front door opens, and you just yell for the guy to come in, and you can keep watching television.

"At night, if you want to go to bed, you take another track into the bedroom, which shoots off on another side, and you just kind of roll out of the chair into the sack. On the ceiling above your bed you have another TV set, so you can watch all night.

Roth is given, apparently, to spinning out long Jean Shepherd stories like this with a very straight face, and he told me all of this very seriously. I guess I didn't look like I was taking it very seriously, because he said, "I have a TV set over the bed in my house right now—you can ask my wife."

I met his wife, but I didn't ask her. The funny thing is, I did find myself taking the story seriously. To me it was a sort of parable of the Bad Guys, and the Custom Sculpture. The Bad Guys built themselves a little world and got onto something good and then the Establishment, all sorts of Establishments, began closing in, with a lot of cajolery, thievery and hypnosis, and thrown into a vinyl Petri dish, the only way left to tell the whole bunch of them where to head in was to draw them a huge asinine picture of themselves, which they were sure to like.

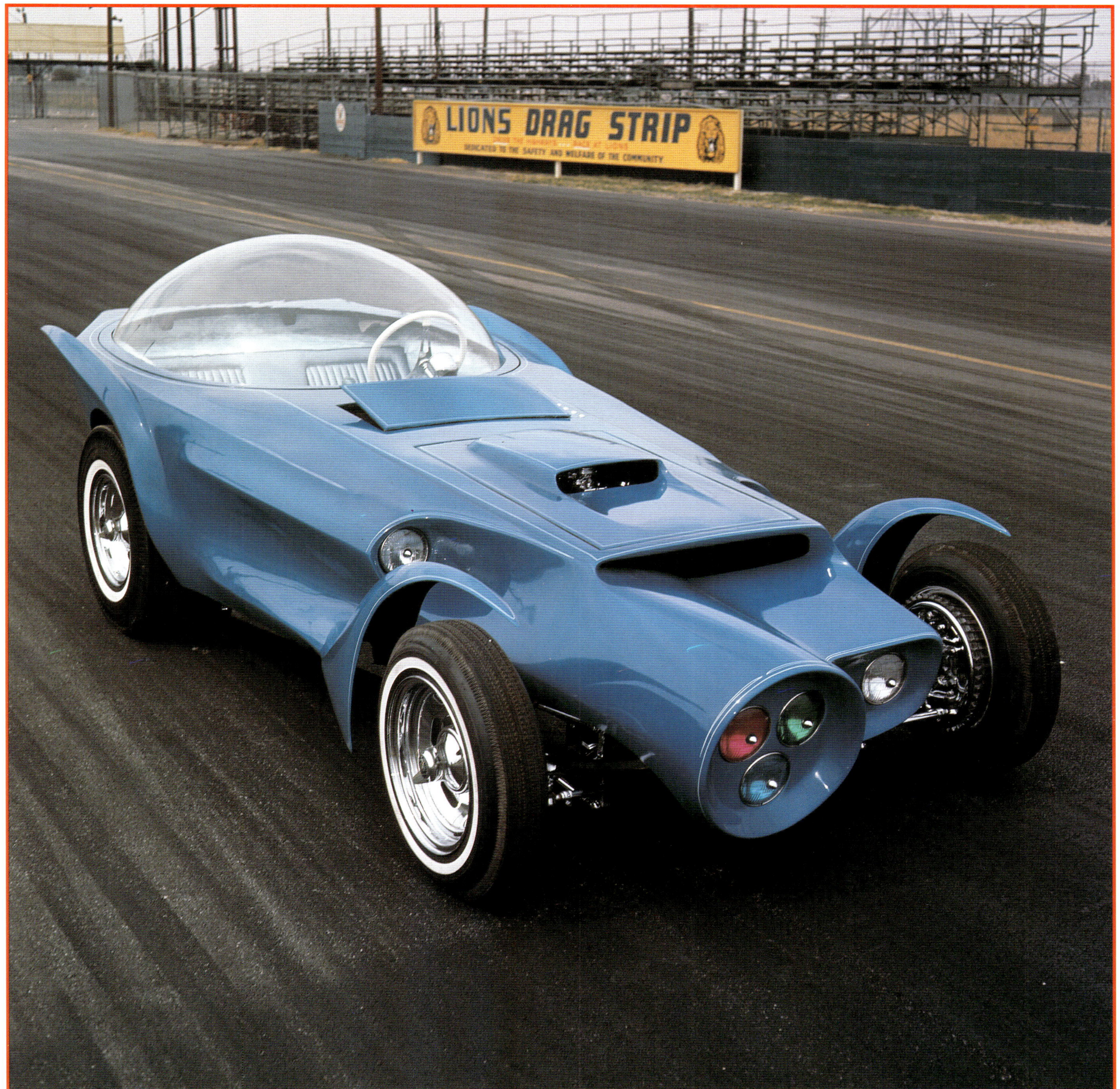
LIONS DRAG STRIP
DEDICATED TO THE SAFETY AND WELFARE OF THE COMMUNITY

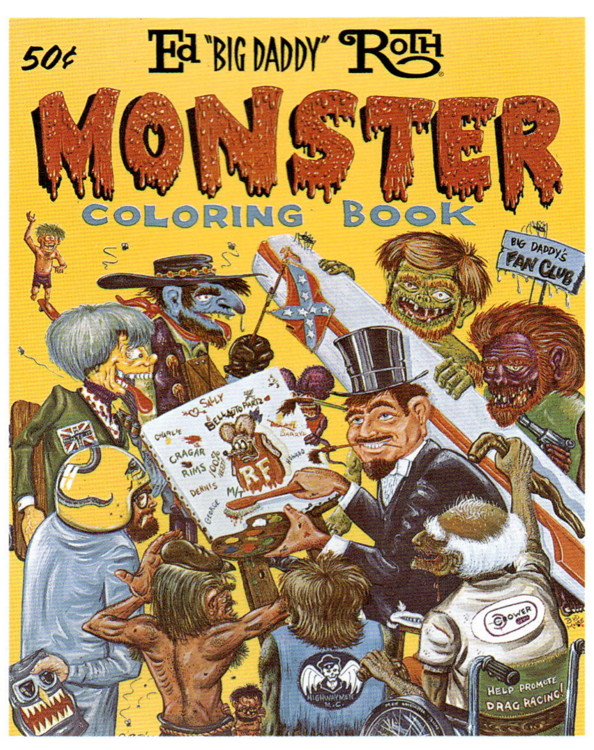

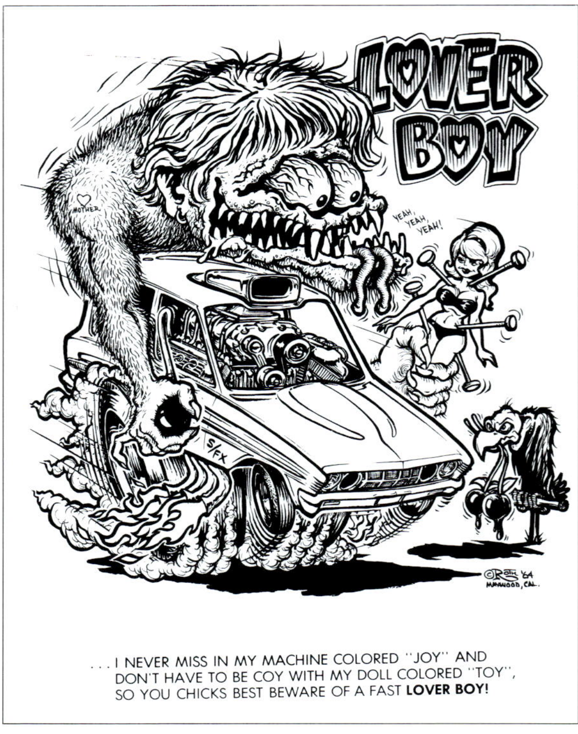

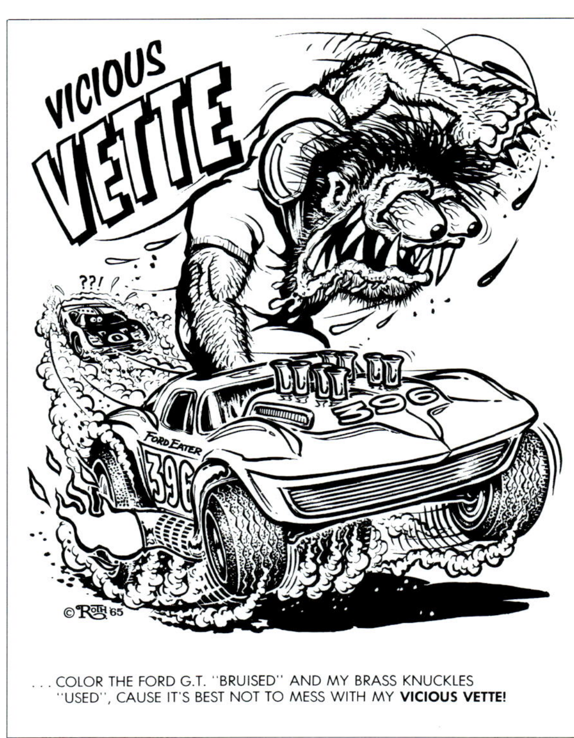

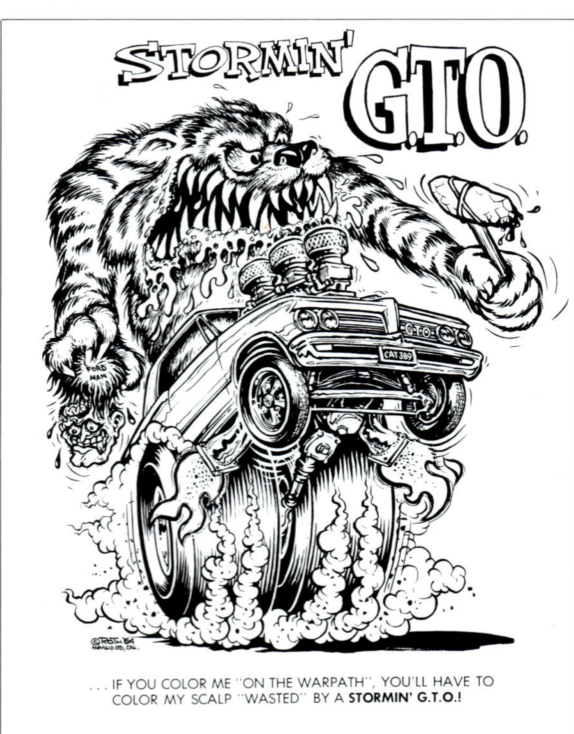

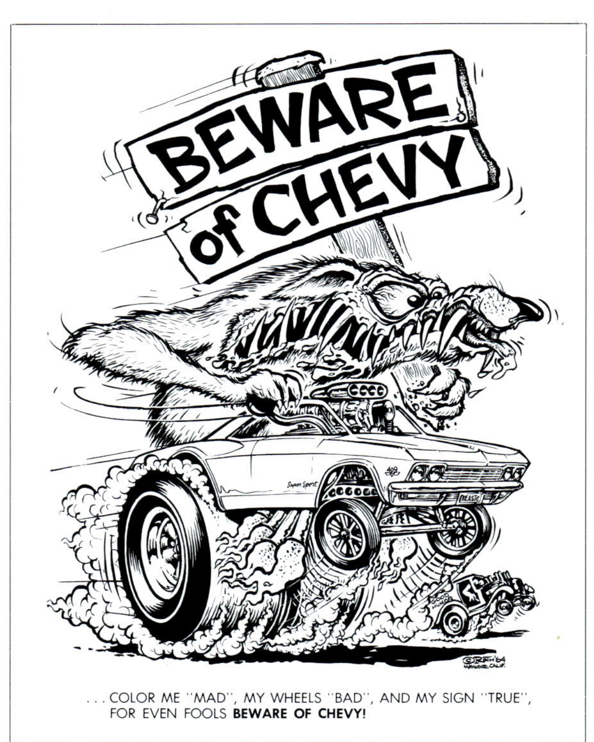

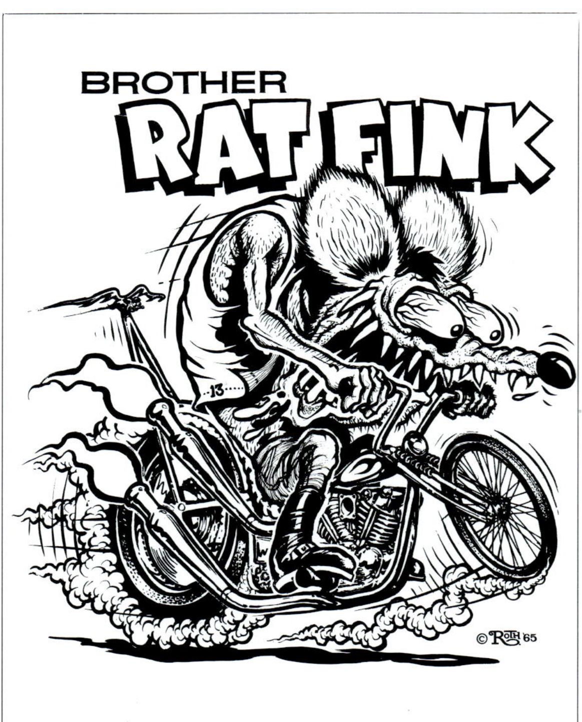

✠ *Ed "Big Daddy" Roth,* Monster Coloring Book, *1964 (magazine, 10¼ x 7 in.; collection of Lynn E. Coleman).*

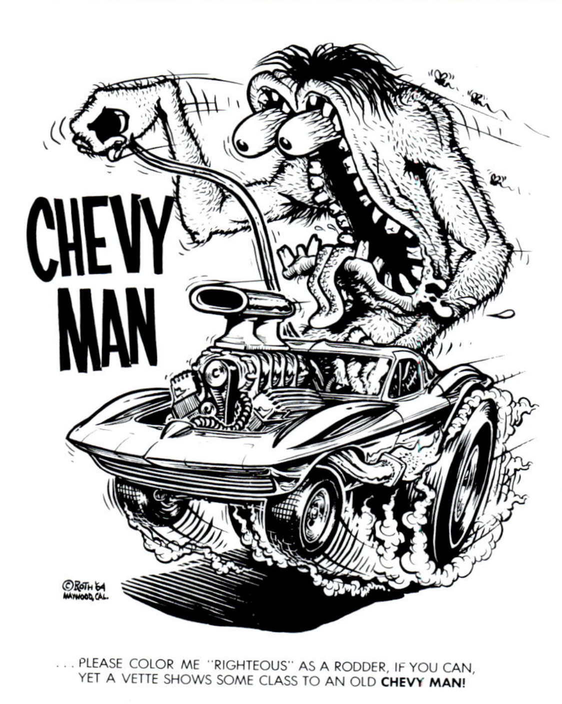

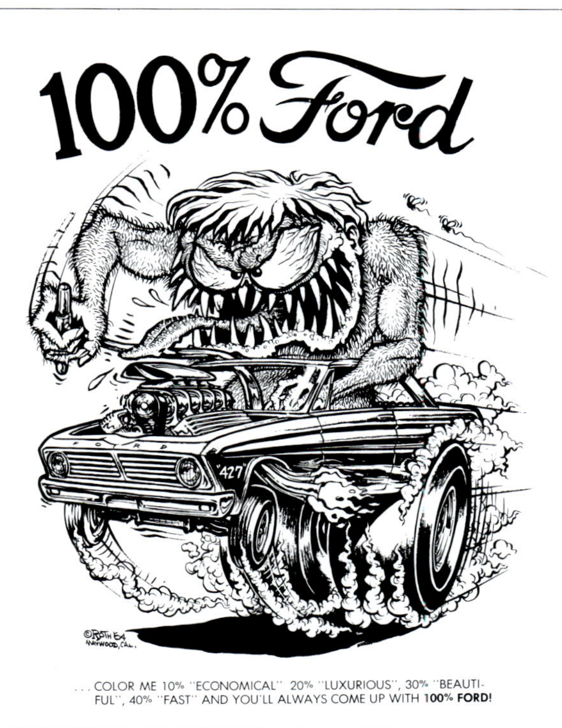

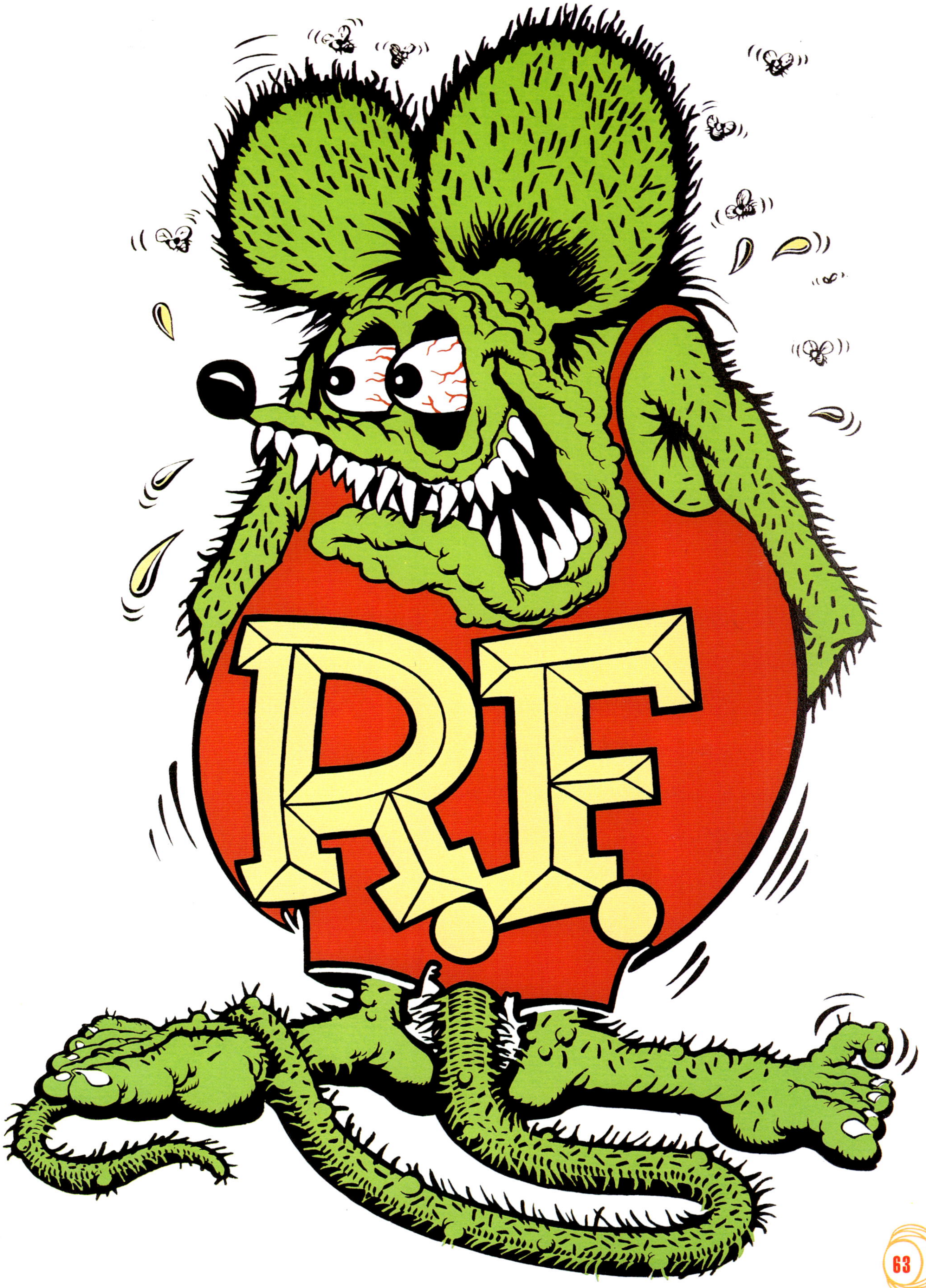

✠ *(Right) Ed "Big Daddy" Roth,* RAT FINK, *1992 (serigraph, 30 x 20 in.; collection of Greg and Kristin Escalante).*

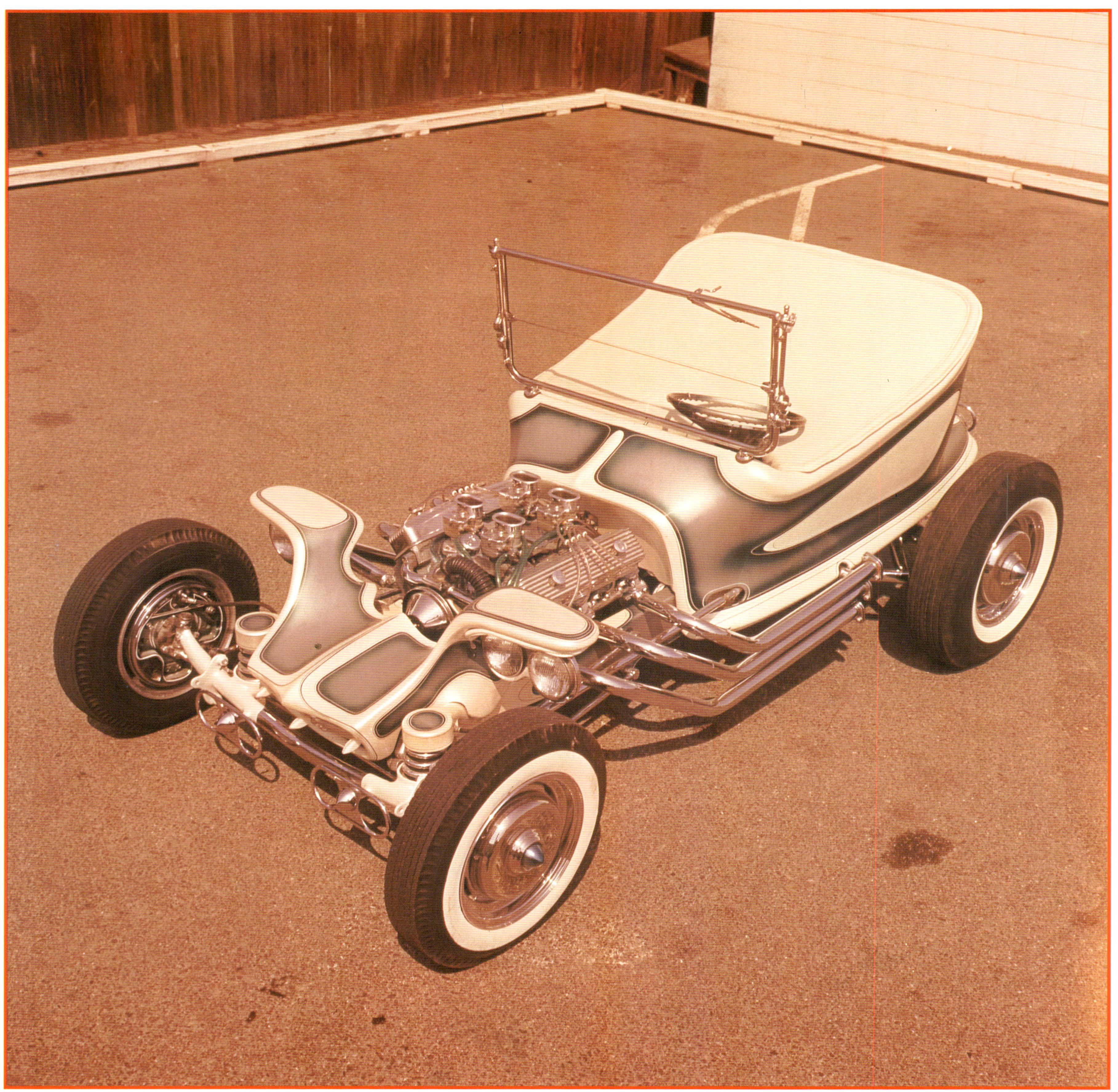

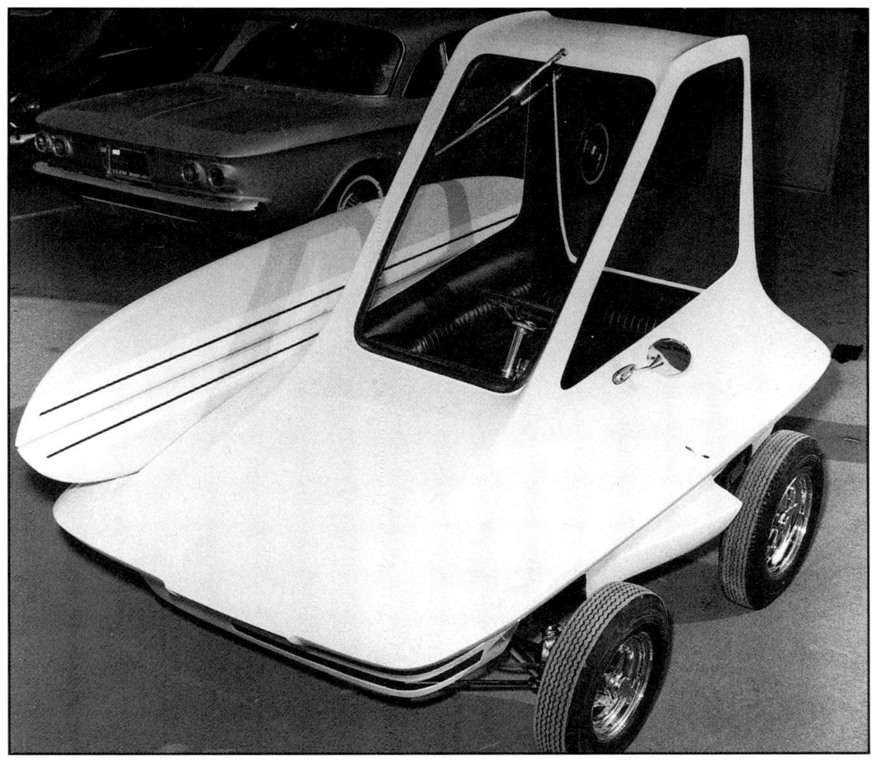

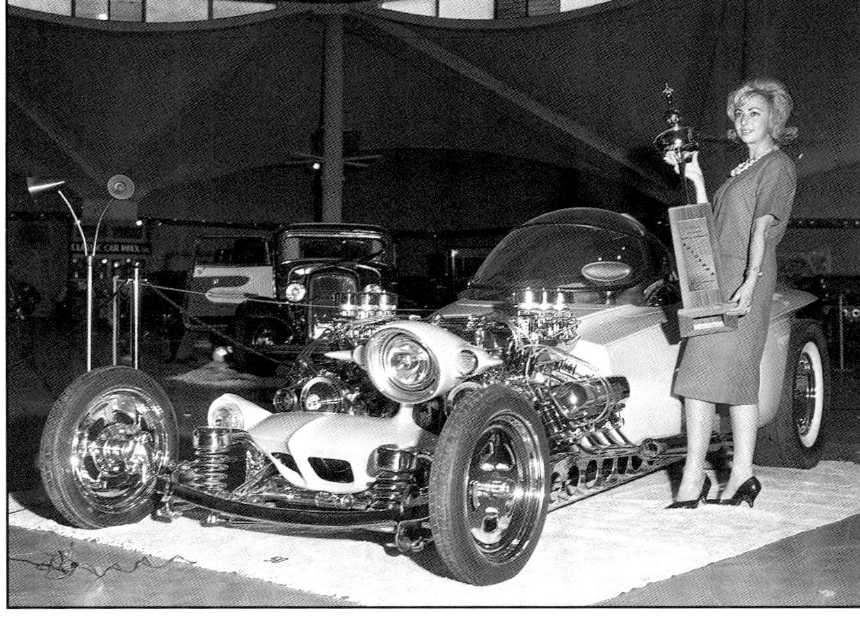

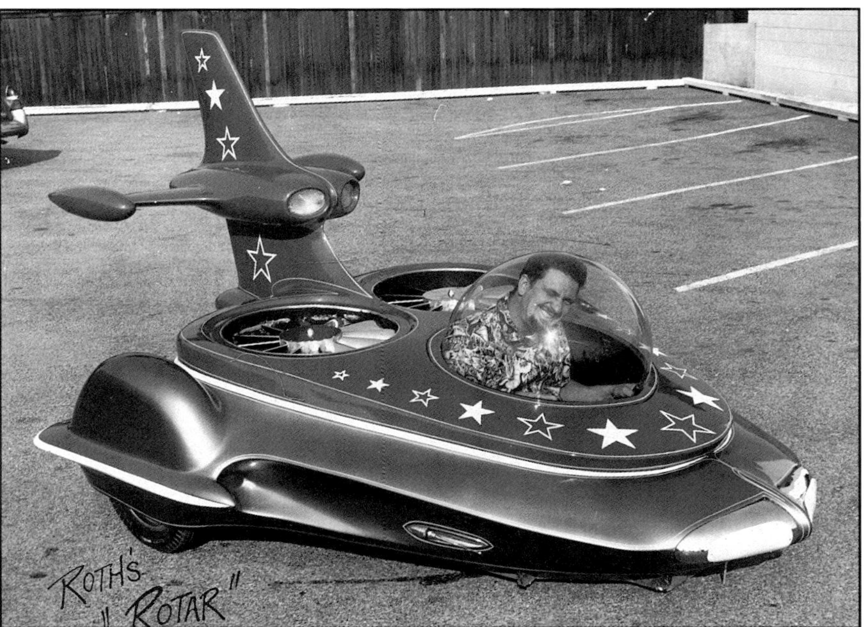

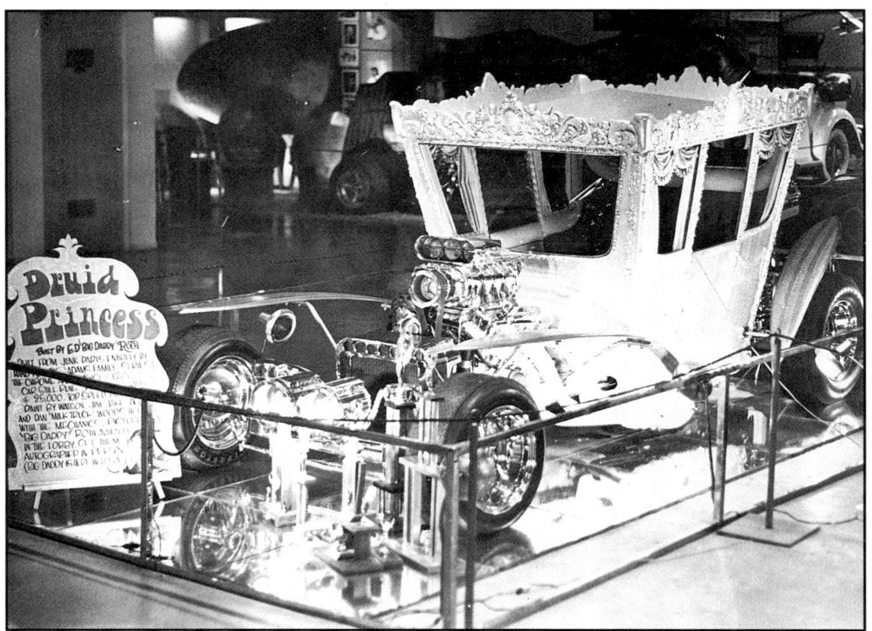

(Opposite) Roth's Outlaw, *1959. Photo courtesy Pat Ganahl.*

Roth vehicles (clockwise from upper left): Surfite, *1962;* Mysterion, *1963;* Druid Princess, *1967;* ✠ Rotar, *1961 (fiberglass, plexiglass, enamel paint and two Triumph motorcycle engines, 68 x 97 x 76 in.; collection of George and Janet Goodrich). Photos courtesy Ed Roth.*

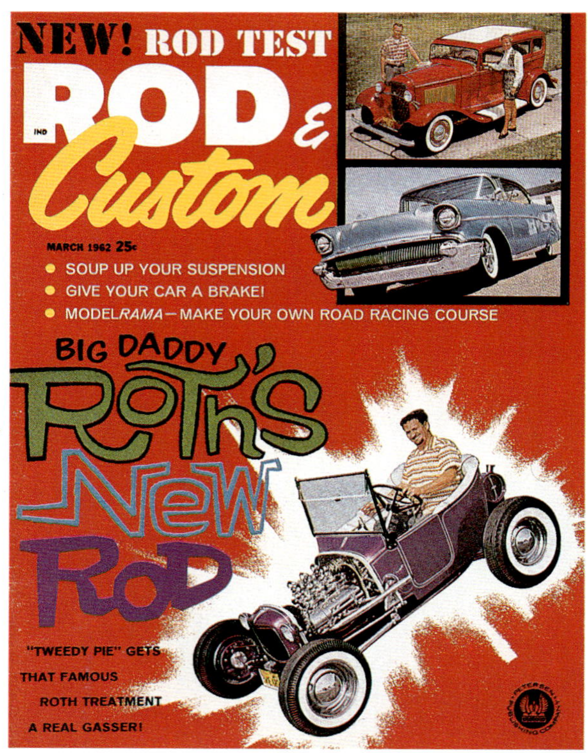

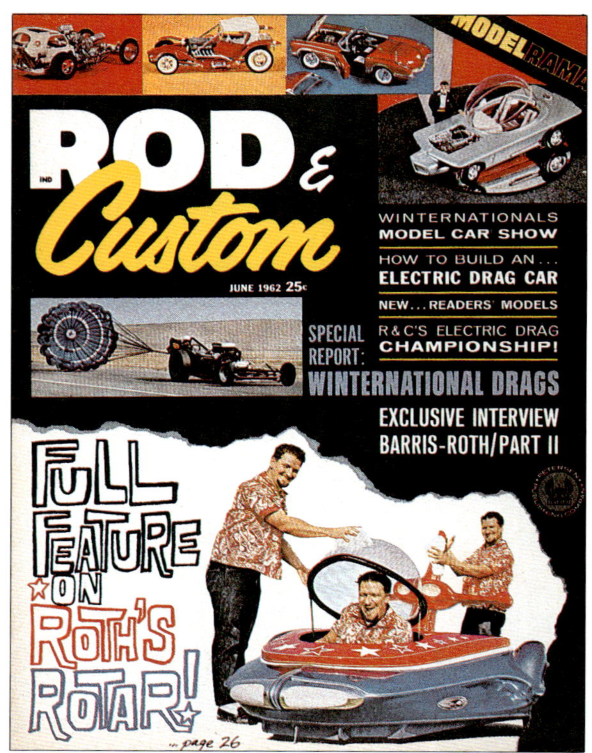

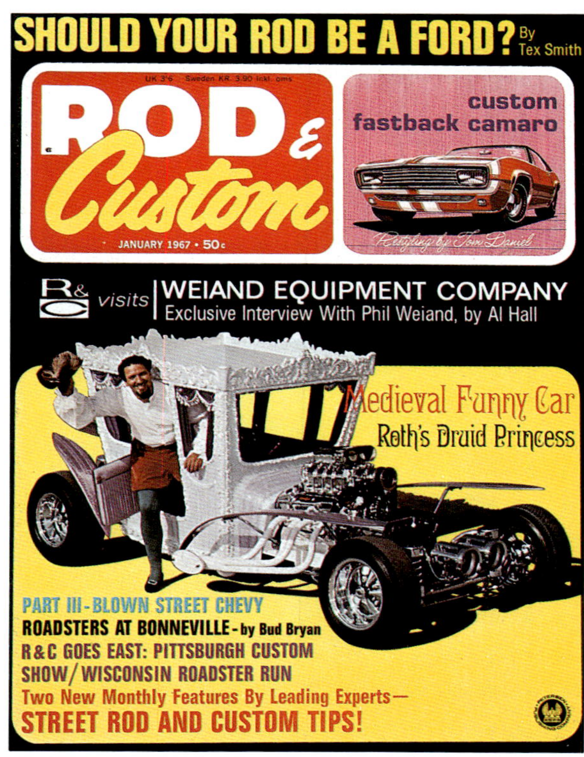

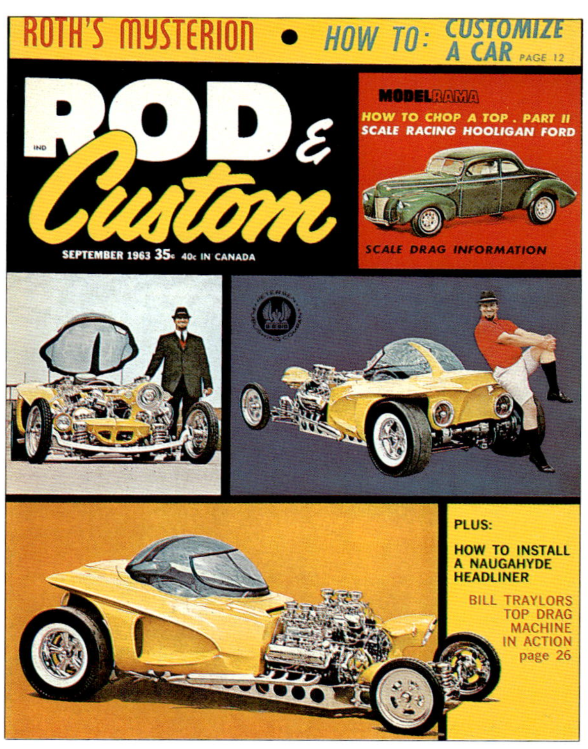

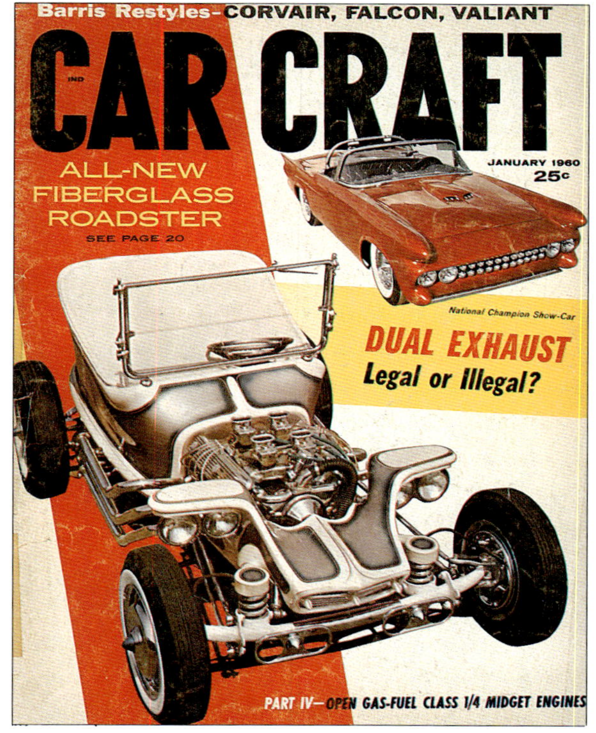

Magazine covers chronicling the introduction of Roth's show cars.

(Opposite) Car Craft cover with the Beatnik Bandit, *1961.*

IND

CAR CRAFT

MAY 1961 25c

New ROTH'S SHOW ROD

The "BEATNIK BANDIT"
Stick Controlled —
Sculptured in Fiberglass

see page 14

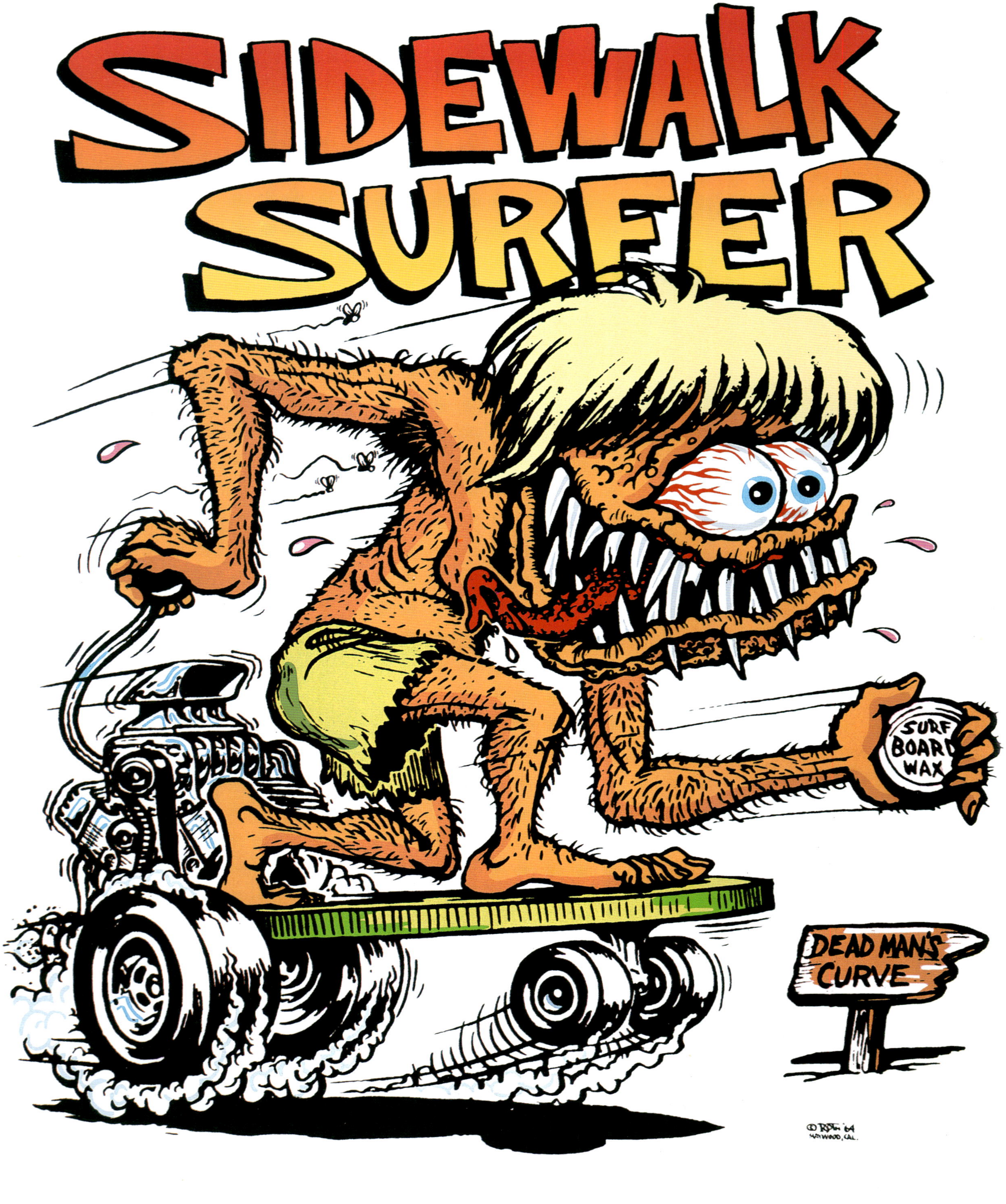

SIDEWALK SURFER

SURF BOARD WAX

DEAD MAN'S CURVE

© RDFink '64
MAYWOOD, CAL.

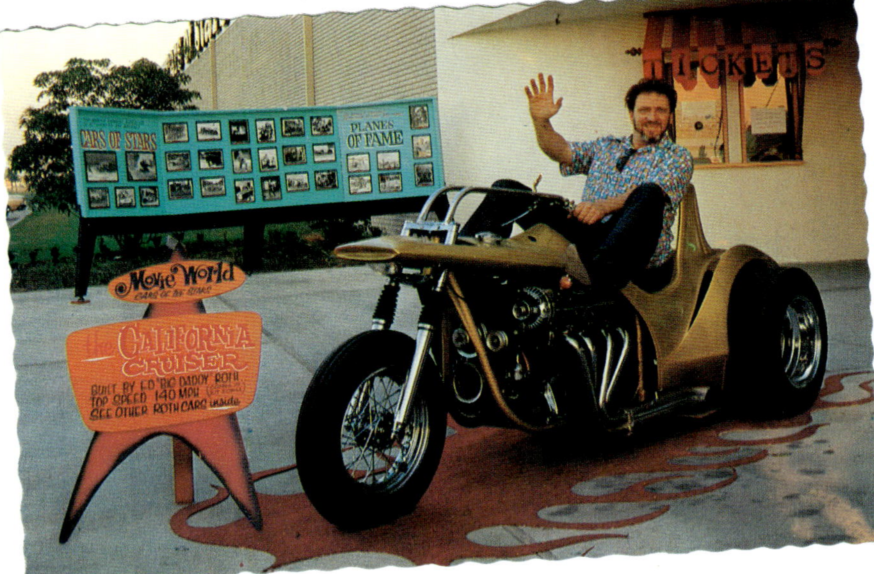

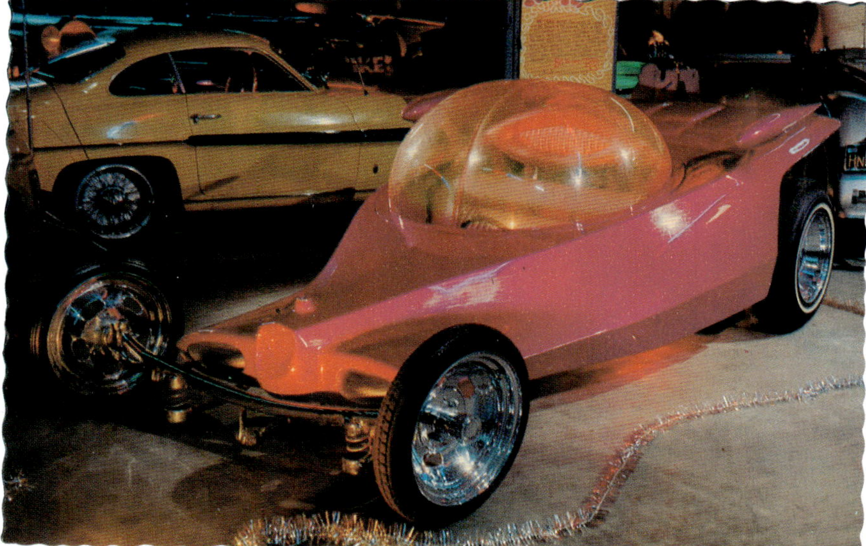

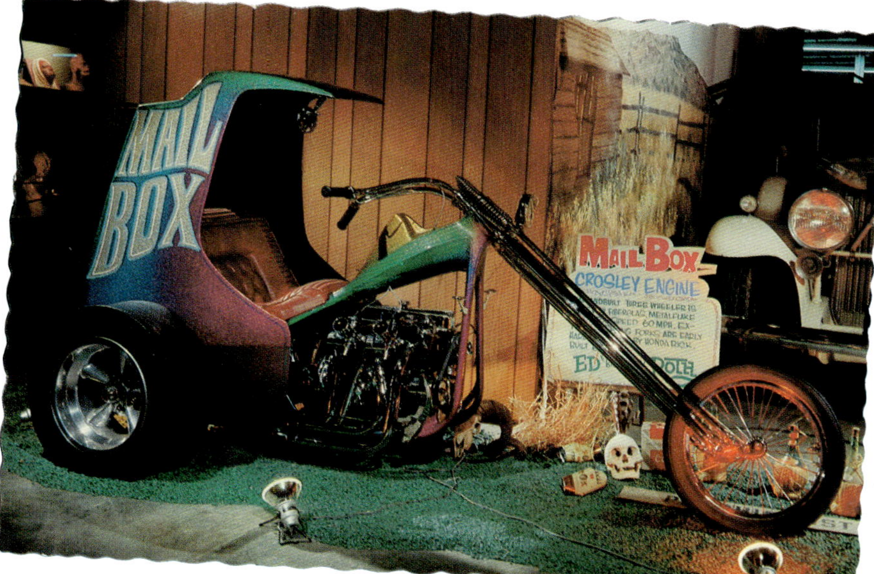

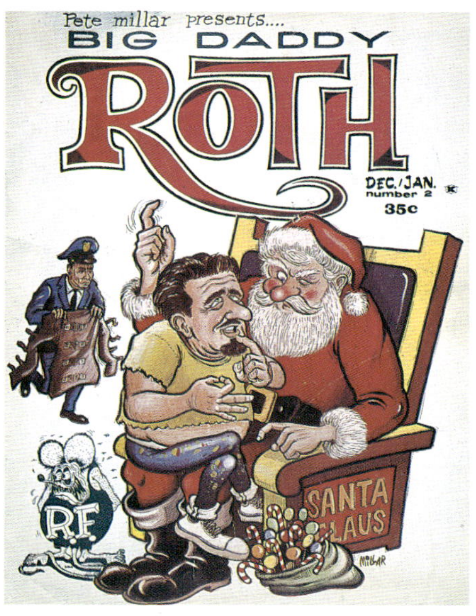

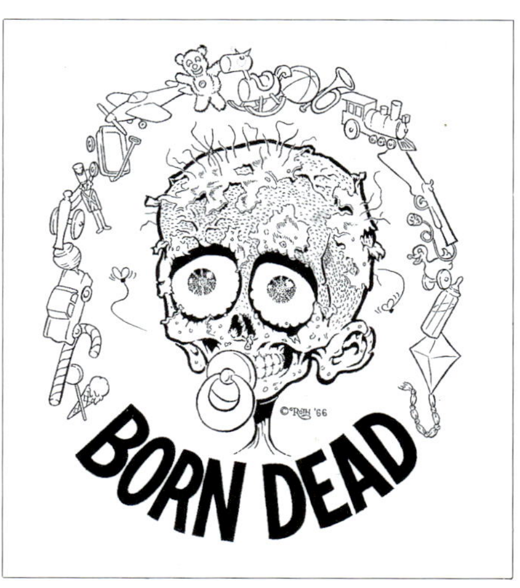

(Left) Postcards from the Movieworld Cars of the Stars and Planes of Fame museum, c. 1960. (Top to bottom): Roth on the California Cruiser; Road Agent; Mailbox.

✠ *(Top) Cover of Big Daddy Roth comic.*

✠ *(Above) Robert Williams, Roth Studio,* Born Dead, *1966 (ink on paper mounted on board, 10 x 8 in.; collection of Suzanne Williams).*

✠ *(Opposite) Ed "Big Daddy" Roth,* Sidewalk Surfer, *1964 (serigraph, 30 x 20 in.; collection of Greg and Kristin Escalante).*

RUBBERNECK MANIFESTO

Robert Williams

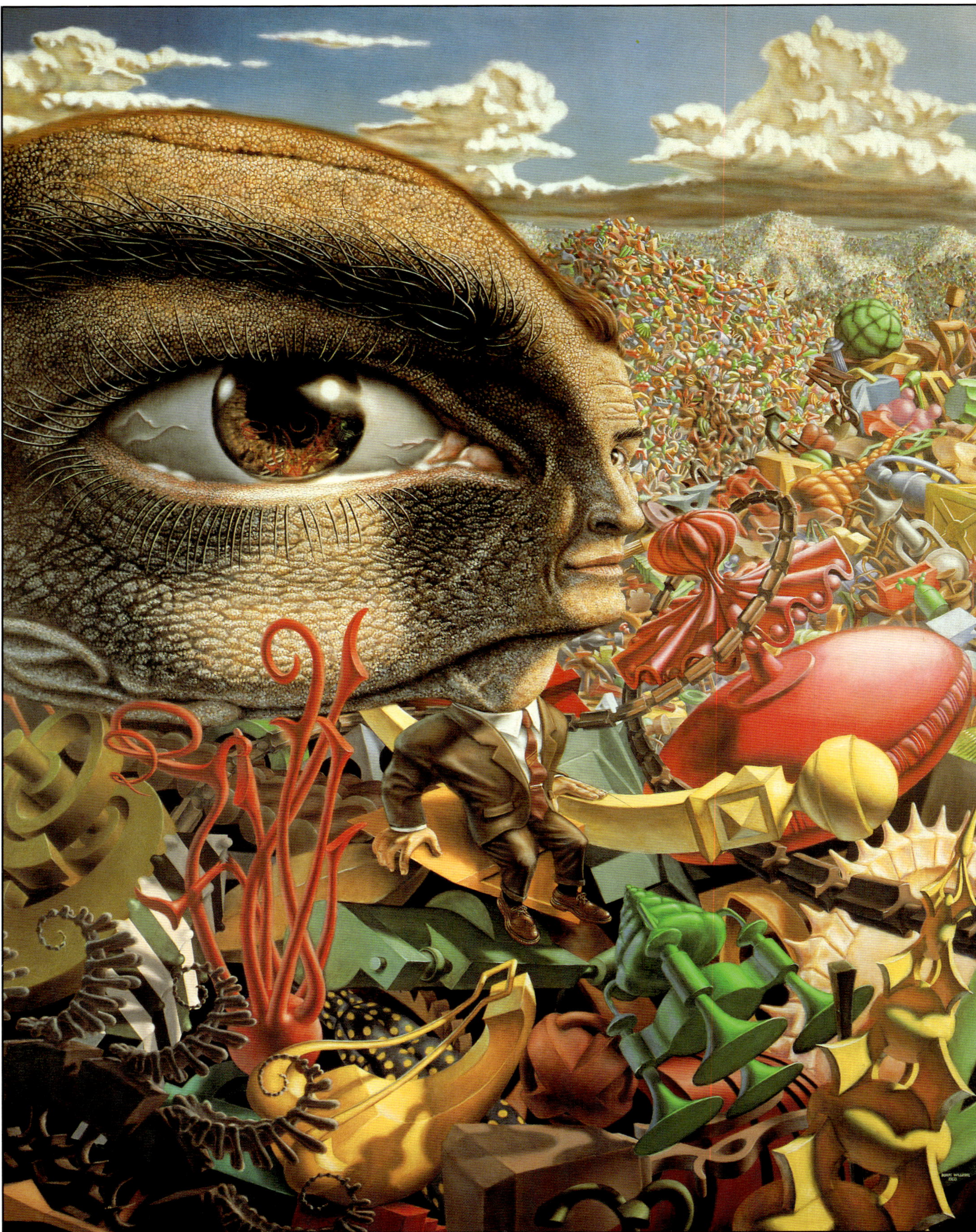

From *Visual Addiction: The Art of Robert Williams.* (San Francisco: Last Gasp, 1989). Reprinted by permission.

ROBT. WILLIAMS

What is the worth of observation? Beyond the practical use of the eye for functioning successfully in everyday life what are these values of simply seeing interesting things and enshrining them as art?

Nietzsche saw art as man's struggle against negative social forces by use of the imagination, which he considered a product of pure ego. Art for him was the highest form of clear lucid thought, a tool for the good. Schopenhauer envisioned art as a device of pleasure. Tolstoy viewed art as propaganda and Oscar Wilde held to a doctrine of "art makes life," meaning art is sometimes more real than reality.

But there exists another facet and here is where I state my dictum, this is the act of simply being attracted to something visually, base curiosity! The purest form of art is to give way to simple visual interest. To look at what you find yourself driven to see. Higher notions of art tend to confine art with lofty moral restrictions. When art is passed off as a quasi- religion which can only be administered and interpreted by a special-order of priestly elites, the system invariably stifles imagination—even when the art is as liberal as blobs, slashes and spatters. Art that has to serve as the instrument of artistic revolution is limited by having to react to a greater force in a continual hope of some overthrow, hence becoming the tool of reaction. Even the great revolt is enslaving.

But when all predetermined prejudices are momentarily set aside and you are one of the many at the scene of the horrible accident your libido will do the looking. Something dead in the street commands more measured units of visual investigation than 100 Mona Lisas. It isn't what you like, it's what the fuck you want to see! Art is not the slave of decoration. Hail the voyeur, the only honest connoisseur!!!

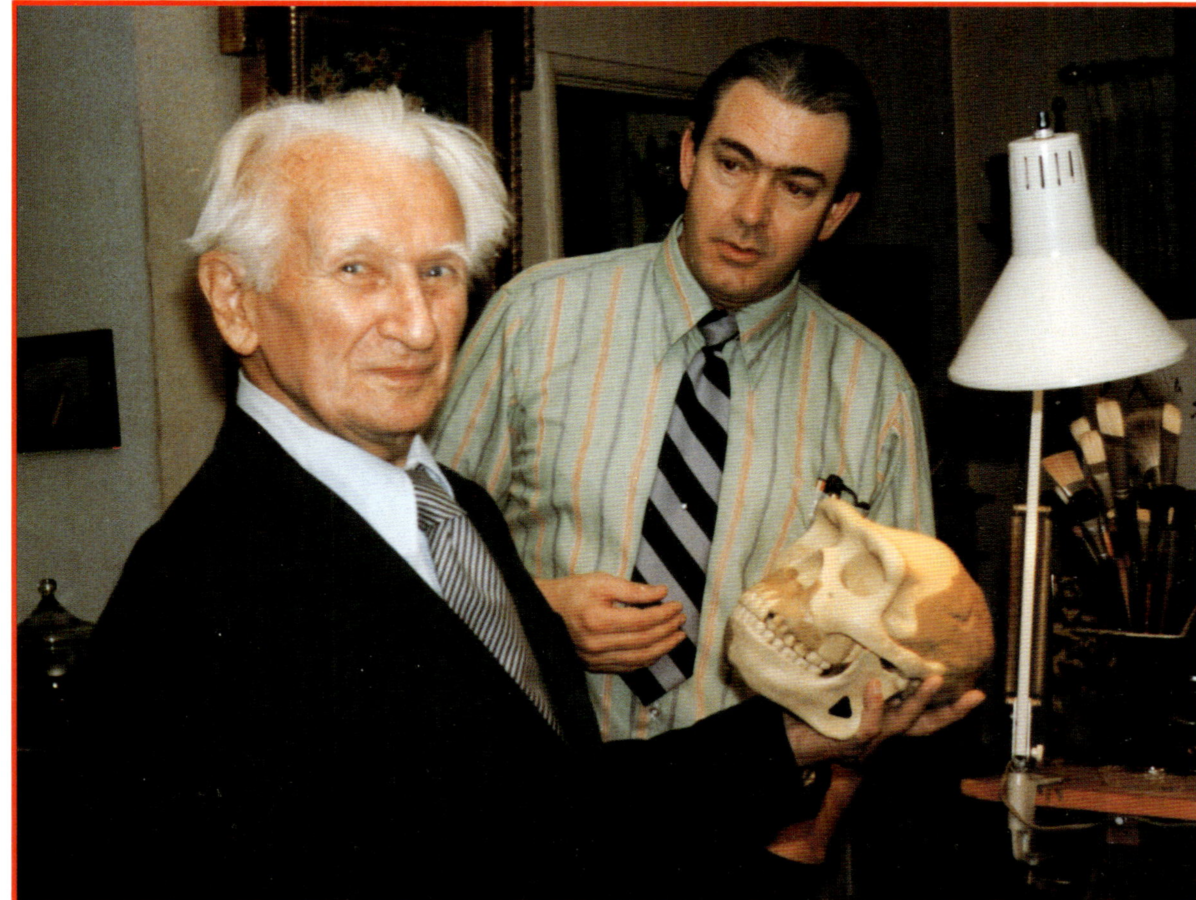

Artist Stanislov Szukalski and Robert Williams, 13 December 1984. Photo by Suzanne Williams.

✠ *(Opposite) Robert Williams,* In the Land of Retinal Delights*, 1968 (oil on canvas, 54¼ x 43½ in.; collection of Jim and Dan Brucker).*

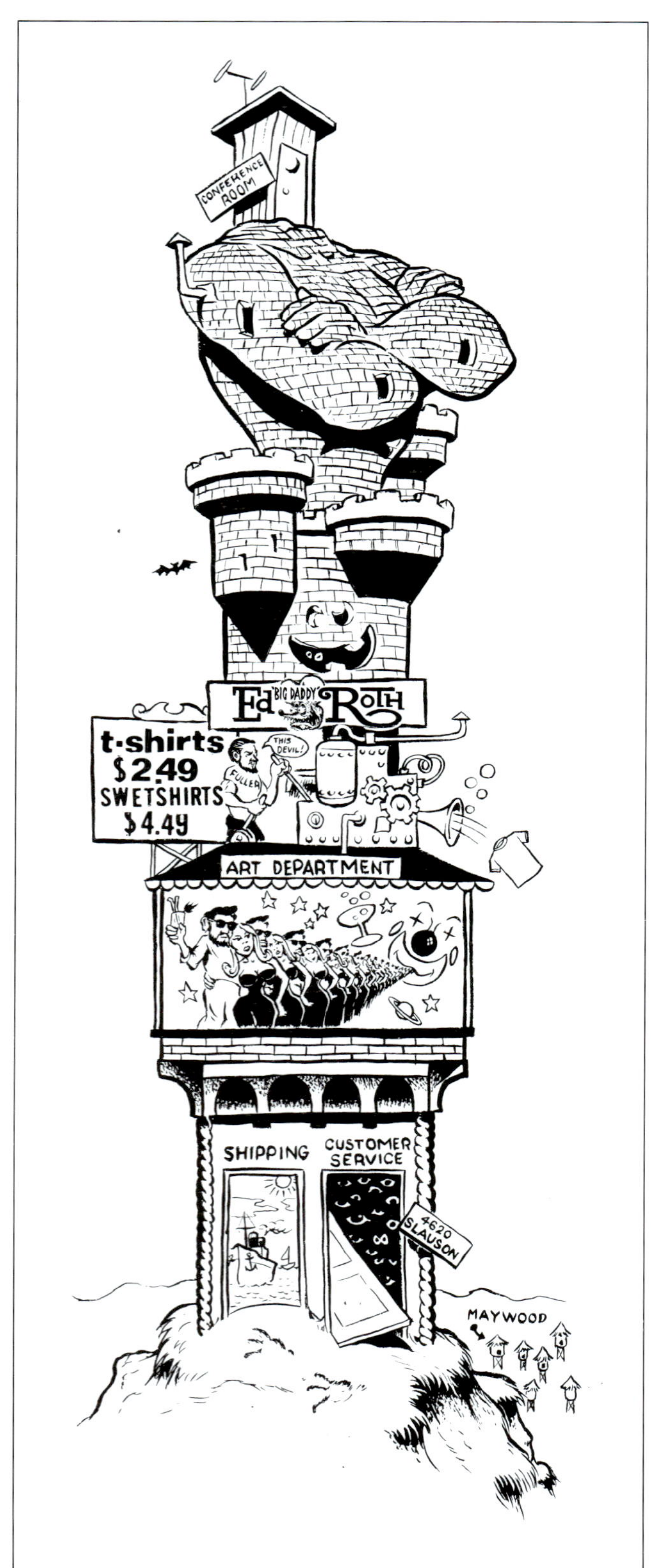
CONFERENCE ROOM
Ed BIG DADDY ROTH
t-shirts
$2.49
SWETSHIRTS
$4.49
THIS DEVIL!
ART DEPARTMENT
SHIPPING
CUSTOMER SERVICE
4620 SLAUSON
MAYWOOD

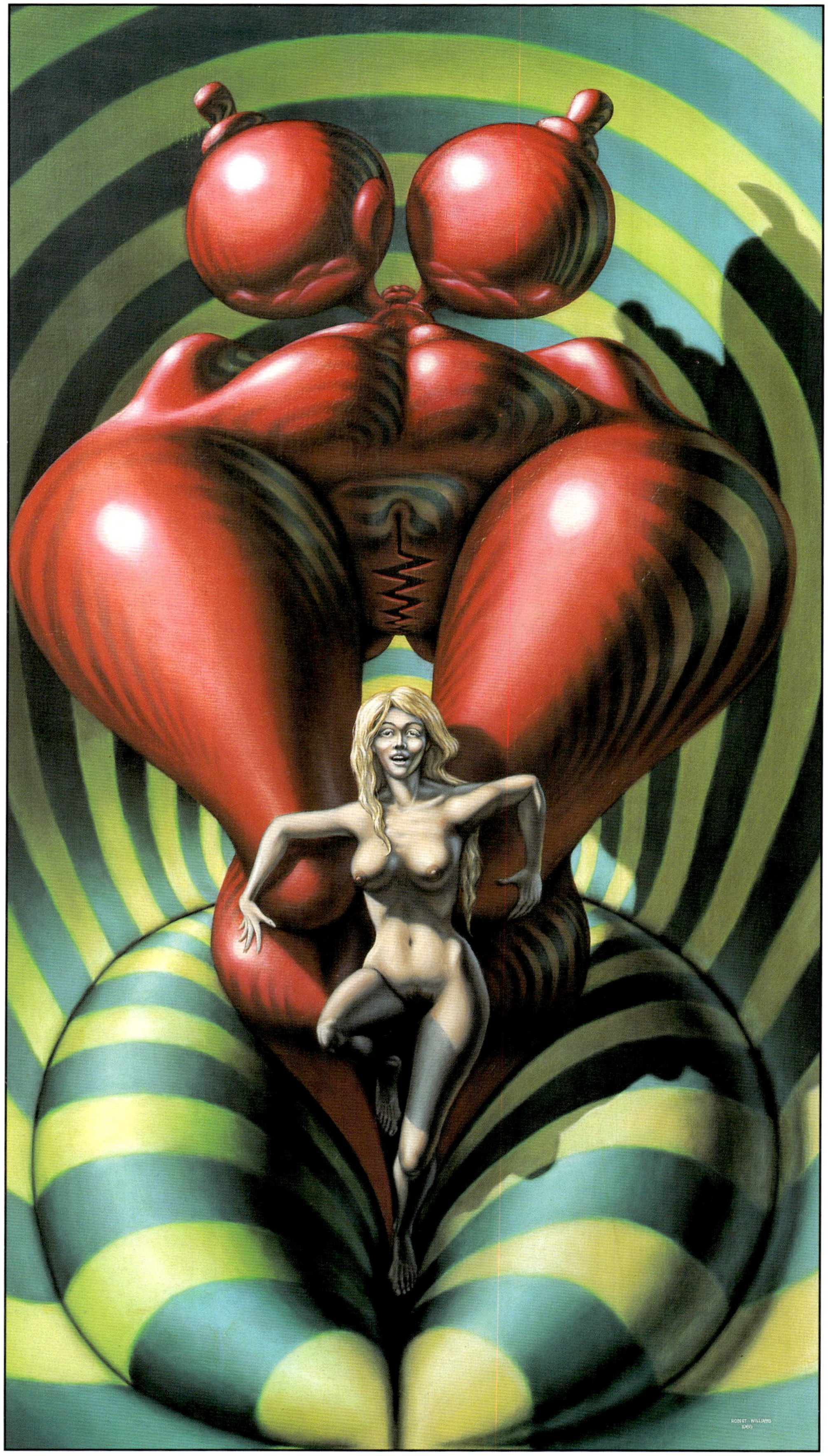

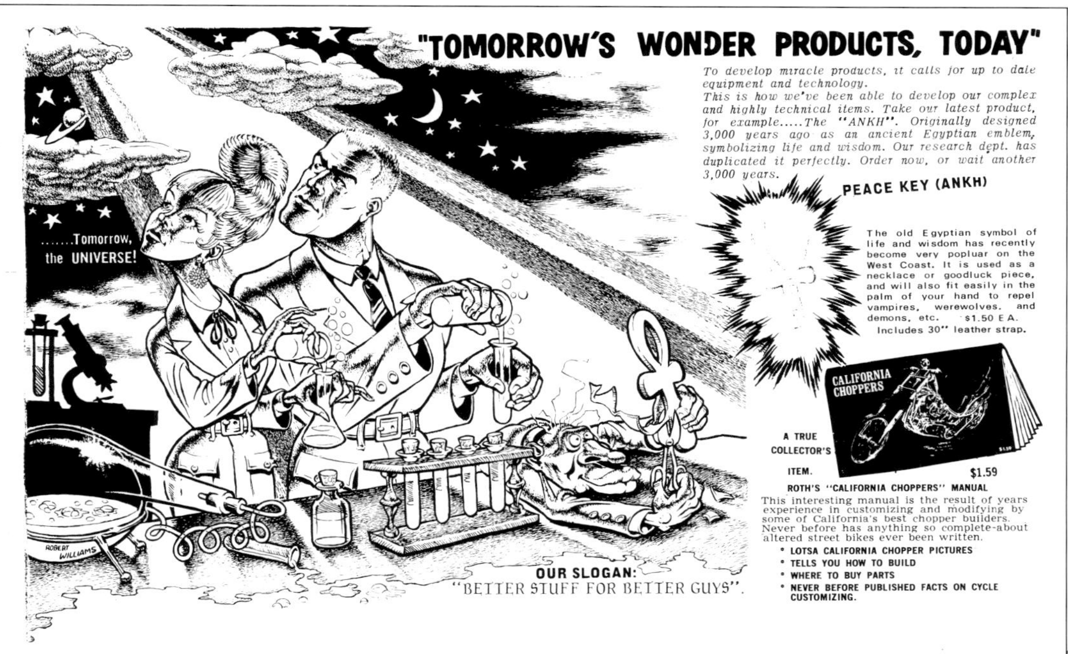

✠ *(Opposite, left) Roth advertisement by Robert Williams,* ART DEPARTMENT, *1967 (ink on paper, 11½ x 4½ in.; collection of Jim and Dan Brucker).*

✠ *(Opposite, right) Robert Williams,* ERNESTINE AND THE VENUS OF POLYETHYLENE, *1968 (oil on canvas, 50¼ x 29½ in.; collection of Judy and Stuart Spence).*

✠ *(Left) Roth advertisement by Robert Williams,* TOMORROW'S WONDER PRODUCTS, TODAY, *1967 (ink on paper, 9⅛ x 5½ in.; collection of Jim and Dan Brucker).*

✠ *(Below) Roth advertisement by Robert Williams,* LET'S STOP THESE NASTY RUMORS ABOUT BIG DADDY ROTH, *1967 (ink on paper, 4¼ x 9⅛ in.; collection of Jim and Dan Brucker).*

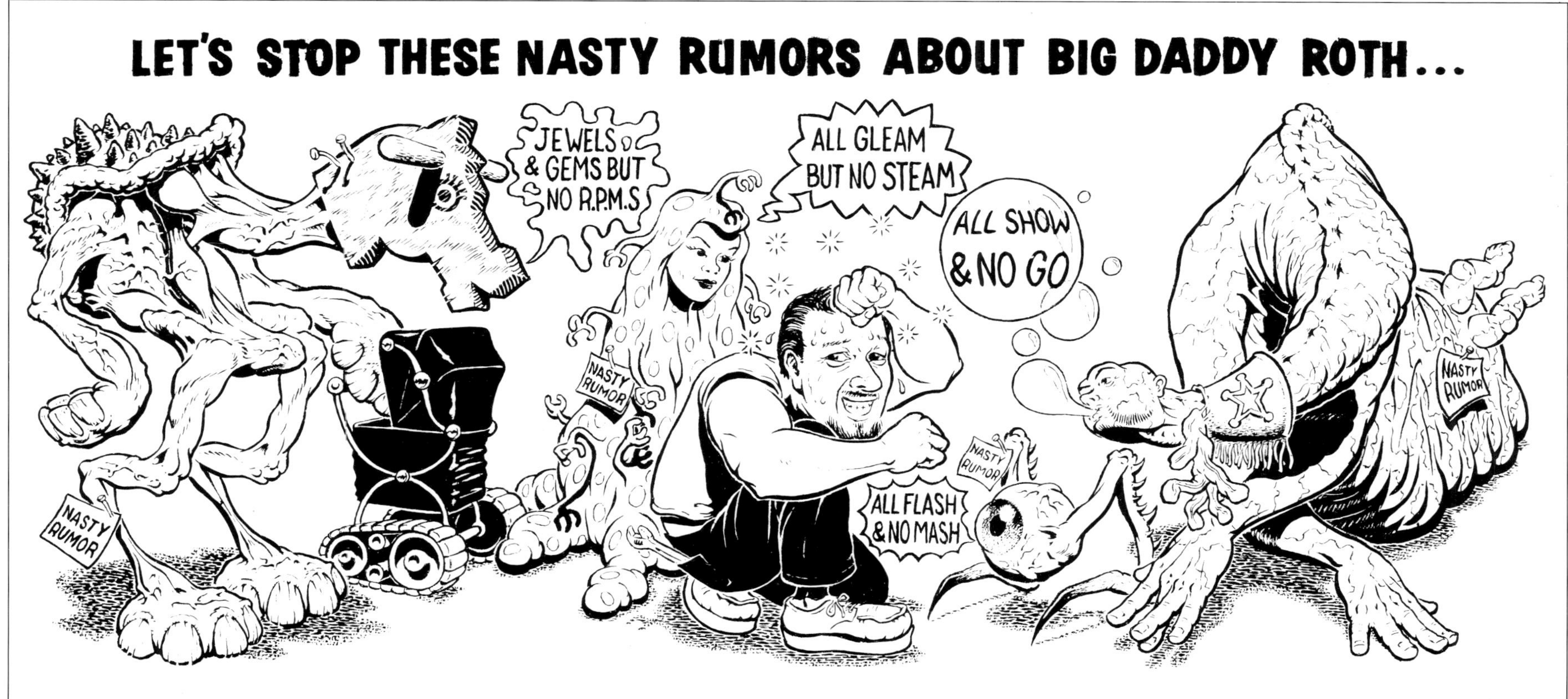

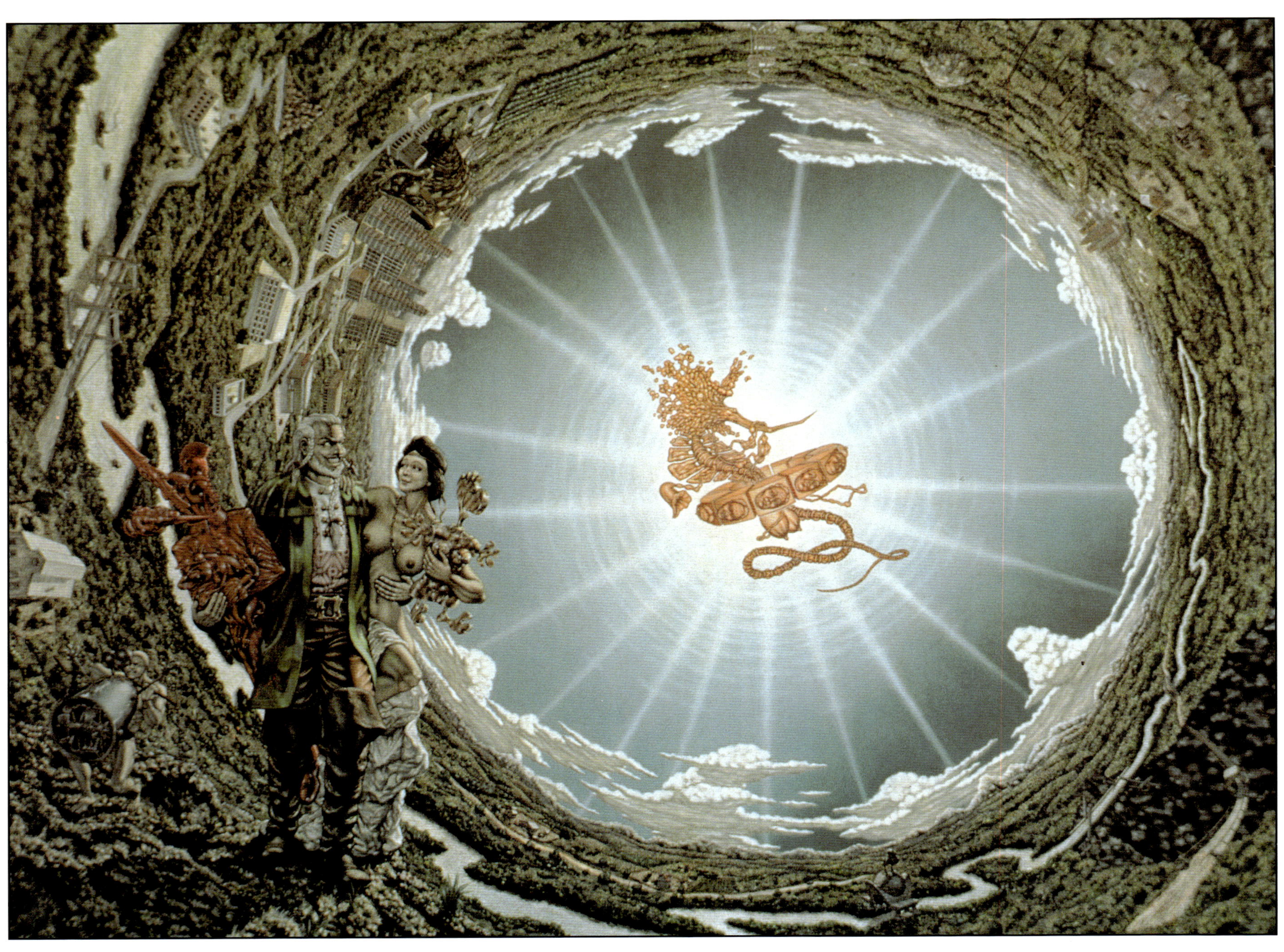

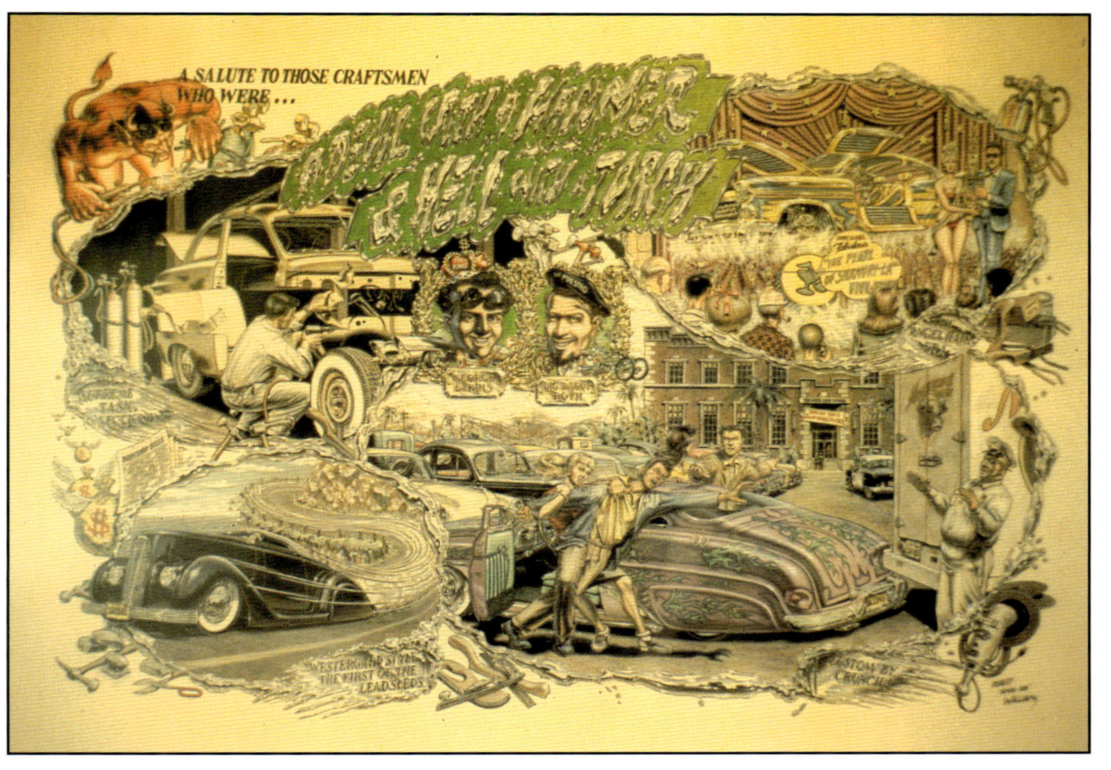

✠ *(Opposite) Robert Williams,* PSYCHIC PEDESTRIANS ON A SPIRAL HORIZON, *1970 (oil on canvas, 40½ x 52⅛ in.; collection of Jim and Dan Brucker).*

✠ *(Left) Robert Williams,* A DEVIL WITH A HAMMER AND HELL WITH A TORCH, *1975 (ink and gouache on paper, 14 x 19¼ in.; collection of Jim and Dan Brucker).*

✠ *(Below) Roth advertisement by Robert Williams,* THE INCREDIBLE MR. PUFF..., *1967 (ink on paper, 5½ x 9¼ in.; collection of Jim and Dan Brucker).*

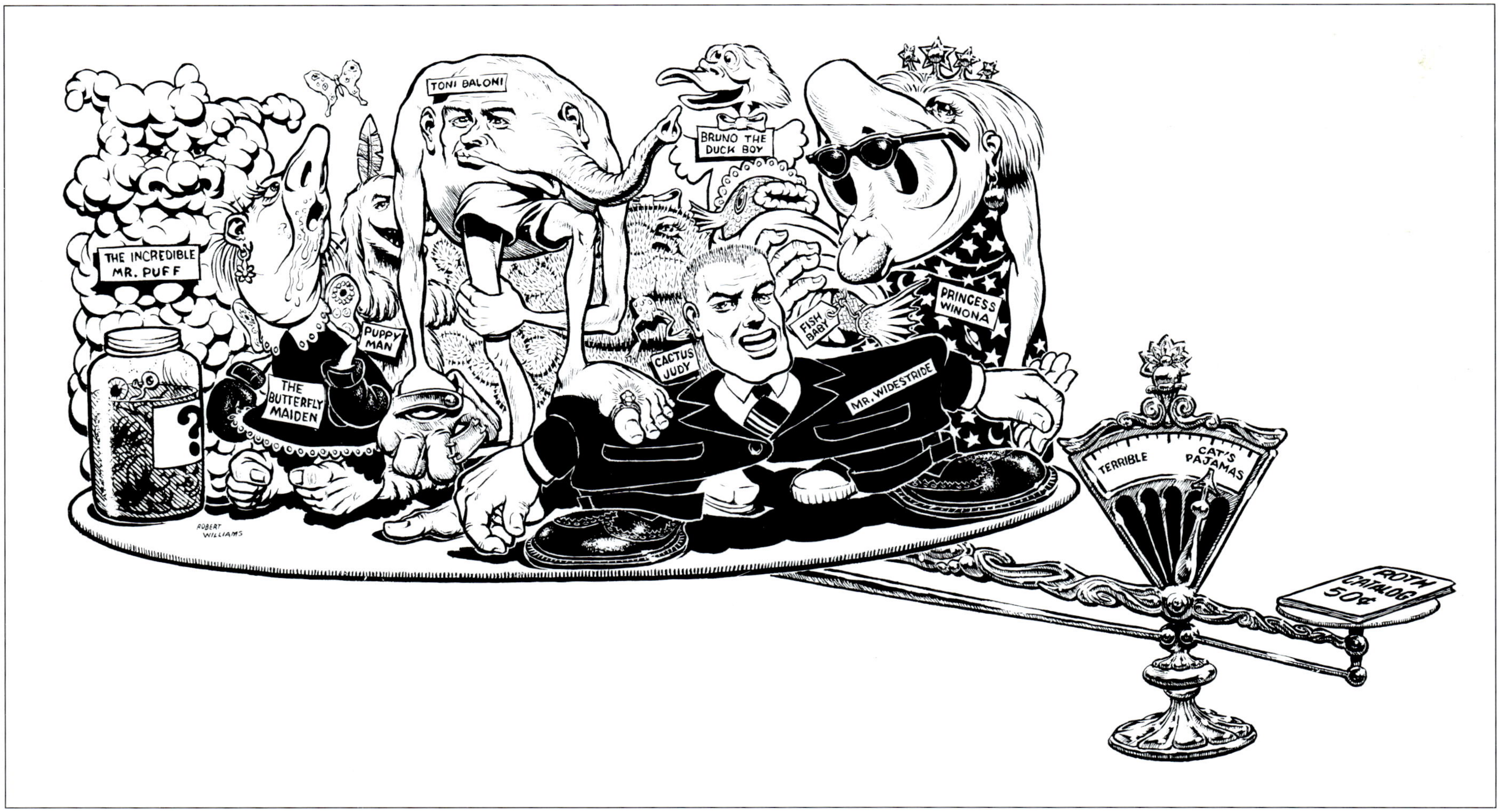

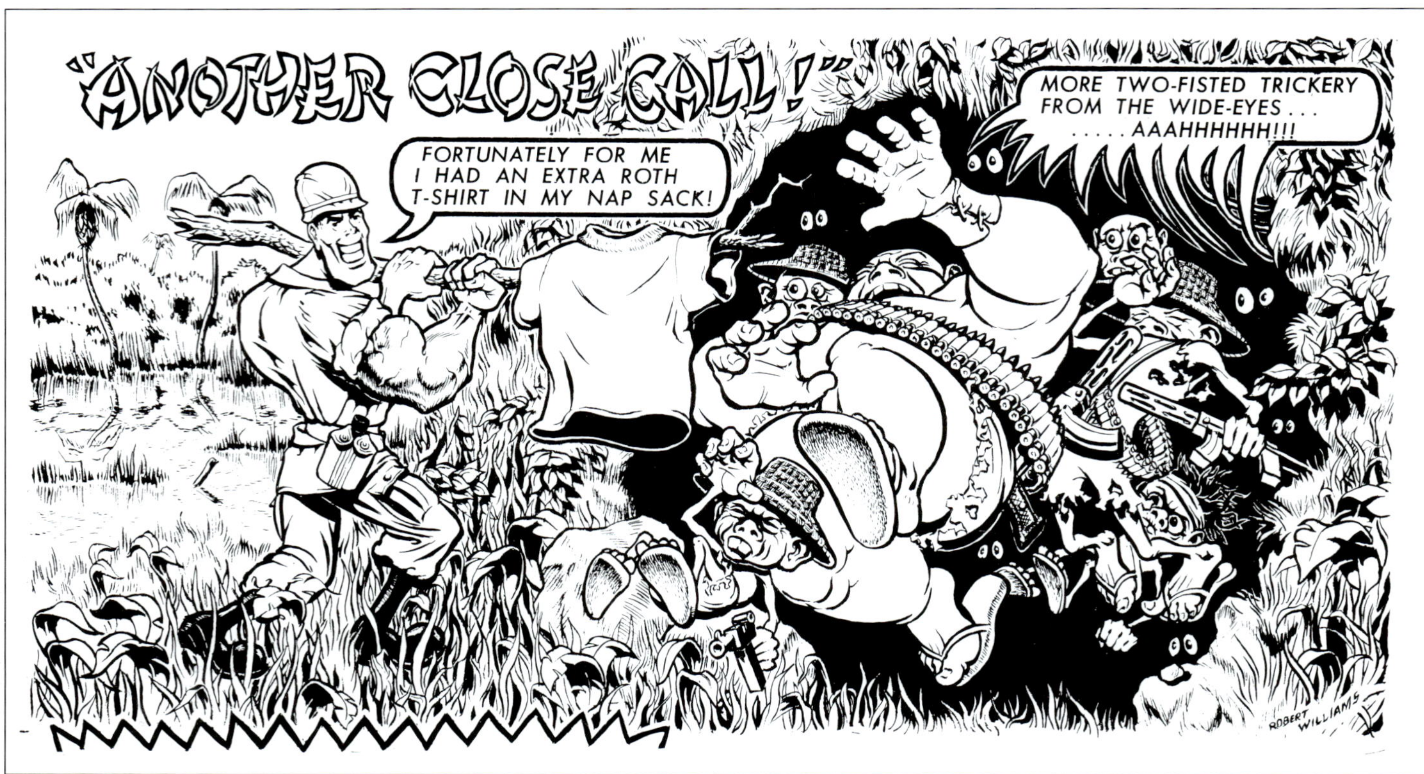

✠ *(Above) Roth advertisement by Robert Williams,* ANOTHER CLOSE CALL, *1967 (ink on paper, 4¼ x 7¼ in.; collection of Jim and Dan Brucker).*

✠ *(Right) Robert Williams,* THE PACHUCO CROSS, *1972 (oil on canvas, 19 x 24 in.; collection of Jim and Dan Brucker).*

✠ *(Opposite) Robert Williams,* HOT ROD RACE, *1976 (acrylic on board, 12¾ x 16¼ in.; collection of Jim and Dan Brucker).*

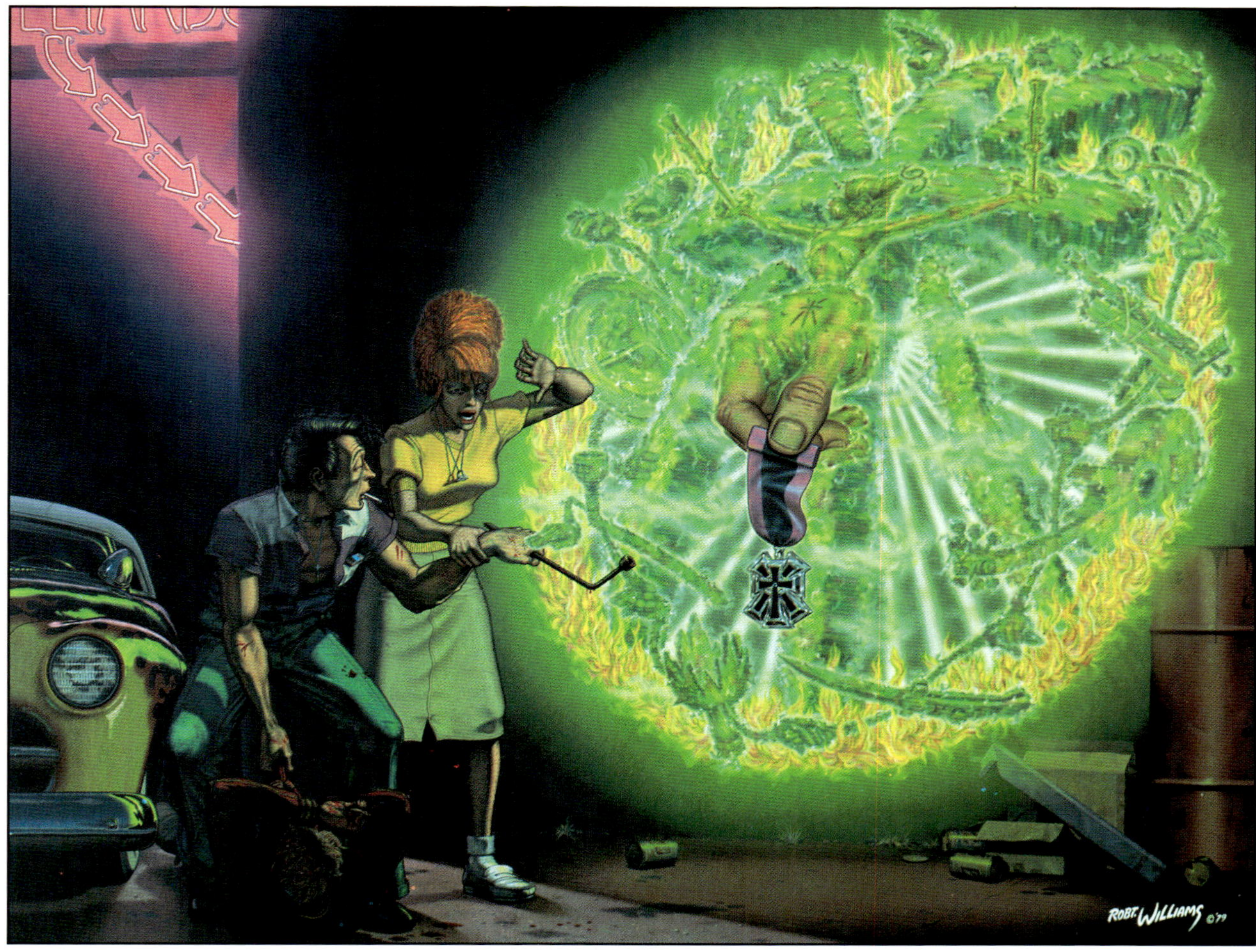

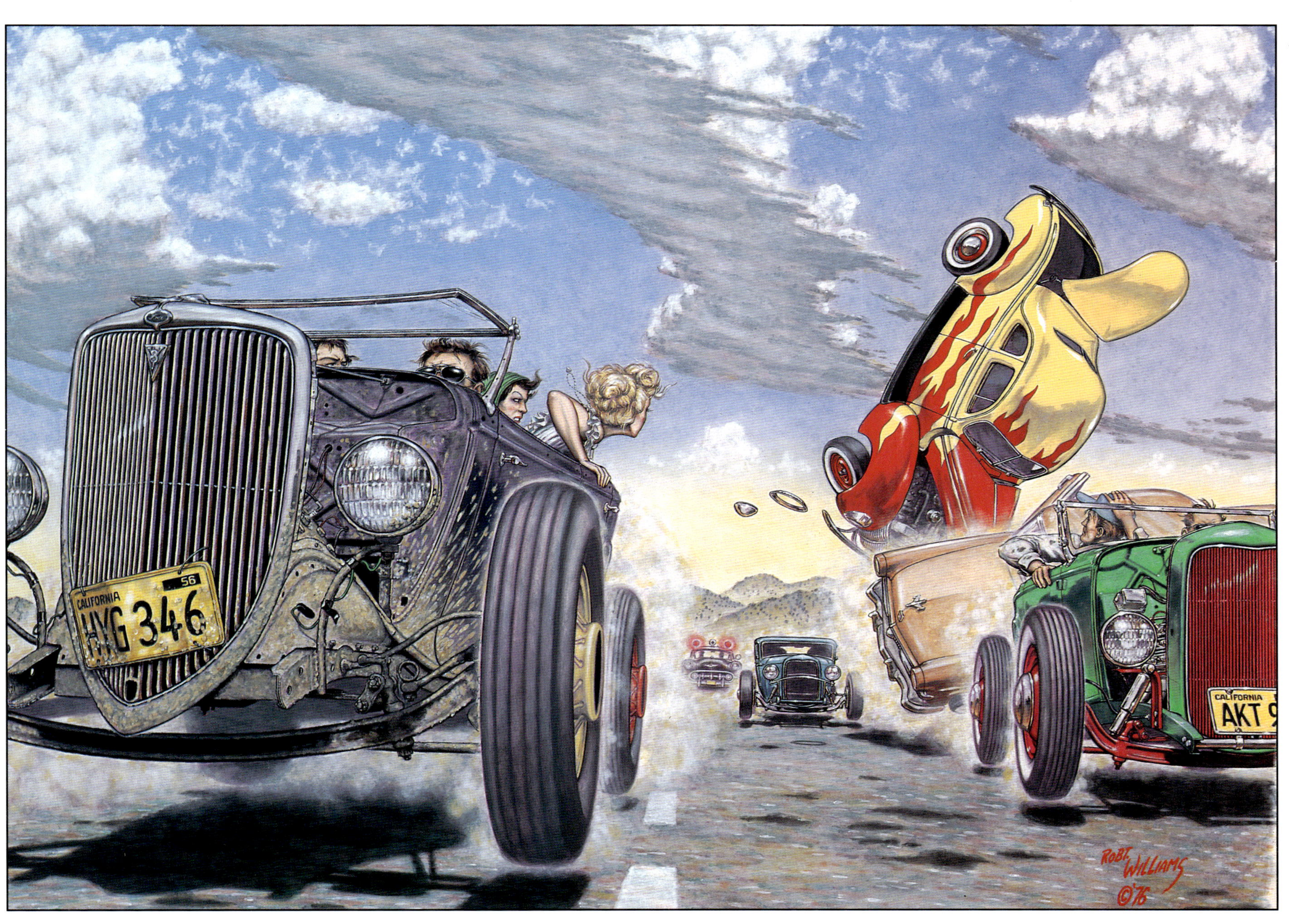
CALIFORNIA
56
HYG 346
CALIFORNIA
AKT 9
ROBT. WILLIAMS
©'76

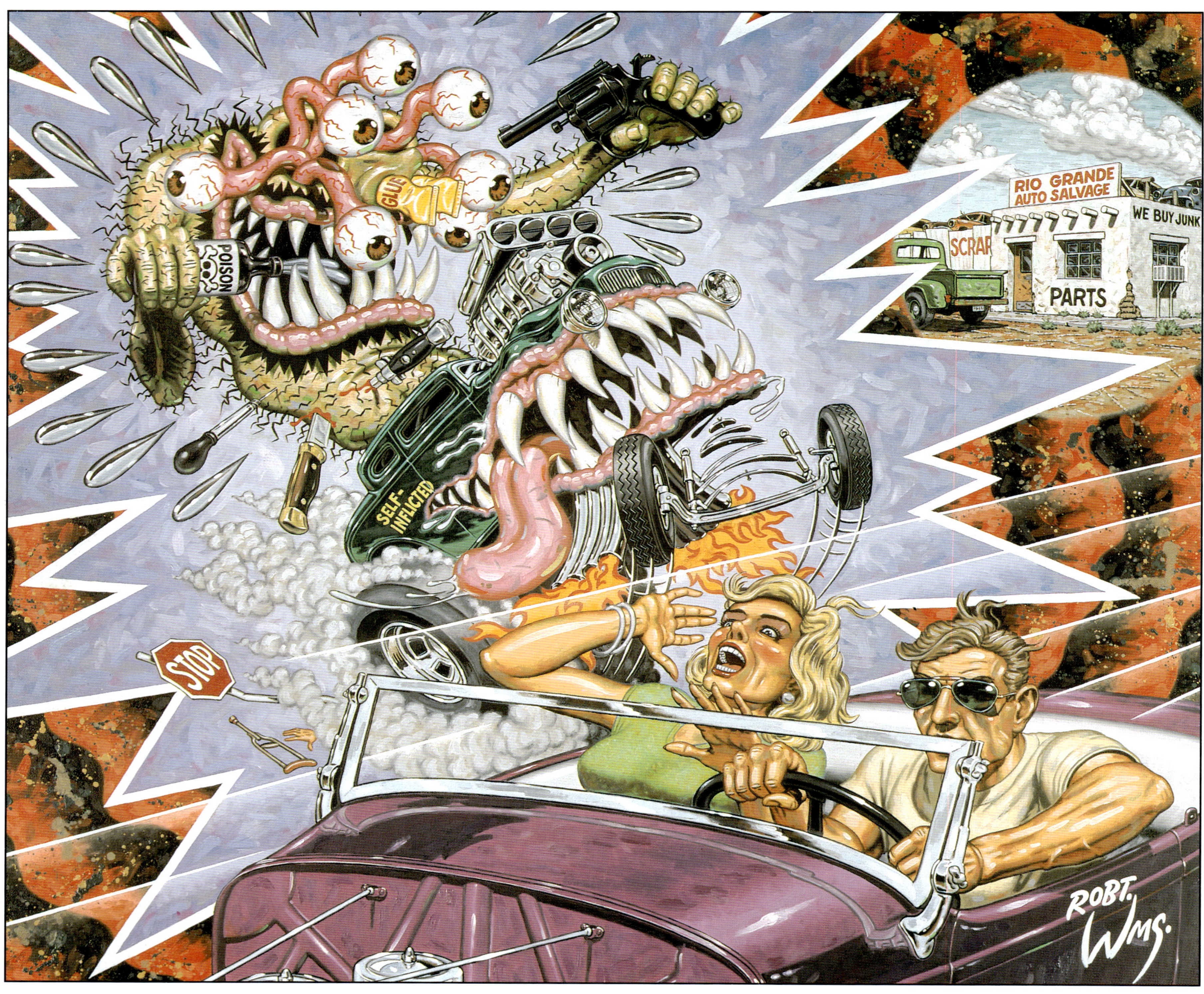

✠ *Robert Williams,* Snuff Fink, *1988.* Museum Catalogue Title: The Exuberance of Youth Bordering on Self-Destruction Lends Romance to the Notion That Acne Is Never Really Cured, It's Just Thrilled into Remission. Colloquial Title: Brodyin' on Feces *(oil on canvas, 30 x 36 in.; collection of Long Gone John).*

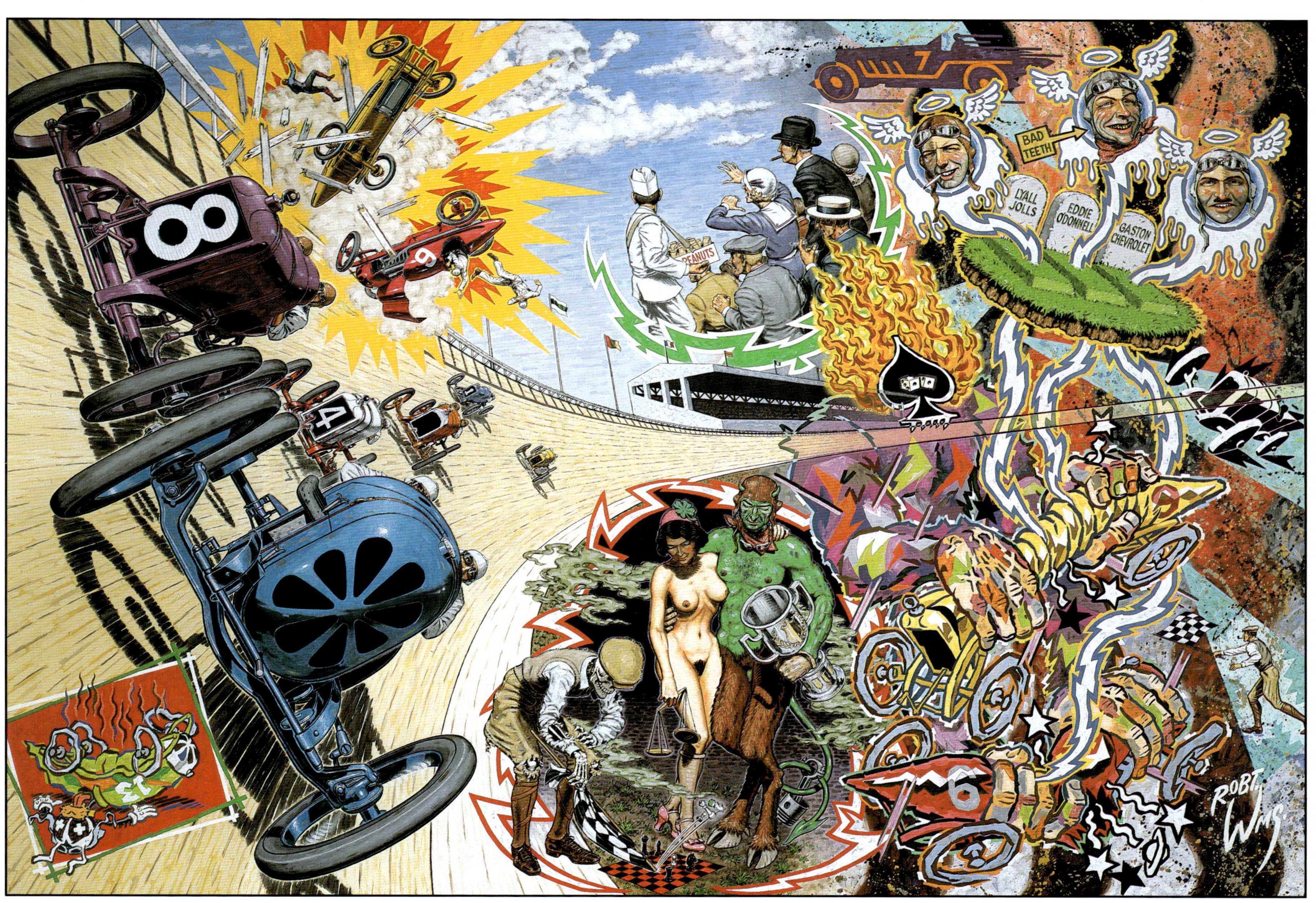

✠ *Robert Williams,* Death on the Boards, *1991.* Scholastic Designation: The Mystery of Indy Winner Gaston Chevrolet and His Death Premonition Which Came True with the Deaths of Two Others at the Plush Beverly Hills Board Track in View of 60,000 Witnesses of Who No Two Gave the Same Account on Thanksgiving Day, Nov. 25, 1920. Remedial Title: Catastrophe at the Greasy Hands of a Duesenberg Jockey with Bad Teeth *(oil on canvas, 60 x 84 in.; collection of Nicolas Cage).*

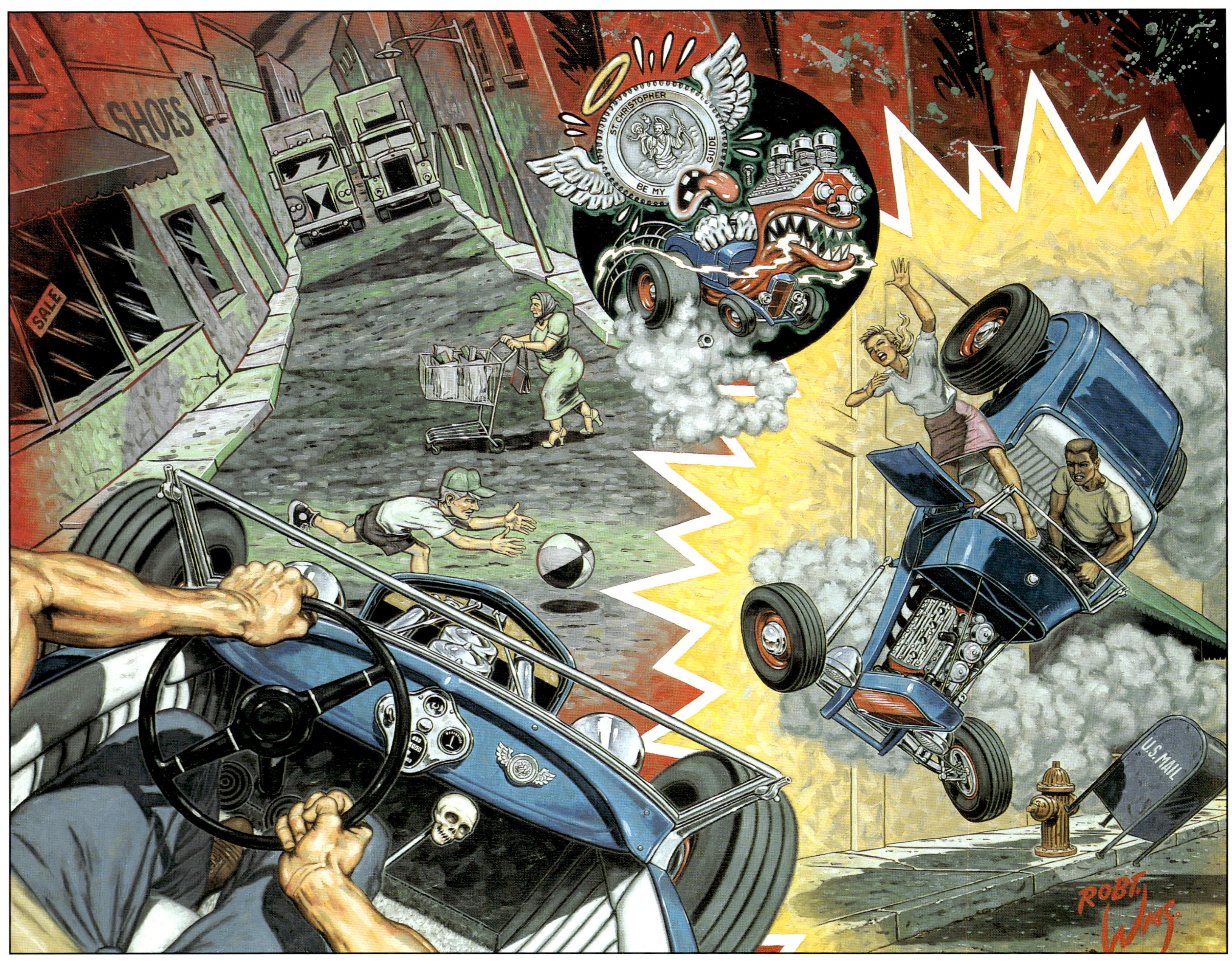

✠ *Robert Williams,* A White-Knuckle Ride for Lucky St. Christopher, *1991.* Scholastic Designation: The Crime of Pure Automotive Thrill Is Exacerbated by the Emotional Dependency on a Lucky Catholic Talisman Commemorating Baby Jesus Fording a River on the Back of an Unlucky Good Samaritan Who Was Later Tortured to Death. Remedial Title: Tearin' a New Ass without the Blessing of the D.M.V. *(oil on canvas, 30 x 36 in.; collection of Terry Maloy).*

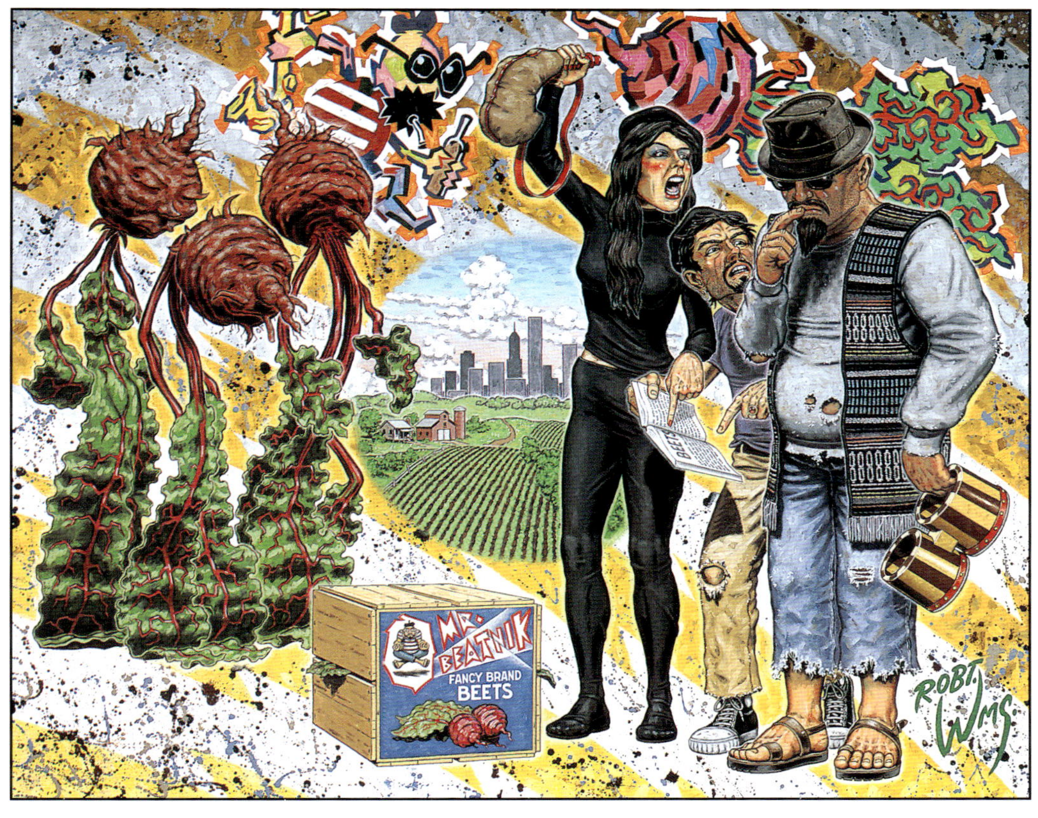

✠ *(Left) Robert Williams,* Beats and Beetniks, *1991.* Scholastic Designation: The Generation of Contemplation Put in Association with the Vegetable of the Same Name, Denotes the Remarkable Similarity between the Philosophy of Passive Inaction and Agrarian Horticultural Osmosis. Remedial Title: Three Zen Bopsters Find Beet Culture in the Farmer's Almanac. *(oil on canvas, 30 x 36 in.; collection of Tom and Jennifer Pollack).*

✠ *(Below) Robert Williams,* Oscar Wilde in Leadville, April 13th, 1882, *1991.* Scholastic Designation: Culture, Unlike War, Moves in a Breeze and Not a Gale, This with Its Slight Persistent Force Has Made a 19th Century Playwright and Sodomite the Messenger of Art to Cretins and is Destined to Be the Doomed Nut in a Three Dollar Fruit Cake. Remedial Title: A Fairy's Kiss for a Syphilitic Lily Sniffer *(oil on canvas, 49½ x 96 in.; collection of Judy and Stuart Spence).*

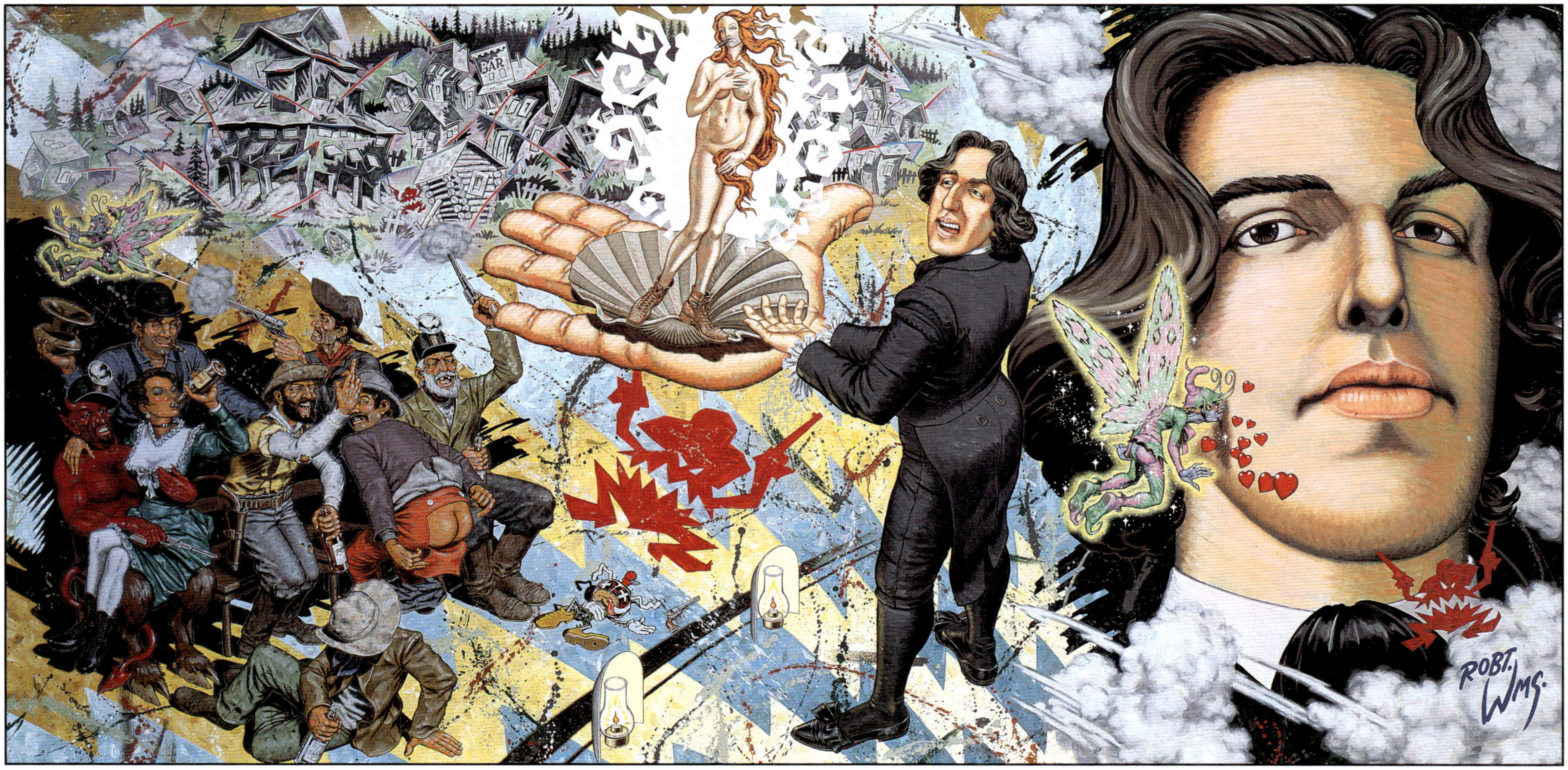

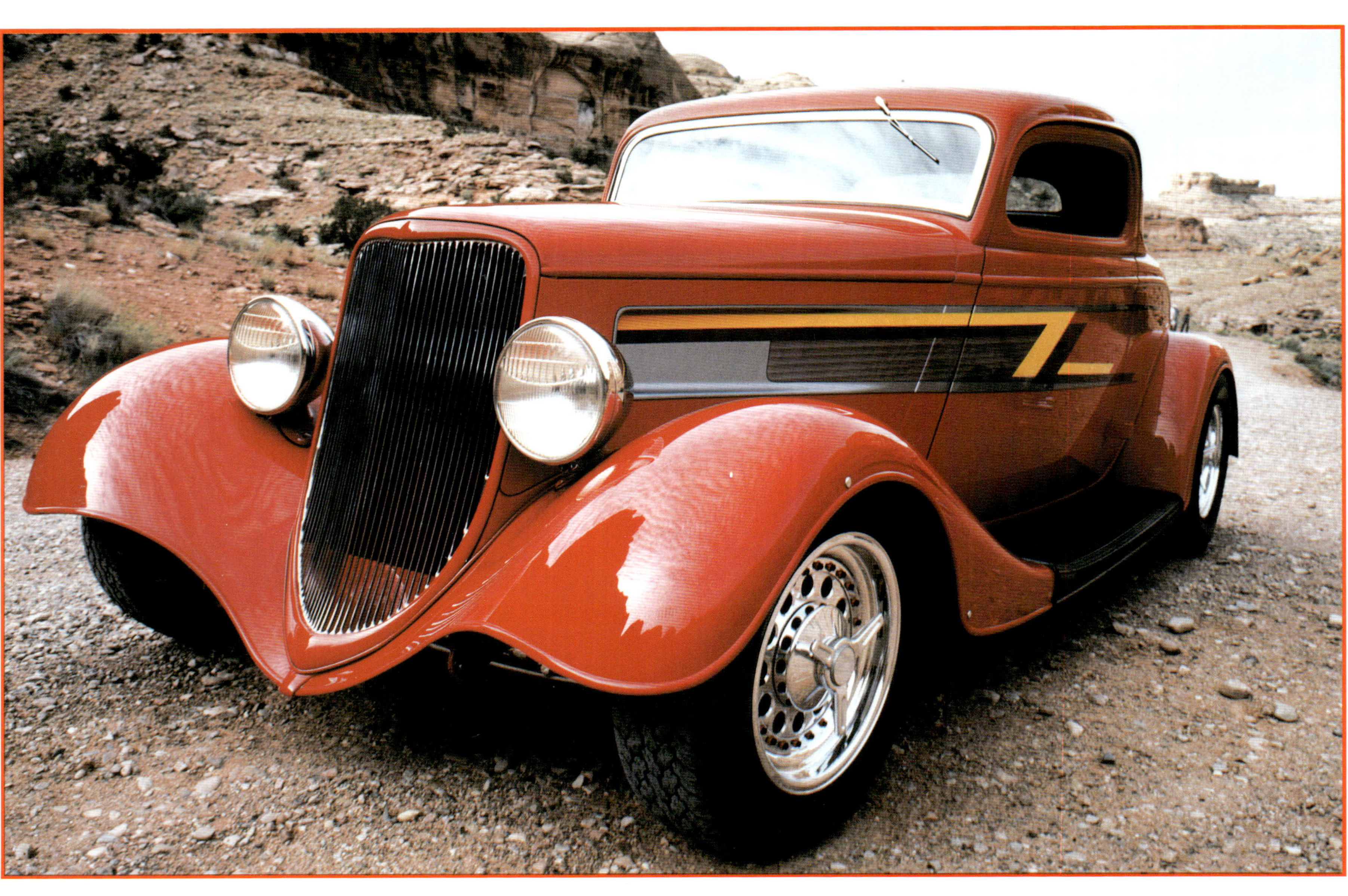

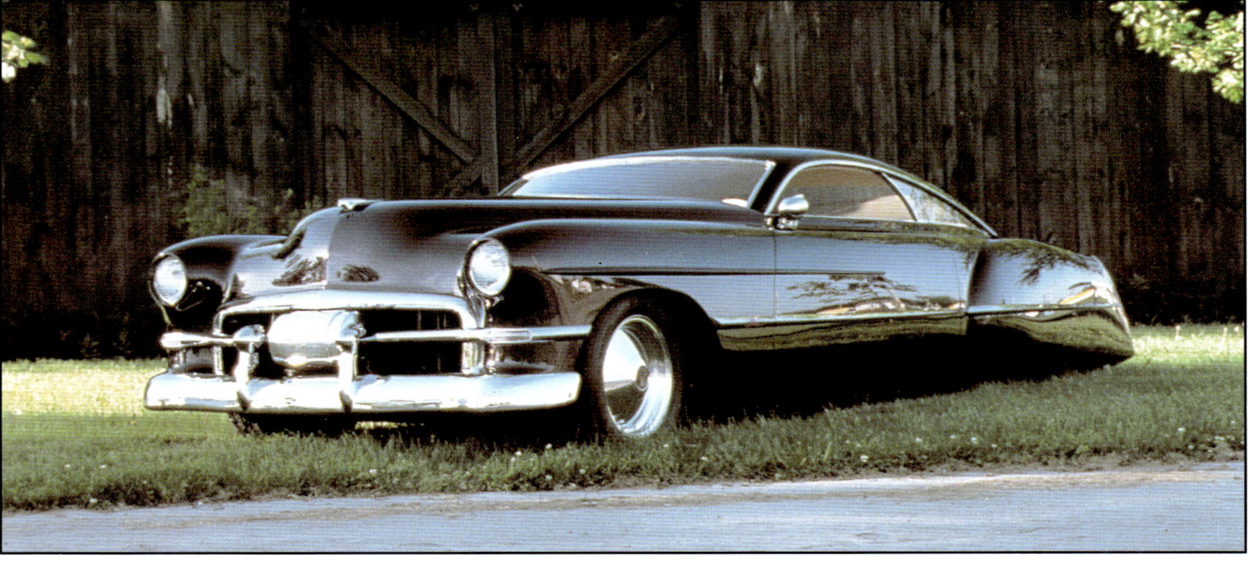

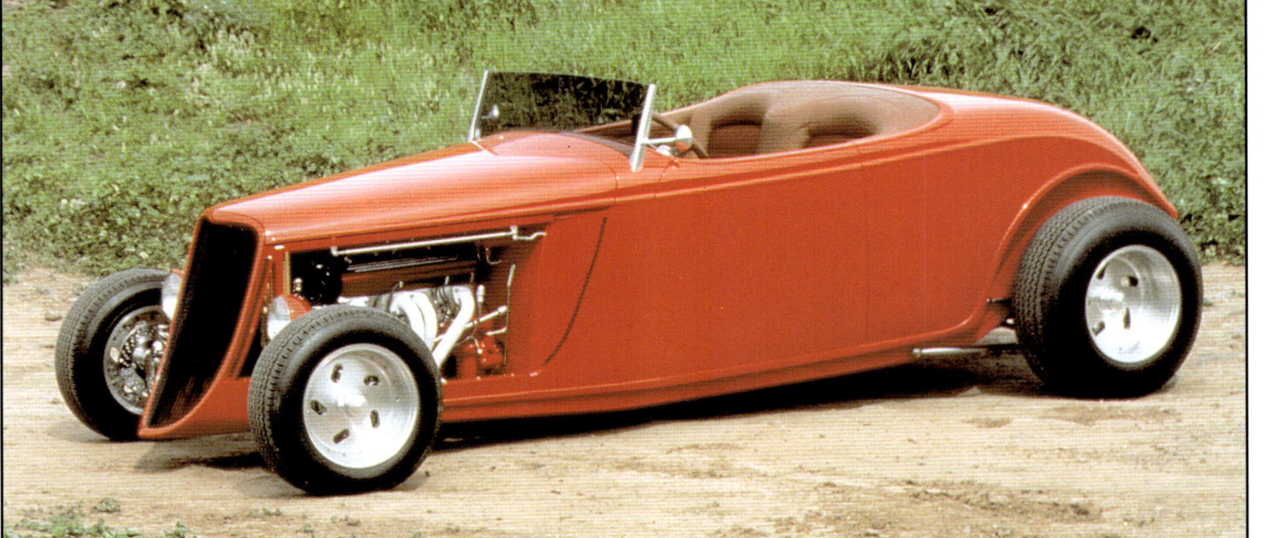

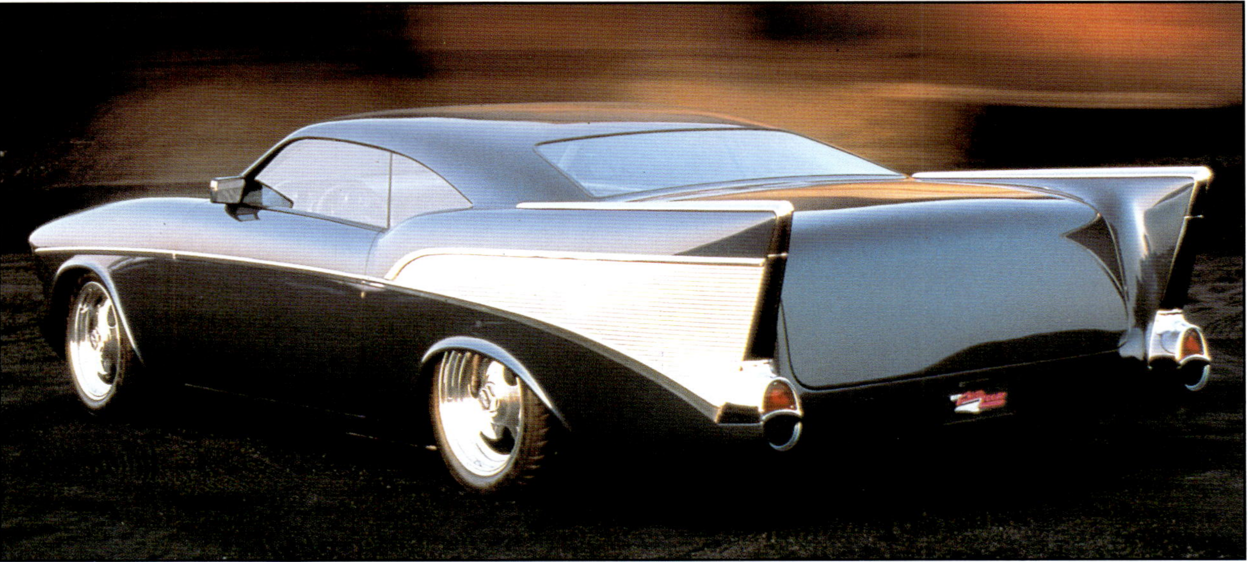

POST-KUSTOM

(This page) Three examples of the work of Boyd Coddington, an automotive stylist whom Ed Roth has called "the guiding light of the day."

(Top) The Cadzzilla *Cadillac Coupe built in 1989 for Billy F. Gibbons.*

(Center) Jamie Musselman's '33 Ford Roadster, winner of the 1982 Oakland Roadster show's top award.

(Bottom) The Chezoom*, 1992, a radically restyled 1957 Chevrolet created for Joe Hrudka.*

Coddington says "All quality rod work being done today builds upon the classic traditions of the established masters. For me personally, Von Dutch and Roth are right at the top."
Photos courtesy of Rod and Custom.

✠ *(Opposite) Don Thelan and Steve Davis,* Eliminator*, 1982 (customized 1933 Ford three-window coupe, steel body and fenders, aluminum hood; collection of Billy F. Gibbons). Photo by Hugh Brown. Courtesy of the Zzilla Tours.*

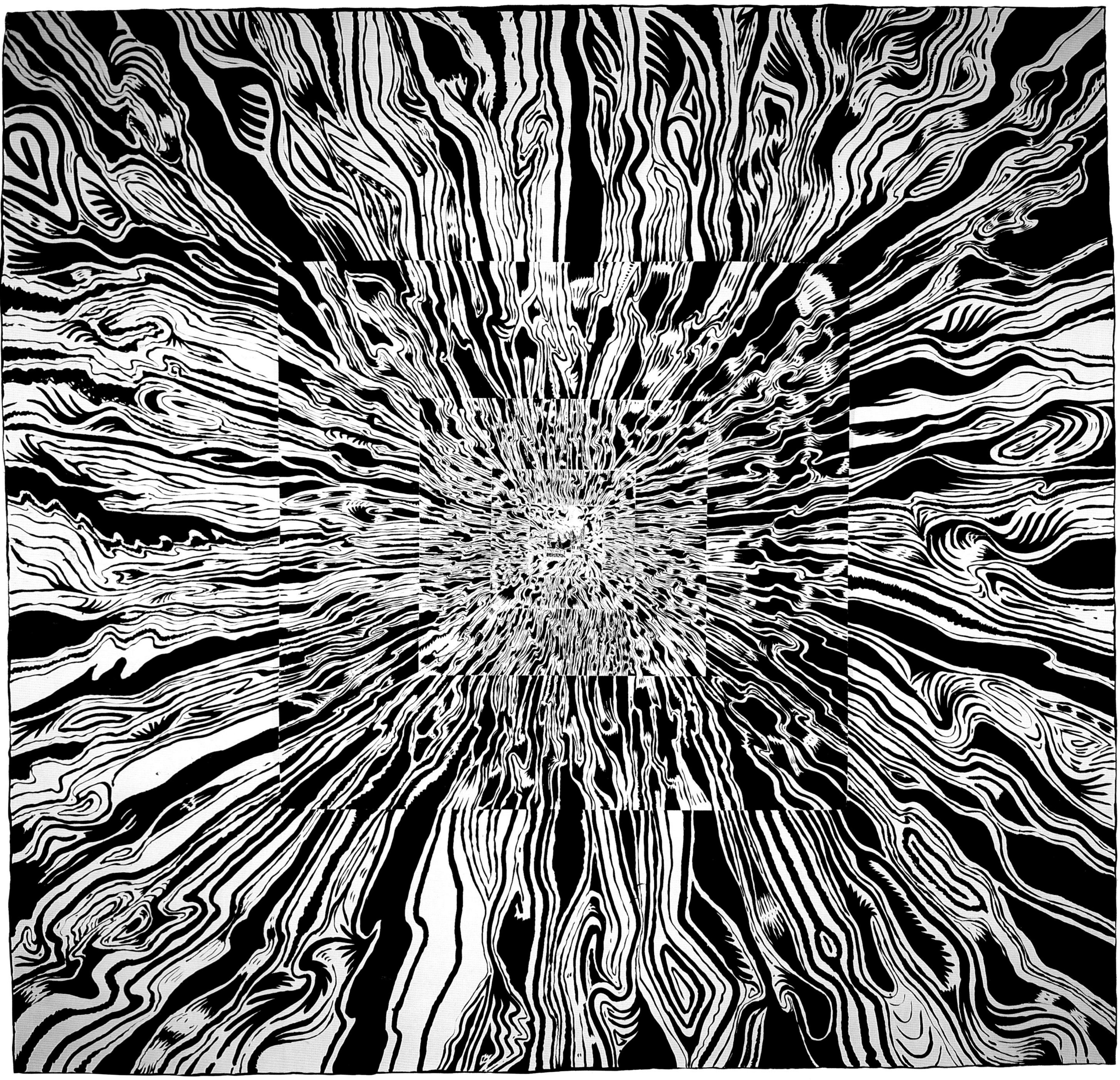

SOME OTHERS

Bolton Colburn

Since the 1950s, Southern Californians have related to the environment primarily through the medium of the car and the freeway. The automobile, with its equation of mobility and personal freedom, has become an outward shell of being, a second persona. It should thus be no surprise that the main influence on the art of Los Angeles in the past four decades has come from car culture.

Even in the loud, fast and garish environment of Los Angeles during the fifties, custom cars were outrageous and provocative. The sensibility of the street, the jargon of the car scene, the shock of seeing bizarre colors, the likes of which you had never seen before, dance in the sun on a car that had been transformed—lowered, chopped, channeled, frenched and decked—had consequences for budding artists that were immediate and lasting. Hanging out at the drive-in, working on their own cars and going to races and car shows imprinted a very specific aesthetic, one which these artists began incorporating into their work, thereby changing notions about the value and importance of Los Angeles popular culture.

Like the Pop artists of the same period, these Californians reacted against Abstract Expressionism, the dominant art movement of the time. Gone were the emotion-laden brush strokes and thickly layered abstract surfaces that spoke of serious art world issues. These were replaced by cool, smooth, transparent finishes, rife with reference to Southern California culture and environment.

Robert Irwin was one of the first artists in Los Angeles to point to auto culture as a seminal influence:

> The car was the key, the pivotal item in the whole ballgame. Everything was wrapped around the car. The car was your home away from home. And you put months and months into getting it just right. Everything was thought out in terms of who you were, how you saw yourself, what your identity was.[1]

Irwin became aware of his own aesthetic sense working on cars. The reductive and additive decisions that he made when modifying a car became a process that could be extended to other realms.[2] Irwin used this approach to explore issues of perception. His line paintings from the early sixties are one phase in a progressively reductive body of work by which Irwin sought to induce in the viewer a sense of absolute presence.

As a result of the aerospace industry build-up in Southern California during World War II, Los Angeles became the center for the development of new materials. High-tech substances, first used by the aircraft industry, were slowly declassified and released to the public. These new materials were extremely potent and could achieve dramatic results. Industrial spray-painting techniques, and materials like Bondo (polyester body filler), gave Southern California artists a different and uniquely regional set of tools. The post-war car culture promoted an artistic emphasis on surface, reflection, the blending of color and form, and the merger of object and environment.

The post-war art community responding to these stimuli included, besides Irwin, Billy Al Bengston, Kenneth Price, Edward Ruscha, Ed Moses, Judy Chicago, Peter Alexander, DeWain Valentine, Larry Bell and Craig Kauffman, all of whom had first-hand experience with the custom car scene. Many owned cars or motorcycles which they either

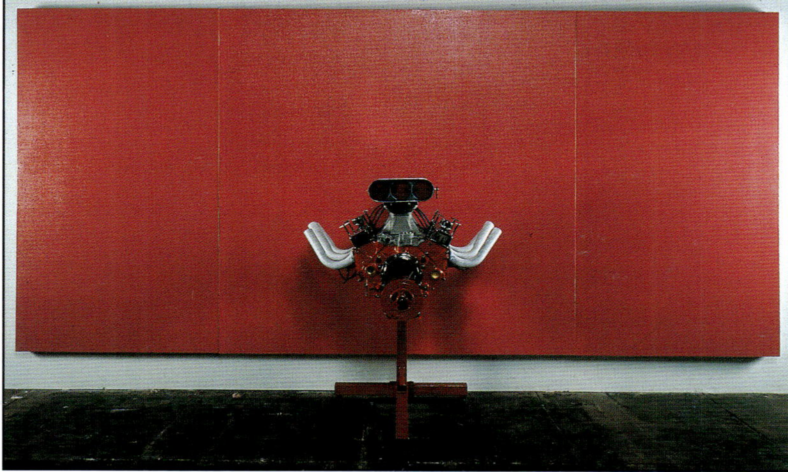

✠ *Tom Henry,* HOT RODS TO HELL, *1990 (Chevrolet 350 cu. in. engine on stand with automotive paint on canvas, 96 x 186 in.; courtesy Galerie Max Hetzler, Cologne, Germany).*

✠ *(Opposite), Mike Kelley,* INFINITE EXPANSION, *1983, partial view (acrylic on canvas, 140 x 140 in.; collection of Eli Broad Family Foundation, Santa Monica).*

1. Lawrence Weschler, ***Seeing is Forgetting the Name of the Thing One Sees: A Life of Contemporary Artist Robert Irwin*** (Berkeley: University of California Press, 1982), 13.

2. Robert Irwin, telephone conversation with the author, 10 January 1993.

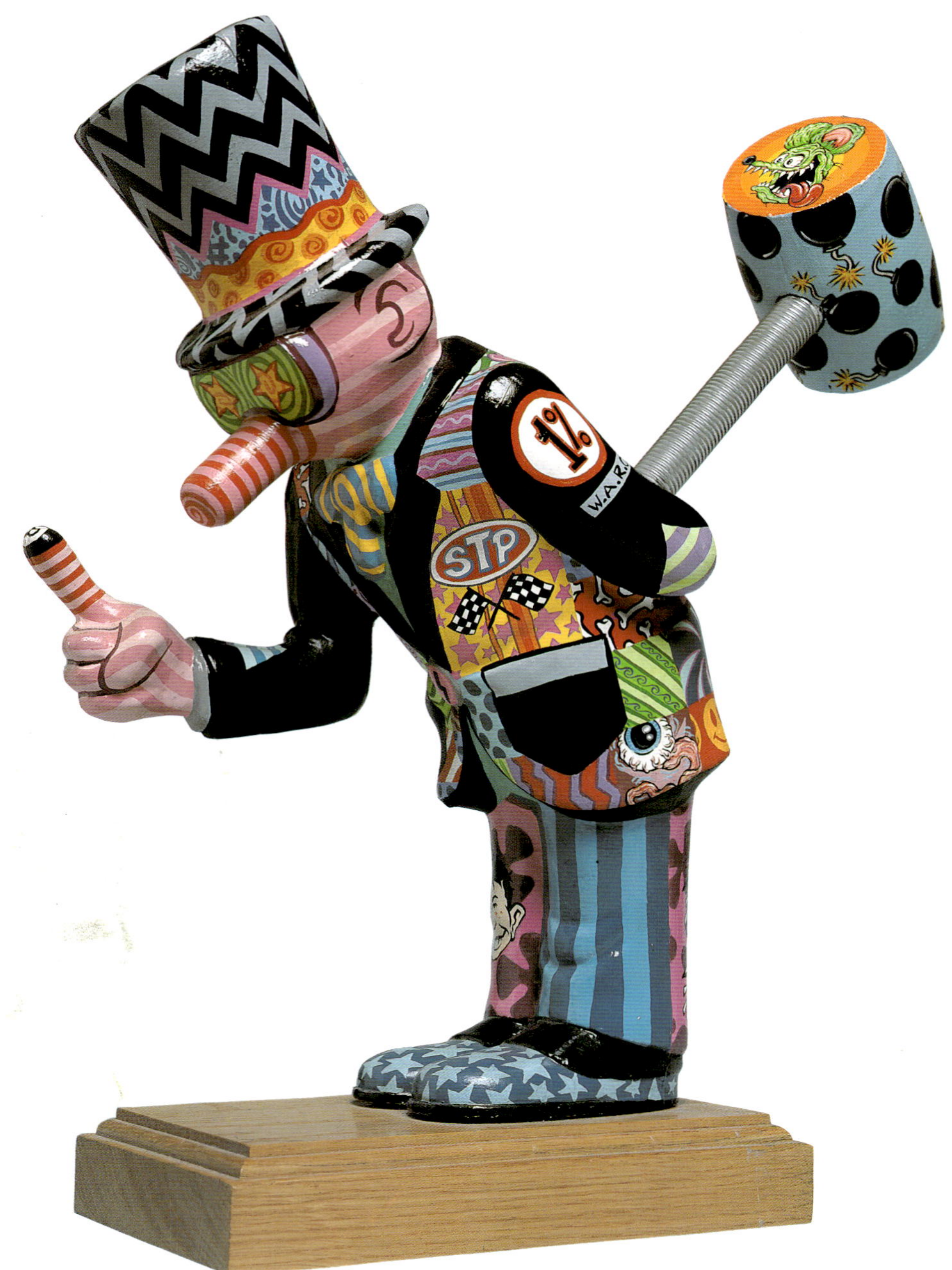
1%
STP

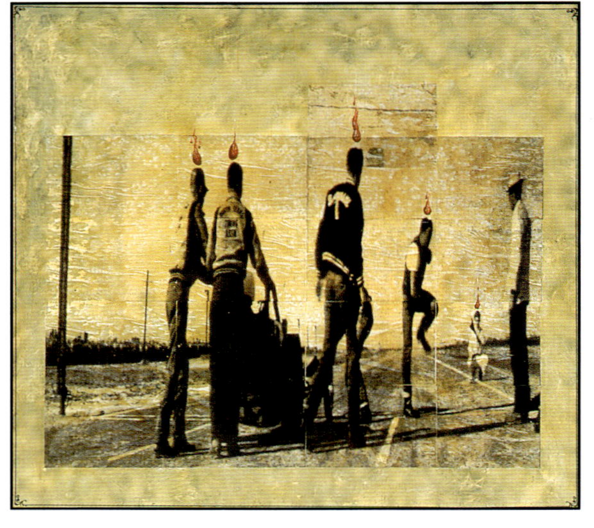

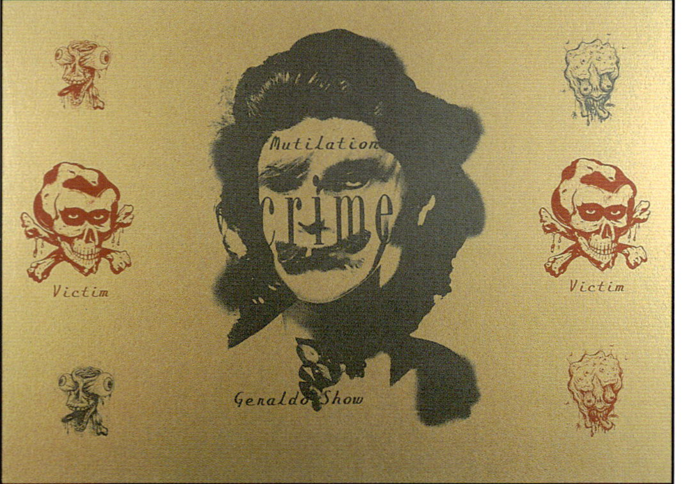
Mutilation
crime
Victim
Victim
Geraldo Show

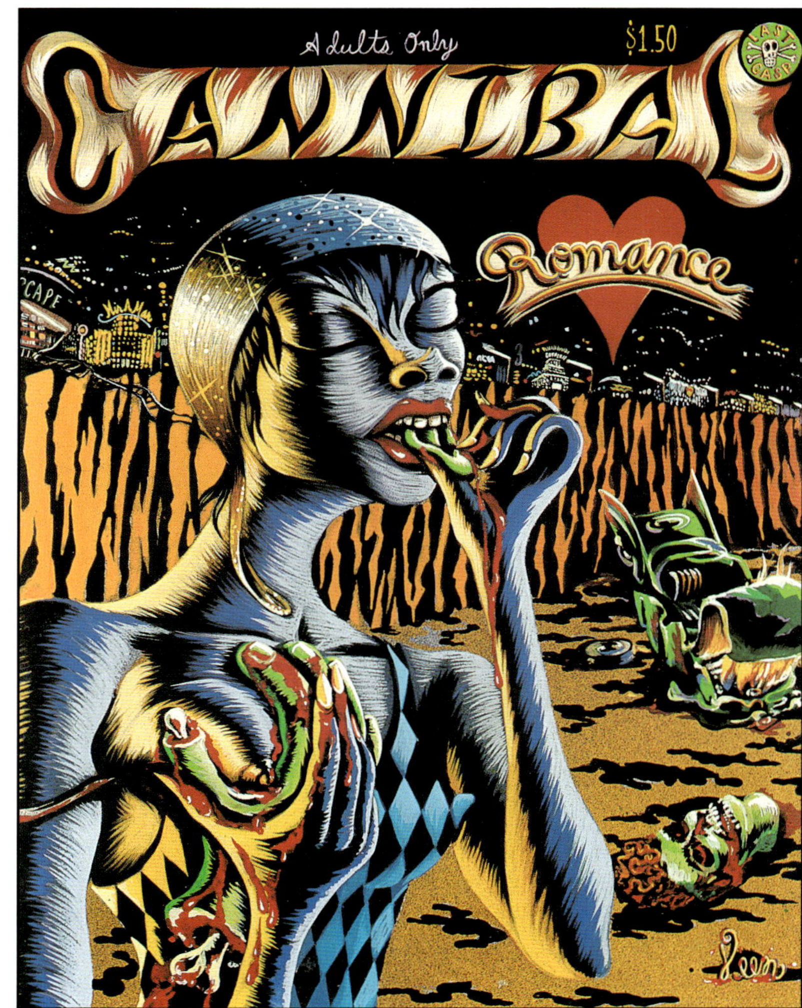
Adults Only
$1.50
CANNIBAL
Romance

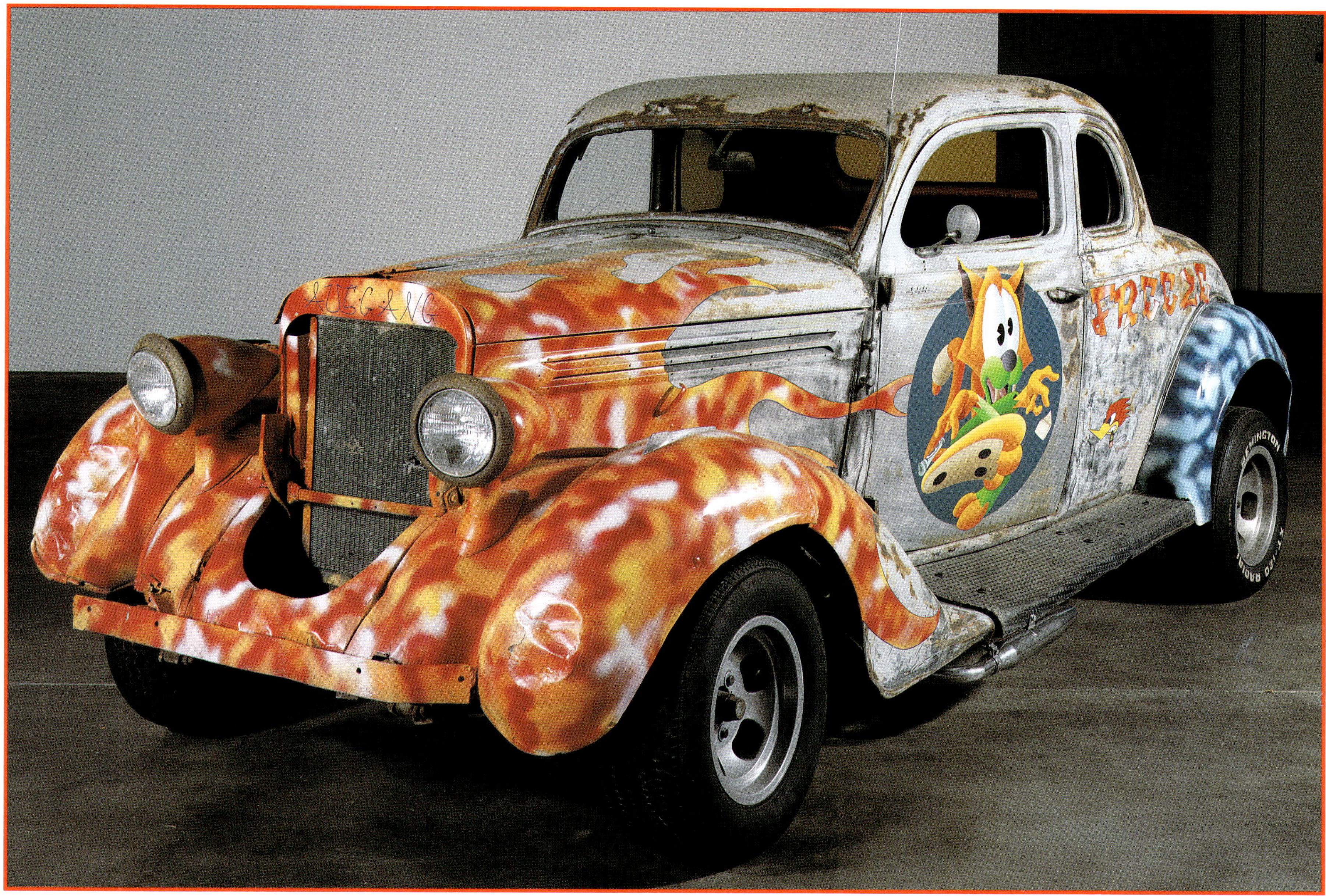

(Facing page)

✠ *(Top left) Alan Forbes,* WESTERN EXTERMINATOR, *1992 (animation cell paint on Western Exterminator logo figure, 25 x 16 x 12 in.; collection of Long Gone John).*

✠ *(Top right) Thaddeus Strode,* CHILDREN OF VIOLENCE, *1990 (laser print, marine varnish, oil and car trim on canvas, 96 x 72 in.; collection of Pablo and Leslie Lawner).*

✠ *(Bottom left) John Souza,* GERALDO SHOW, *1989 (custom color transfers on poster board, 22 x 30 in.; courtesy Sue Spaid Fine Art). Photo by James Franklin.*

✠ *(Bottom right) Georganne Deen,* CANNIBAL ROMANCE, *1986 (acrylic and gouache on board, 13 x 10 in.; collection of Danny Elfman).*

✠ *Anthony Ausgang,* NINTH LIFE, *1992 (acrylic and enamel on 1935 Plymouth, 67 x 165 x 65 in.; collection of the artist).*

painted themselves or had Los Angeles's most infamous customizer, Von Dutch, stripe for them. Most also showed at the Ferus Gallery (where Von Dutch was offered a one-man show)[3] and hung out at Barney's Beanery in West Hollywood. They went to car shows and drag races, and in some cases worked in commercial auto shops and raced motorcycles.

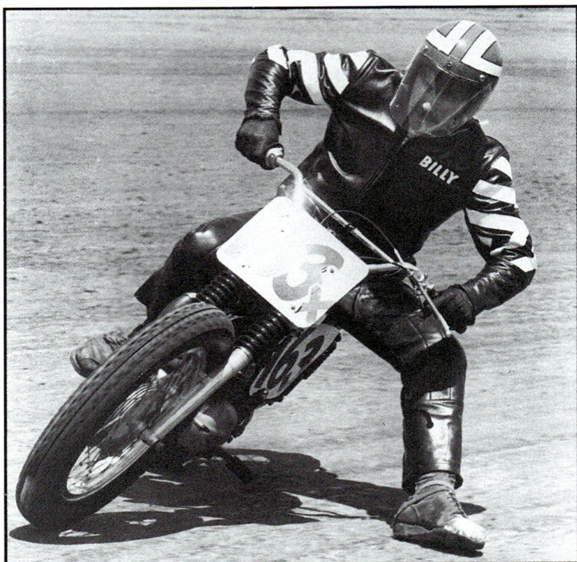

Artist Billy Al Bengston as a professional motorcycle racer, Ascot Park, Los Angeles, 1967. Photo courtesy Billy's Studio.

✠ *(Opposite) Billy Al Bengston,* Lady For a Night, *1970 (lacquer on aluminum, 36 x 34 in.; collection of the artist).*

Bengston was one of the first to adapt the materials and techniques of the car culture to his art practice. Working at LeBard and Underwood's motorcycle shop, he would paint, repair and race motorcycles. More interested in their performance than their visual aspect, Bengston nevertheless would freshly paint his machines weekly. He kept abreast of every new surface coating developed at the time, from nitrocellulose lacquer to a special concoction released by the Defense Department, popularly called "trick-shit paint." He not only experimented with these materials himself, but also introduced them to the artists around him.

Bengston had a car customizing pro named Molly (Roland Sanders) paint the clear coats on some of the works for which he is most famous, a series of Dentos—dented squares of sheet metal spray-painted with rich colors. One such Dento, *Lady for a Night* (1970), contains all the materials and techniques that Bengston employed in his automotive work—lacquer on aluminum with fades, rich background colors and heraldic patterns—placing this piece a scant breath away from the customized cars of the period.

The custom car scene was male driven, the car being perceived by men as a device to attract women. Judy Chicago was one of the few woman artists to adopt the use of auto-decorating techniques in her work. Having finished her graduate degree in art at UCLA in 1964, Chicago felt that to compete with her male counterparts and to be taken seriously in the male-dominated art world, she would have to learn something about "masculine" crafts and techniques. She ended up taking spray-painting lessons from customizer Percy Jeffries. Urged toward abstracting her "too direct" imagery (which referred to phalluses, vaginas, testicles, wombs, and other body parts) by her teachers in graduate school, Chicago used her newfound skills to produce large autobiographical abstractions based on the body, like *Car Hood.* Instead of denying or obscuring the meaning of her motifs, like her male counterparts, Chicago spoke about pieces like *Car Hood* in direct terms.

> In *Car Hood,* which I made at auto body school, the vaginal form, penetrated by a phallic arrow, was mounted on the "masculine" hood of a car, a very clear symbol of my state of mind at this time.[4]

By the forties, Chicanos in Los Angeles had established their own customizing traditions. The "lowrider" became a stylistic symbol and a component of Zootsuit sensibility. The car became a central focus in the paintings of Carlos Almaraz, Gilbert Lujan and Frank Romero. Lujan was particularly interested in imagery celebrating the Chicano lifestyle, and the lowrider was a key metaphor for that lifestyle. Growing up on *Hot Rod* magazine and car shows, Lujan became familiar with Von Dutch in the late fifties. Dutch's pinstriping had a major impact on Lujan, which he says inspired in his own work a graphic line combining elements of graffiti and car striping. Lujan's modified 1957 Chevrolet, *Our Family Car*, which sports a custom flame paint job, links ideas about travel with a flying couple representing Chicano youth.

At the same time, unlikely subcultures like surfing were being influenced in similar ways. The king of surf-illustration and sixties album covers, Rick Griffin, discovered an abandoned car in 1958 that was painted with a flying eyeball.[5] Subsequently Griffin became familiar with the art of Von Dutch and incorporated his own version of the flying eyeball in his "Murphy" series, a progression of increasingly psychedelic cartoons detailing the adventures of a mythic surfer, published in *Surfer Magazine*. Griffin's flying eyeball—illustrated in works like *Yowza!*—emblematized the pure surf experience and inspired hundreds of young surfers to begin drawing.

3. Walter Hopps, the former director of the Ferus Gallery, says Dutch turned down several offers of an exhibition before offering to construct a suit of armor. The project never proceeded, however, as Dutch insisted on payment up front. (Walter Hopps in a conversation with Charles Desmarais, Houston, Texas, 20 March 1993)

4. *Through the Flower: My Struggle as a Woman Artist*, Judy Chicago, Doubleday & Company, Inc., 1975, page 36-37.

5. A story recounted by Gordon McClelland—author of *Rick Griffin*—2 March 1993.

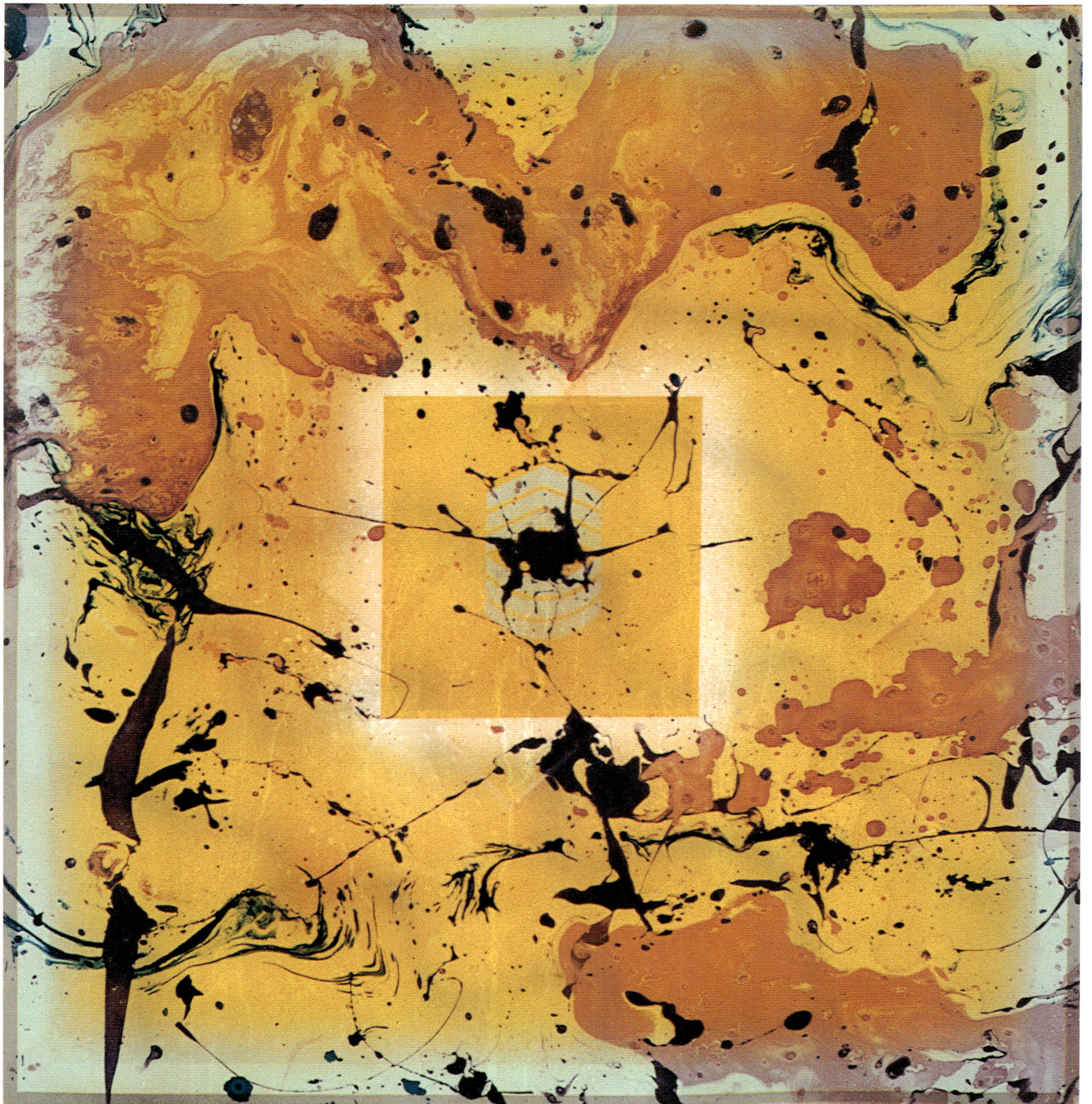

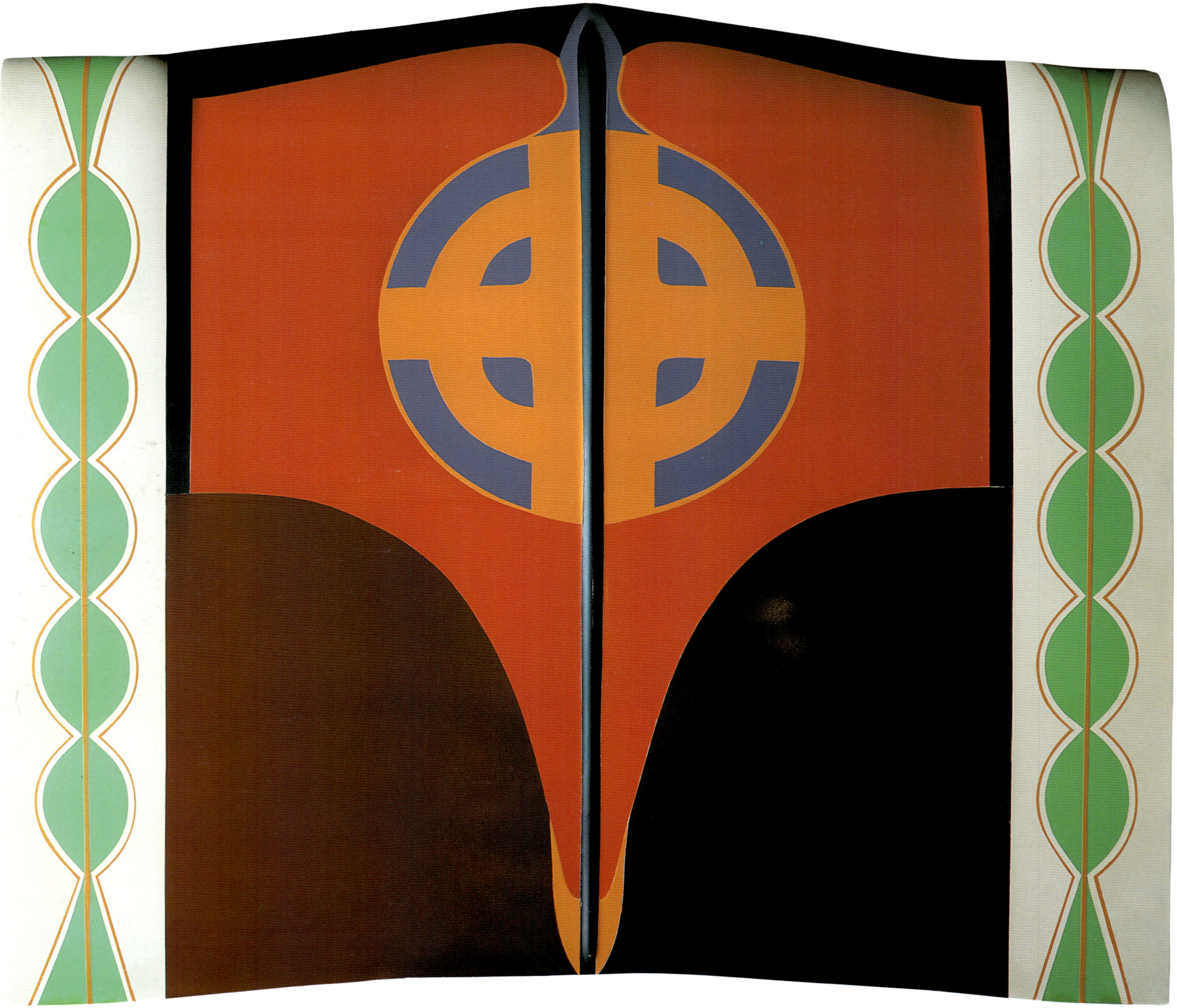

✠ *Judy Chicago,* Car Hood, *1964*
(sprayed acrylic lacquer on 1964 Corvair hood, 48 x 48 x 5 in.; collection of Elaine F. and Radoslav L. Sutnar).

(Facing page)

✠ *(Top left) The Pizz,* Surf Trog, *1993 (oil on canvas, 36 x 24 in.; collection of the artist). Photo by Kip Duff.*

✠ *(Bottom left) Basil Wolverton,* Dr. Spocktor Proctor, Surgeon, Has Rearranged His Head to Suit Himself. He Has Hung His Eyes Out His Nostrils So That He Can See Better Than over His Nose, and Has also Routed a Branch of Wind Pipe Out an Ear in Case Eyeballs Retract and Plug His Nostrils. An Opening above His Adam's Apple Makes It Possible to Inject Food He Wants Only to Taste but Not Reach His Stomach. Besides, the Changes Improve His Looks, *1972 (ink on illustration board, 14 x 11 in.; collection of Suzanne Williams).*

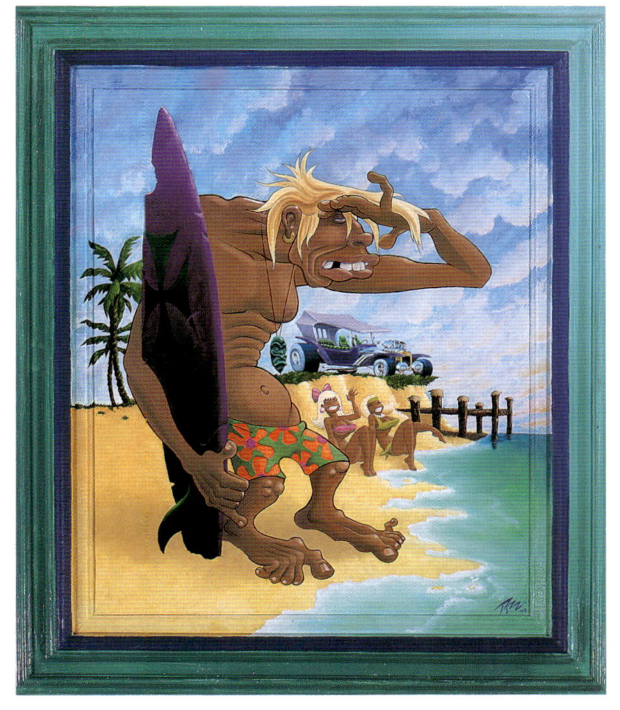

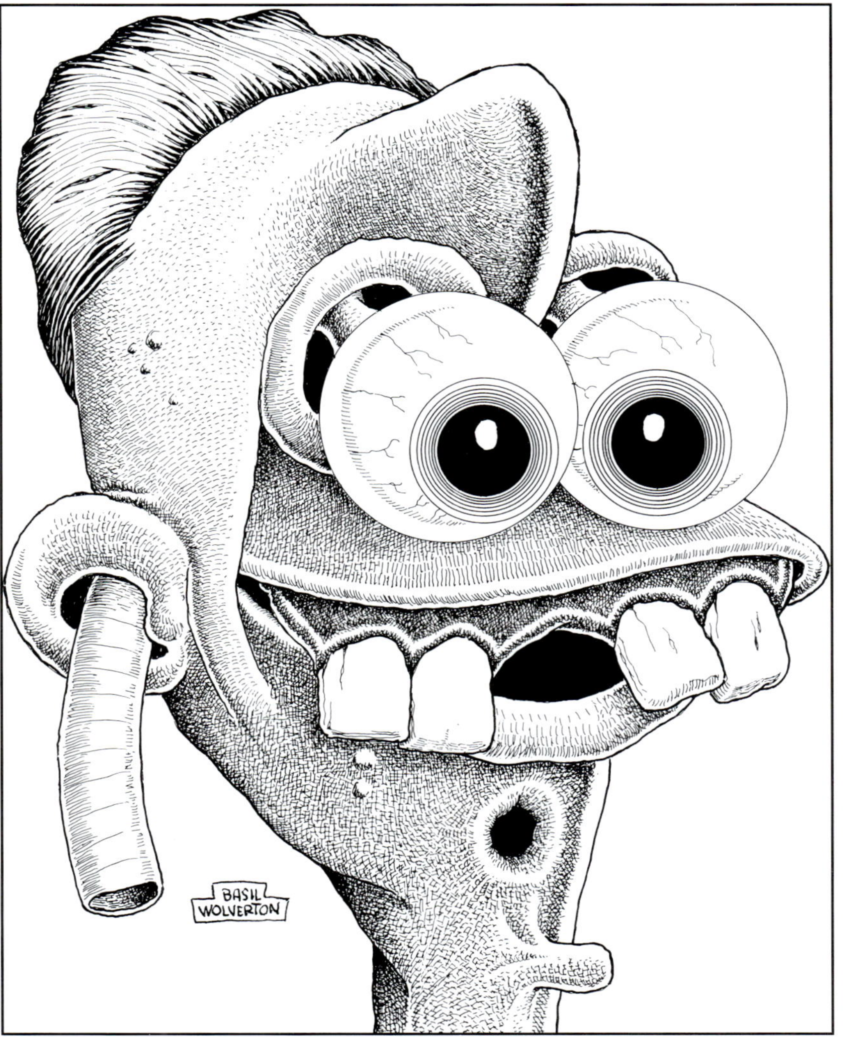

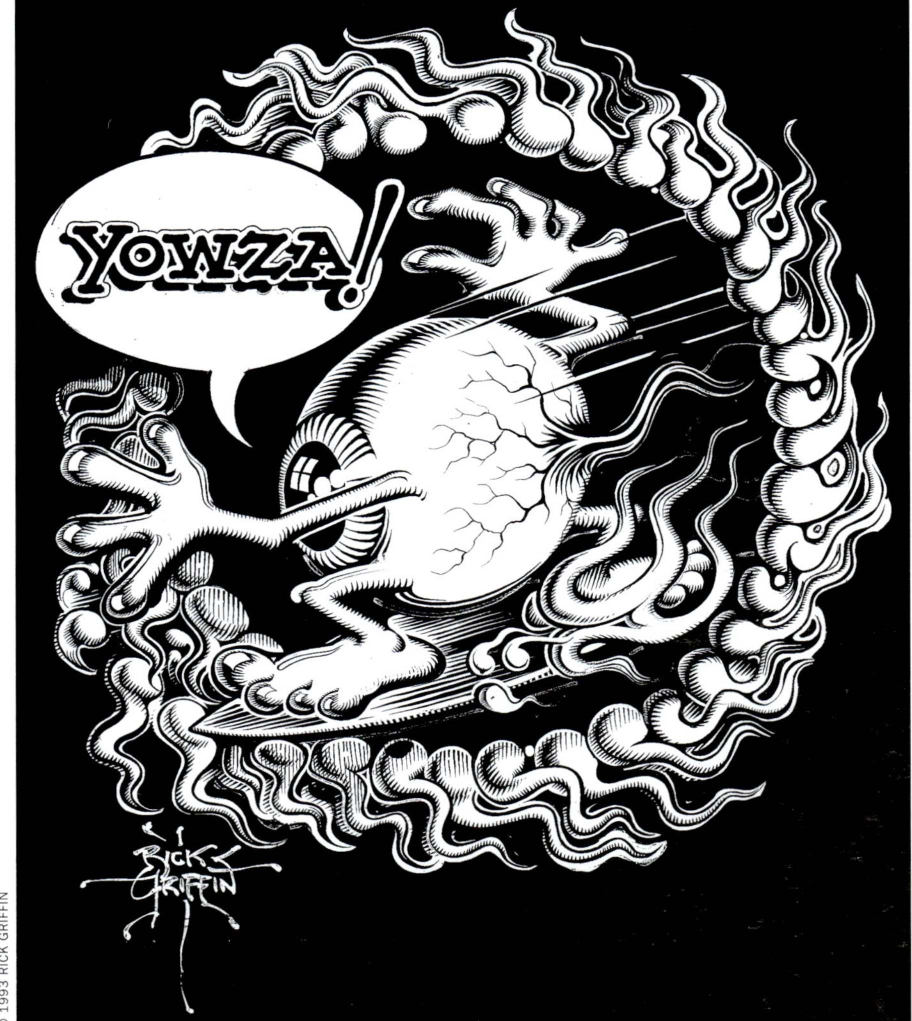

✠ (Above) Rick Griffin, YOWZA!, 1972 (ink and wash on illustration board, 17¾ x 13¾ in.; private collection).

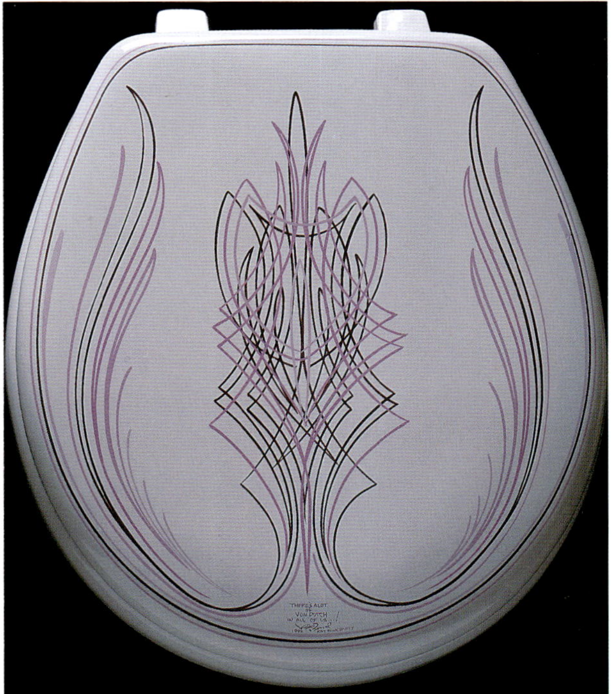

✠ (Right) Bob Bond, THERE'S A LOT OF VON DUTCH IN ALL OF US...!, 1992 (enamel on toilet seat, 15¾ x 14½ in.; private collection).

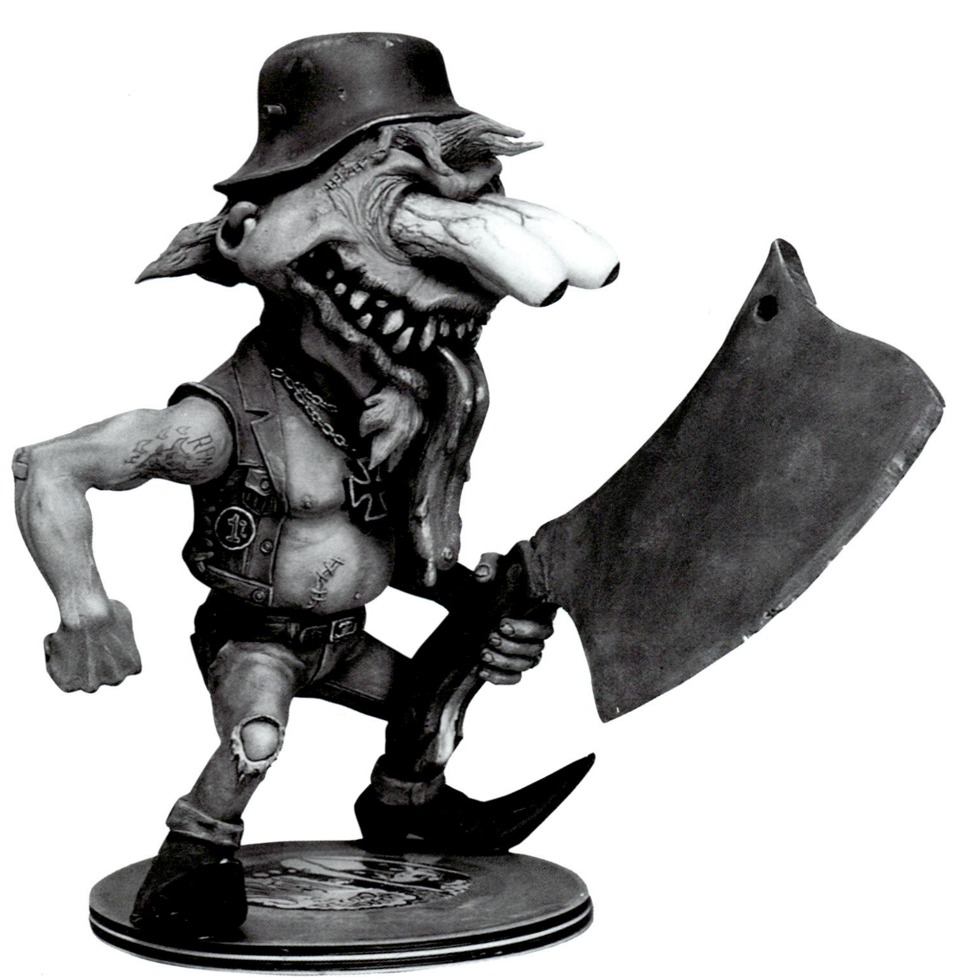

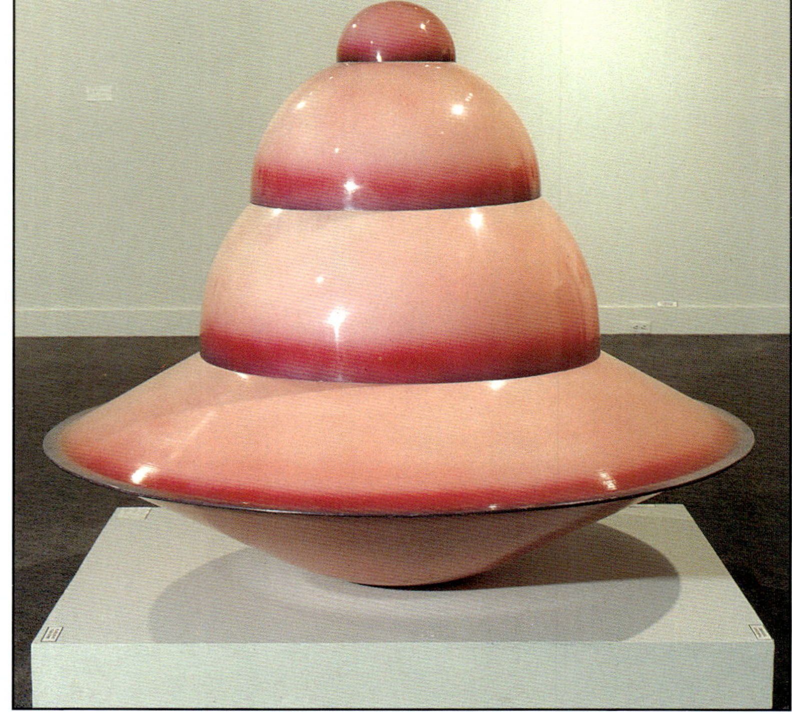

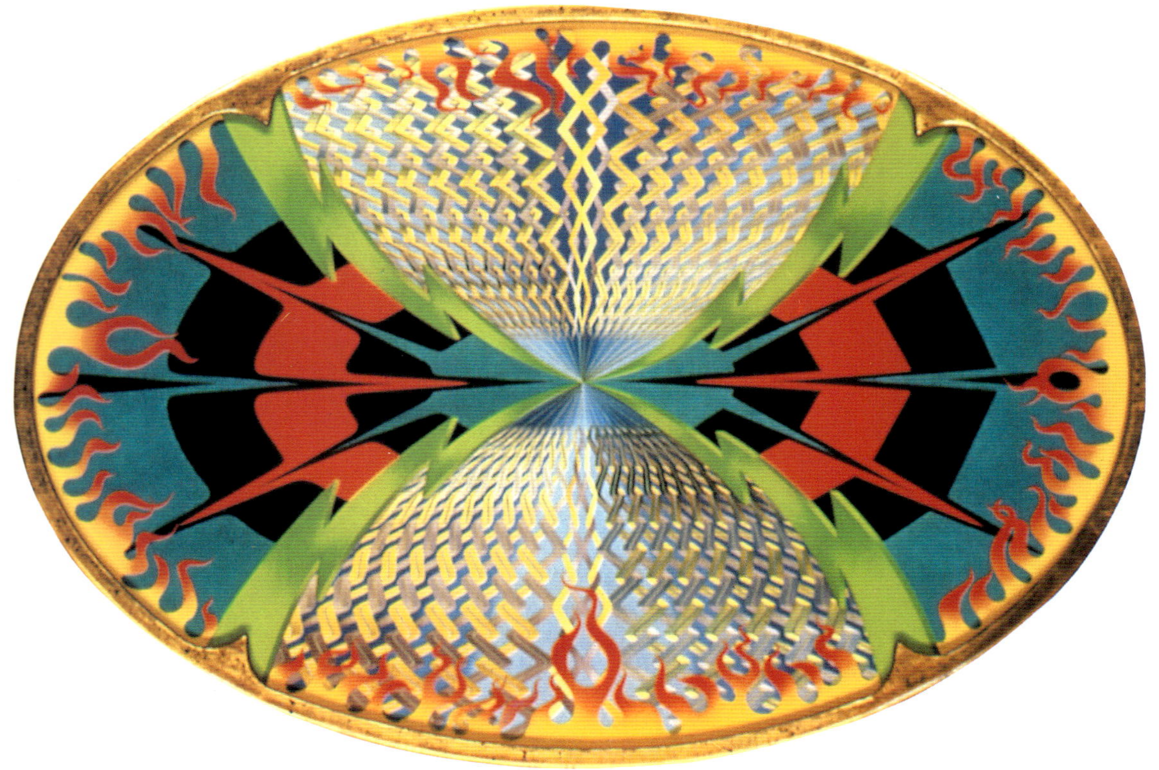

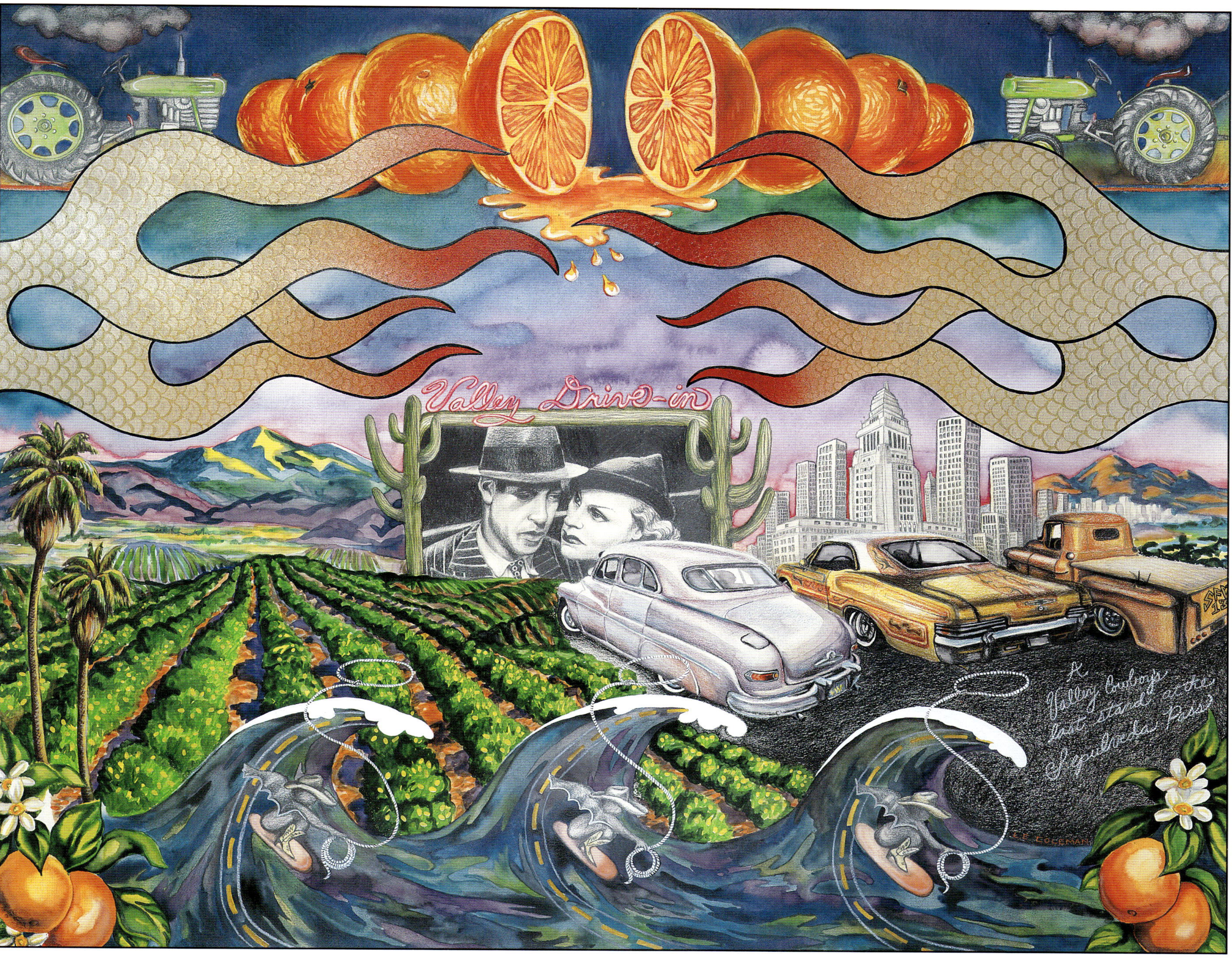

(Facing page)

✠ (Top left) *The Pizz, Long Gone John and Tom Kuntz,* ELDRIDGE CLEAVER, *1991 (cast resin and acrylic, 10 x 6 x 8 in.; collection of Long Gone John).*

✠ (Top right) *DeWain Valentine,* PINK TOP, *1967 (lacquer and acrylic on plexiglass, 55 x 76 dia. in.; collection of Laguna Art Museum, gift of Herbert Hirsh from the estate of Pauline Hirsh).*

✠ (Bottom) *Suzanne Williams,* SCALLOPS AND STRIPES CONFINED WITHIN AN OVAL OF FLAMES, *1975 (oil on canvas, 19 x 25 in.; collection of the artist).*

✠ *Lynn E. Coleman,* A VALLEY COWBOY'S LAST STAND AT SEPULVEDA PASS, *1975 (mixed media, 23 x 29 in.; collection of the artist).*

If the artists who grew up in the late forties and fifties had direct knowledge of Von Dutch and experienced the car culture at its height, then the generation who grew up in the sixties knew about their predecessors primarily through their products. Much stranger than today's Teenage Mutant Ninja Turtles were the Revell™ models of Rat Fink, the Hot Wheels reproduction of the *Beatnik Bandit*, and characters in magazines such as *Mad* and *Zap*. Rat Fink, the mutating, seething "thing" described by Ralph Rugoff as "Mickey Mouse turned inside out,[6]" completely contradicted the notion of a standardized reality and introduced the possibility of the weird to thousands of adolescents across the United States. More importantly, Rat Fink characterized, in a humorous way, the custom car fanatic, giving lower and middle-class kids a character they could relate to and an instant entryway into art. Rat Fink and company provided a break with the norm for American youth, a personification of the more unsavory and grotesque aspects of adolescence—those least likely to be acknowledged (in fact, likely to be suppressed).

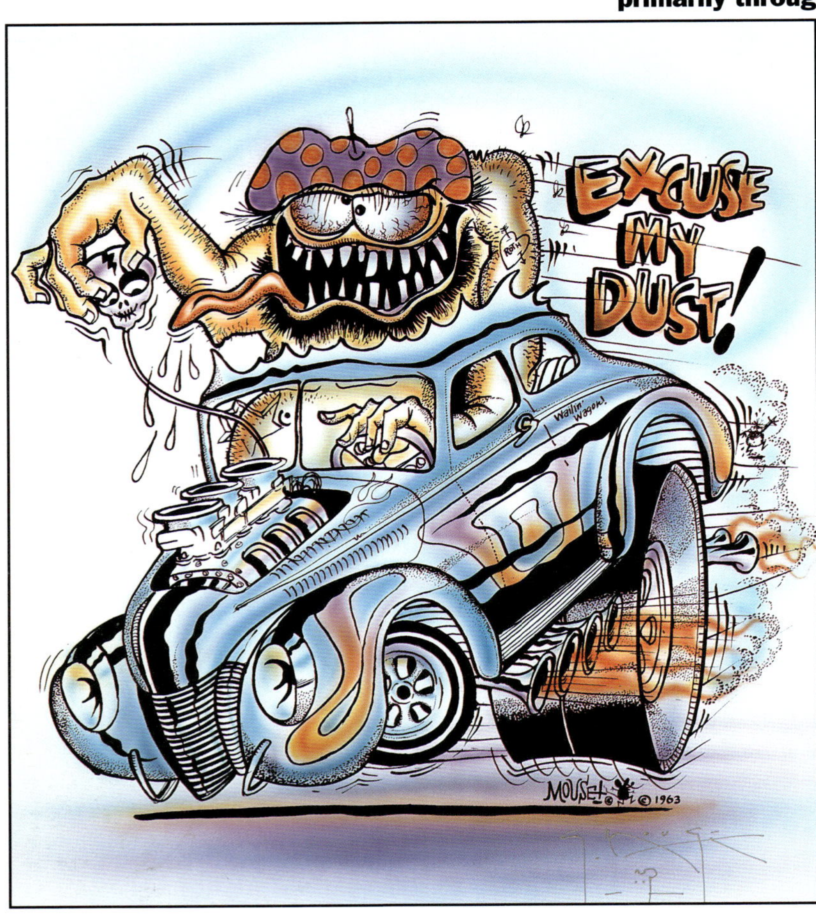

✠ *Stanley Miller Mouse,* Excuse My Dust!, *1963 (airbrushed silkscreen, 24 x 20 in.;collection of Douglas A. Nason).*

✠ *(Opposite) Gilbert Sanchez "Magu" Lujan,* Our Family Car, *1985-1986 (1951 Chevy two-door sedan, 57 x 204 x 87 in.; collection of the artist). Photo by Tom Vinetz.*

The progenitors of these visual excesses, Ed "Big Daddy" Roth and Robert Williams, influenced countless young artists. Among the more prominent working in the Los Angeles area today are Jim Shaw, Jeffrey Vallance, Mike Kelley, Chris Wilder, John Souza, Georganne Deen, Marcy Watton, Anthony Ausgang and Lynn Coleman. These artists have not only adopted the punk cartoon styles of Roth and Williams but claim as their subject matter our society's stew of materialism, sex and violence.

Growing up in Detroit, the center of car manufacture, Mike Kelley remembers being particularly interested in Ed "Big Daddy" Roth and Stanley Mouse (a Detroit car artist) as a kid. Alienated by the mainstream car culture around him, Kelley was attracted to its extremes, and can recall such memorable times as the controversy over Robert Williams's *Flash in the Pan* illustration, published in *Zap* magazine during his junior high school years. In graduate school at California Institute of the Arts, Kelley adopted a plain illustrative graphic style, which he set off with words to create a schism between content and image. In works like *Infinite Expansion*, Kelley adopts a psychedelic sixties, low-brow style to provoke comparisons with eighteenth-century ideas about the sublime.

Georganne Deen, another Cal Arts graduate to adopt the underground comic-book style, has been the only woman to exhibit consistently alongside Roth and Williams. Very much influenced by Roth, Deen published her work in Art Spiegelman's magazine *Raw*. Deen's *Cannibal Romance* suggests the tendency of people to consume one another in relationships, as well as our vulnerablity to being consumed by our love affair with the automobile. Deen takes the sexist aspects of the work of Williams and turns them upside down, by making the women the consumers and men the consumed.

The development of the custom car, Chicano and surf subcultures was of tremendous importance to art in Los Angeles. The Los Angeles custom car scene encouraged individuals to take a generic industrial product and change it, thereby expressing aspects of their own personalities and the personality of their particular local tribe.

While Pop artists elsewhere were acting like mirrors, reflecting back the commodified, corporate and media-dominated America they saw around them, Los Angeles artists dispensed with the reiteration of popular simulacra and instead forged icons of their own, based on the techniques and practices of the subcultures of which they were part.

6. *Exterminating Angel*, Ralph Rugoff, *L.A. Weekly*, October 18-24, 1985, page 51.

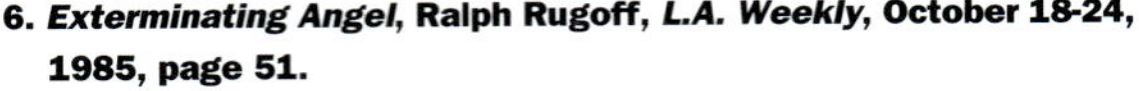

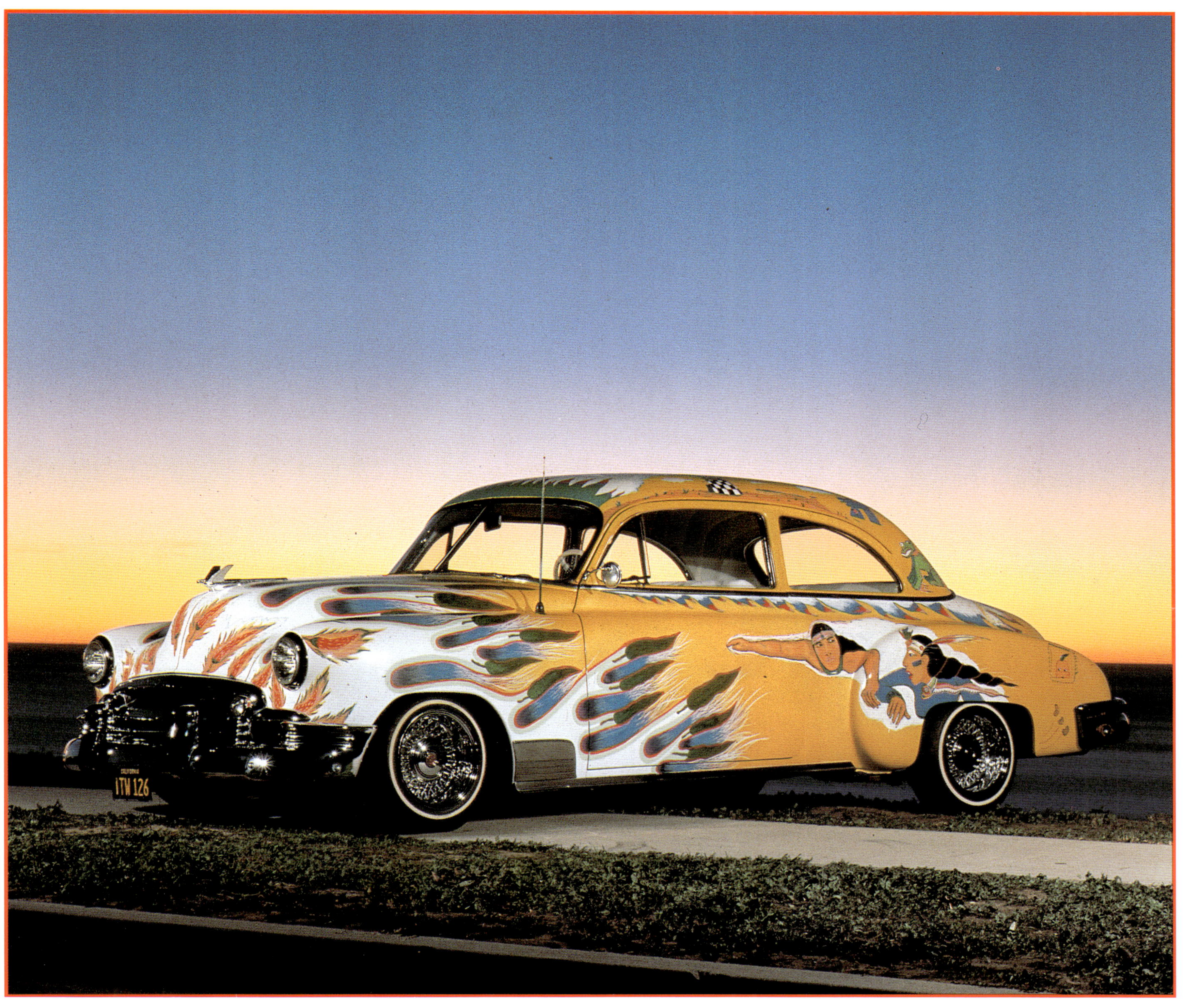
1TW 126

LAGUNA ART MUSEUM

STAFF

Charles Desmarais, *Director*

Susan M. Anderson, *Curator of Exhibitions*
Serge Armando, *Exhibition Designer/Preparator*
Winston Bao, *Museum Store*
Lisa Buck, *Curatorial Assistant*
Vanessa Cao, *Museum Store*
Colleen M. Callinan, *Assistant to the Director*
Sergio Carranza, *Maintenance*
Bolton Colburn, *Curator of Collections*
Jacqueline Collin, *Museum Store*
Vaughn Custer, *Chief of Security*
Teresa Ferreira, Manager, *Museum Stores*
Bonnie Brittain Hall, *Endowment Campaign*
Gloria Grant, *Museum Store*
Nancy Hightower, *Finance Officer*
Holly Jenks, *Museum Store*
Susan Landauer, *Adjunct Curator*
Margaret A. Maynard, *Curator of Education*
Carolyn H. Moody,
Development Officer/Individual Giving
Carole Reynolds, *Librarian/Archivist*
Alexandra Rudoff, *Museum Store*
Sue Henger, *Interim Public Relations Officer*
Susan Shadwick, *Museum Store*
Gayle Simmonds,
Development Assistant/Special Events
Mike Stice, *Security*
John Winning, *Security*
Holly Wisneski, *Director of Development*

Bob Zoell, invitation graphic for the Western Exterminators exhibition, 1985.